THE TOTAL BUSINESS PLAN

HOW TO WRITE, REWRITE, AND REVISE

THE TOTAL BUSINESS PLAN

HOW TO WRITE, REWRITE, AND REVISE

Patrick D. O'Hara

John Wiley & Sons

New York • Chichester • Brisbane • Toronto • Singapore

Editor: Michael Hamilton
Managing Editor: Linda Indig
Copy Editor: Sheck Cho
Design and Production: Lenity Himburg and Rob Mauhar, The Coriolis Group

Library of Congress Cataloging-in-Publication Data

O'Hara, Patrick D.
The total business plan : how to write, rewrite, and revise / by Patrick D. O'Hara.
p. cm.
ISBN 0-471-52450-6
1. Corporate planning--Handbooks, manuals, etc. 2. Business enterprises--Planning--Handbooks, manuals, etc. 3. Business enterprises--Finance--Handbooks, manuals, etc. I. Title.
HD30.28.035 1990
658.4'012--dc20 89-77520
CIP

Printed in the United States of America
90 91 10 9 8 7 6 5 4 3 2 1

CONTENTS

PREFACE

This book is the product of the author's experiences in researching and writing business and marketing plans for numerous start-up ventures and businesses seeking borrowed capital. It is compiled from material created and used in successful capital seeking activities and from public information sources knowledgeable of capital sources and the methodology of approaching them. The objective of this book is to assist the entrepreneur in planning a successful business venture from start-up through growth and expansion.

Provided herein are full conceptual explanations of the total business planning processes such as market planning, strategizing, research sources, pricing concepts, as well as specific questions the entrepreneur must answer when preparing for the presentation of the resulting plan to its targeted audience—management, a lender, or the investment community. Suggested business and marketing plan outlines are given and each sections' reasoning explained; with full knowledge that each plan is unique in its presentation and must be the creation of the entrepreneur and his or her selected management team participants.

I have put this book together for you—the entrepreneur. Complete information on the concepts of business planning and a guide to some of the research resources necessary for you to write and present your proposition successfully to your selected audience is provided. I have made it as simple yet as thorough as I have found necessary in my own experience. I sincerely hope you find it helpful in your planning process.

I want to thank my wife, Betty, for her patience and encouragement in the writing of this book which took many hours away from our time together. Also, a special thanks to Fred Seddiqui of MCI, Inc. and my editor, Michael Hamilton, and his staff at John Wiley & Sons for their advice and assistance in getting this book to print.

Patrick D. O'Hara
Fremont, CA.

1 INTRODUCTION

PLANNING

The planning function is the first function of any business operation to be performed, since it allows you to define what it is your business will offer in the way of a product or service. It also allows you to show how the product or service will be offered.

It is presumed that you have an idea that you believe has business potential. This idea must be available prior to starting the planning function. If not, you have nothing to plan around.

The planning function should permit you to plan an organization that is both dynamic and flexible, and has the capability of growth built in. Thus, through this process, you can evaluate your human resource needs and construct an organization chart with these thoughts in mind. Job descriptions for each function on the chart should be written that encourage top performance. However, you will not actually staff all positions immediately. Since, initially, you and maybe one or two others will be performing all of the functions. However, with a business plan you will know when you should hire personnel to fill various functions, what these functions are, and how you can acquire top quality personnel to fill them.

The Business Plan

You can create and control your company according to the plan of action. The plan of action, when written, is the "business plan." Before actually beginning the operation of your business, it is a good idea to write a plan. It should be as detailed as possible, but something you are comfortable with. If it is to be used to attract capital investment, it must also be comfortable to your potential investors or lenders. However, remember, the business plan is just that, a plan, and should be thought of as being as adaptable as the experience of operating the business dictates.

Some reasons for preparing a business plan are: to bring closure to the planning process, to communicate to the firm the seriousness of the planning process and its outcomes, to provide tangible framework for managing the firm, and to give lenders and investors a real sense of assurance that the company can perform financially as is claimed.

A typical business plan will contain much of the following, depending on its intended audience.

I. Company organization and product/service description.
 a. Company charter

b. Organization
1. Officers functional descriptions
2. Founders and officers resumes
c. Product/service description (product plan)

II. Market analysis.
a. Product market overview
b. Competition
c. Product pricing
d. Product market potential

III. Revenue distribution.
a. Marketing plan
b. Departmental budget development
c. Income and cash flow

The Marketing Plan

Another plan that supplements the business plan is the "marketing plan." The marketing plan contains some of the information contained in the business plan but provides expanded details of the expected revenue dynamics of the proposed business. A typical plan will contain most of the following.

I. Market analysis.
a. Product market overview
b. Competition study
c. Pricing (based on material and labor cost data)
d. Product market potential

II. The market.
a. Total size (units and dollars)
b. Product versus competition (past 5 years)
1. Sales (by units and dollar value)
2. Sales by distribution outlet (units and dollar value)
3. Potential market share
c. Potential consumption
1. Demographics
2. Season
3. Geographic market area

III. Advertising (product versus competition).
a. Media costs (past 5 years)
b. Creative strategies (past 3 years)
1. Sample of advertising
2. Analysis of competitive advertising

IV. Sales promotion (same analysis as advertising but on sales promotion activity).

V. Public relations (analysis of public relations activity).

VI. Financial data.
a. Product price and profit structure
b. Profit and loss (last 5 years)

This dynamic process, once initiated, becomes the process of managing the business. You will have set goals, and now you can review actual results versus plans and take action when actual results do not meet established goals. This may require changes in actions to cause results to move closer to the goals or, possibly, the goals need changing. The decisions regarding the changes to be made are the act of managing the business. This book is designed to guide you through these analyses and decision processes.

These actions will probably be communicated to your financial resource carriers (investors, banks, etc.) and, when your team grows, to all employees, customers, and suppliers as necessary.

The primary use of this book is as a reference source to develop, implement, and work your plan in a logical and controlled manner. In this way you will have greater chance of success.

USES OF A BUSINESS PLAN

In general, a business plan is necessary to provide a logical and rational sense of direction for a firm.

A working definition of a *business plan* is that it is a set of management decisions focusing on what a firm will do to be successful. It must address both what a firm will do and how it will do it.

The overall purpose of a business plan is to provide a logical, rational sense of direction and to provide a framework for guiding and evaluating the firm's accomplishments. Beyond this overriding purpose, a business plan can have several different objectives that, in turn, relate very closely to the intended uses of the plan. It can have both internal and external uses.

The differences between internal and external uses of a business plan are: (1) Internal uses focus on guiding and improving performance of the firm; and (2) External uses focus on relations with significant outside parties, such as investors and competitors.

Internal Uses

A business plan can provide several internal benefits for a firm. First, it can improve performance by identifying both the strengths and weaknesses of the firm's operation and potential or emerging problem areas. Improved performance will also result from developing strategies that simultaneously build on the firm's strengths and correct its weaknesses. Second, a business plan can communicate to management and staff clear expectations regarding the firm's performance and priorities. Third, for firms with multiple divisions, units, or points of management responsibility, a business plan can effectively coordinate and ensure consistency in the plans and operations of the various units or divisions. Fourth, a business plan provides a solid basis for measuring performance of the overall firm and of individual units and managers. It establishes a standard for deciding if actual performance is good, bad, or indifferent. It also establishes a framework for making key decisions in the ongoing management process of the firm. As new developments and opportunities arise, a business plan provides rational structure for evaluating the impact of the developments or opportunities on the operations and performance of the overall firm and its individual units.

Finally, and perhaps most important, a business plan and the process of developing it can be used to educate and motivate the key personnel of a firm. Through participation in analyzing past performance, evaluating the impact of trends and developments, and developing action plans for the future, managers and other key personnel tend to learn more about the total operation of a firm and the relationship of their specific area(s) of responsibility toward the achievement of the firm's goals. This increased level of understanding and involvement generally leads to increased commitment to achieving the firm's goals and, in turn, generates a higher level of motivation.

Thus a business plan is used internally to communicate expectations to and of staff, coordinate activities across functions or departments, measure and evaluate performance (variance analysis), provide a framework for making key decisions, and educate and motivate key personnel.

External Uses

A business plan has several uses in relationship with significant parties outside the firm. First, it can be used to educate outside parties regarding the objectives, structure, and performance of a firm. This use becomes important if the support—either financial or nonfinancial—of outside parties is important to a firm's success. A clear example is the support of current or potential stockholders or investors. A less clear but equally significant example is the support of regulatory or legislative bodies. Second, a business plan can be used to secure funding from outside investors—either individual or institutional. If this is an intended use of the business plan, it is important to identify the issues and types of information that are of primary concern and interest of the potential investor group(s) in advance.

Planned actions can also be communicated through a business plan. This use relates to deflecting competitive or regulatory moves that may be under consideration by outside parties. By formalizing intentions in a business plan, a firm is committing itself to action. By communicating this commitment to selected, significant outside parties, a firm may preempt actions that could have a negative impact on its own plans and actions.

Thus some of the external uses of a business plan are to educate outside parties about the firm and its objectives, communicate to outside parties planned actions of the firm that may affect them, preempt actions by competitors, and secure funding.

The desirability and need to distribute a business plan, or any parts thereof, to parties outside a firm is a decision of the firm's management.

Obviously, there are many different objectives and uses of a business plan. Although there is a standard content for a properly constructed plan, the specific structure and content should and will be affected by the intended uses and target audience.

WHAT MAKES AN EFFECTIVE BUSINESS PLAN

The standard components of a business plan are: organization and staffing (management and administration) strategy, marketing or revenue-generating strategy, and research and development strategy, if applicable.

In order for this information to be acted on effectively the following suggestions for creating such a plan should be considered and implemented where applicable.

- The business planning process and the development and use of a business plan must have the commitment and involvement of a firm's management, including top management.
- The planning process and the resulting objectives and strategies must address all of the significant factors that affect a firm's short- and long-term performance.
- The planning process must be forward looking, particularly regarding trends and developments in a firm's marketplace and operating environment.
- The goals, strategies, and performance objectives should be consistent across all functions of a firm and provide a clear sense of direction to the firm's staff regarding future and important performance goals.
- Key management and staff who are responsible for implementing a business plan should be actively involved in its development.
- A business plan should include specific contingency planning provisions that indicate courses of action to be taken if key assumptions underlying the plan prove invalid.

The key element that makes an internal business plan effective is the willingness of management to use it to manage a firm's operations.

In an external business plan, the key element that makes it effective is management's familiarity with the target audience which is normally a financier—lending organizations and/or investors of various types.

Internal business plans are very much akin to the budgetary process and focus on the internal processes of the organization and their costs and revenue generation.

External business plans must focus on how the organization plans to be profitable—meet the criteria of the outside party—so the payback of a loan or the return on the investment is very evident and assured by the logic and background study of the plan.

We will focus on the creation and evolution of the external plan—both the lender's and the investor's plan. Thus, the first objective is to get to know your audience. We will begin by acquiring an understanding of money sources and what is important to those sources.

2

UNDERSTANDING MONEY SOURCES

MONEY

Never enough money! How many times have you heard that expression. You need money (capital) to get sales, buy inventory, pay employees, purchase assets, pay taxes, you name it you need money for it. Your need for capital is a continuing one. To remain in business or to expand, the business owner needs capital, but where do you get it?

Regardless of where the business person goes to acquire capital some sort of business plan will be requested and probably required—some more detailed than others.

Available Sources

In order to secure the capital business owners need they must understand the various sources of money that are available to them. For example:

- Capital generated internally.
- Capital available from trade creditors.
- Borrowed money.
- Sale of an ownership interest in the business to equity investors.

Each of these capital sources has unique characteristics. These characteristics must be fully understood by the business owner so that he or she will know available sources and which source is best suited to the needs of the business.

This section is designed to help the business person in the following ways:

- Recognize those situations that create a need for additional capital.
- Identify the capital sources that are normally available to the business owner.
- Manage the business judiciously to take full advantage of the capital that can be generated internally.
- Establish a plan to permit you, the client, to take full advantage of trade capital without jeopardizing credit status.
- Identify various specific sources of debt and equity capital.
- Identify collateral that can be used to secure loans.
- Identify potential compensation to equity investors such as opportunities for dividends, capital gains, or a future public offering that could attract equity capital.

CAUSES OF ADDITIONAL CAPITAL NEEDS

There are many factors that can create a need for additional capital. Some of the more common are as follows:

- Sales growth requires inventories to be built to support the higher sales level.
- Sales growth created a larger volume of accounts receivable.
- Growth requires the business to carry larger cash balances in order to meet its current obligations to employees, trade creditors, and others.
- Expansion opportunities such as a decision to open a new branch, add a new product, or increase capacity.
- Cost savings opportunities such as equipment purchases that will lower production costs or reduce operating expenses.
- Opportunities to realize substantial savings by taking advantage of quantity discounts on purchases for inventory, or building inventories prior to a supplier's price increase.
- Seasonal factors, where inventories must be built before the selling season begins and receivables may not be collected until 30 to 60 days after the selling season ends.
- Current repayment of obligations or debts may require more cash than is immediately available.
- Local or national economic conditions which cause sales and profit to decline temporarily.
- Economic difficulties of customers that can cause them to pay more slowly than expected.
- Failure to retain sufficient earnings in the business.
- Inattention to asset management may have allowed inventories or accounts receivable to get out of hand.

Frequently, the need for additional capital cannot be entirely attributed to any one of the factors described, but results from a combination. For example, a growing, apparently successful business may find that it does not have sufficient cash on hand to meet a current debt installment or to expand to a new location because customers have been slow in paying.

SHORT- AND LONG-TERM CAPITAL

Capital needs can be classified as either short or long term. Short-term needs are generally those of less than 1 year. Long-term needs are those of more than 1 year.

Short-Term Financing

Short-term financing is most common for assets that turn over quickly such as accounts receivable or inventories. Seasonal businesses that must build inventories in anticipation of selling requirements and will not collect receivables until after the selling season often need short-term financing for the interim. Contractors with substantial work-in-process inventories often need short-term financing until payment is received. Wholesalers and manufacturers with a major portion of their assets tied up in inventories and/or receivables also require short-term financing in anticipation of payments from customers.

Long-Term Financing

Long-term financing is often associated with the need for fixed assets, such as property, plant, and equipment, where the assets will be used in the business for several years. It is a practical alternative in many situations where short-term financing requirements recur on a regular basis.

A series of short-term needs could often be more realistically viewed as a long-term need. The addition of long-term capital should eliminate the short-term needs and the crises that occur if capital were not available to meet a short-term need.

Whenever the need for additional capital grows continually without any significant pattern, as in the case of a company with steady sales and profit from year to year, long-term financing is probably more appropriate.

INTERNAL VERSUS EXTERNAL SOURCES OF CAPITAL

Internal sources of capital are those generated within the business. External sources of capital are those outside the business such as suppliers, lenders, and investors. For example, a business can generate capital internally by accelerating collection of receivables, disposing of surplus inventories, retaining profit in the business, or cutting costs.

Capital can be generated externally by borrowing or locating investors who might be interested in buying a portion of the business.

Internal Financing Sources

Before seeking external sources of capital from investors or lenders, a business should thoroughly explore all reasonable sources for meeting its capital needs internally. Even if this effort fails to generate all of the needed capital, it can sharply reduce the external financing requirement, resulting in less interest expense, lower repayment obligations, and less sacrifice of control. With a lower requirement, the business' ability to secure external financing will be improved. Further, the ability to generate maximum capital internally and to control operations will enhance the confidence of outside investors and lenders. With more confidence in the business and its management, lenders and investors will be more willing to commit their capital.

There are three principal sources of internal capital. These are:

- Increasing the amount of earnings kept in the business.
- Prudent asset management.
- Cost control.

Increased Earnings Retention

Many businesses are able to meet all of their capital needs through earnings retention. Each year, shareholders' dividends or partners' drawings are restricted so that the largest reasonable share of earnings is retained in the business to finance its growth.

As with other internal capital sources, earnings retention not only reduces any external capital requirement, but also affects the business's ability to secure external capital. Lenders are particularly concerned with the rate of earnings retention, since the ability to repay debt obligations normally depends on the amount of cash generated through operations. If this cash is used excessively to pay dividends or to permit withdrawals by investors, the company's ability to meet its debt obligations will be threatened.

Asset Management

Many businesses have nonproductive assets that can be liquidated (sold or collected) to provide capital for short-term needs. A vigorous campaign of collecting outstanding receivables, with particular emphasis on amounts long outstanding, can often produce significant amounts of capital. Similarly, inventories can be analyzed and those goods with relatively slow sales activity or with little hope for future fast movement can be liquidated. The liquidation can occur through sales to customers or sales to wholesale outlets, as required.

Fixed assets can be sold to free cash immediately. For example, a company automobile might be sold and provide cash of $2000 or $3000. Owners and employees can be compensated on an actual mileage basis for use of their personal cars on company business. Or if an automobile is needed on a full-time basis, a lease can be arranged so that a vehicle will be available.

Other assets such as loans made by the business to officers or employees, investments in nonrelated businesses, or prepaid expenses should be analyzed closely. If they are nonproductive, they can often be liquidated so that cash is available to meet the immediate needs of the business.

On a long-term basis, the business can minimize its external capital needs by establishing policies and procedures that will reduce the possibility of cash shortages causes by ineffective asset management. These policies could include the establishment of more rigorous credit standards, systematic review of outstanding receivables, periodic analysis of slow-moving inventories, and establishment of profitability criteria so that fixed-asset investments are more closely controlled.

Cost Control

Careful analysis of costs, both before and after the fact, can improve profitability and therefore the amount of earnings available for retention. At the same time, cost control minimizes the need for cash to meet obligations to trade and other creditors.

Before cost analysis, a business can establish buying controls that require a written purchase order and competitive bids on all purchases above a specified amount. Decisions to hire extra personnel, lease additional space, or incur other additional costs can be reviewed closely before commitments are made.

After cost analysis, management should review all actual costs carefully. Expenses can be compared with objectives, experience in previous periods, or with other companies in the industry. Whenever an apparent excess is identified, the cause of the excess should be closely explored and corrective action taken to prevent its recurrence.

Trade Credit

Trade credit is credit extended by suppliers. Ordinarily, it is the first source of extra capital that the small business owner turns to when the need arises.

Informal Extensions

Frequently, this is done with no formal planning by the business. Suppliers' invoices are simply allowed to "ride" for another 30 to 60 days. Unfortunately, this can lead to a number of problems. Suppliers may promptly terminate credit and refuse to deliver until the account is settled, thus denying the business access to sorely needed supplies, materials, or inventory. Or, suppliers might put the business on a C.O.D. (cash on delivery) basis, requiring that all shipments be fully paid in cash immediately on receipt. At a time when a business is strapped for cash, this requirement could have the same effect as cutting off deliveries altogether.

Planning Advantages

A planned program of trade credit extensions can often help the business secure extra capital that it needs without recourse to lenders or equity investors. This is particularly true whenever the capital need is relatively small or short in duration.

A planned approach should involve the following:

- Take full advantage of available payment terms. If no cash discount is offered and payment is due on the 30th day, do not make any payments before then.
- Whenever possible, negotiate extended payment terms with suppliers. For example, if a supplier's normal payment terms are net 30 days from the receipt of goods, these could be extended to net 30 days from the end of the month. This effectively "buys" an average of 15 days.
- If the business feels that it needs a substantial increase in time, say 60 to 90 days, it should advise suppliers of this need. They will often be willing to accept it, provided that the business is faithful in its adherence to payment at the later date.
- Consider the effect of cash discounts and delinquency penalties for late payment. Frequently, the added cost of trade credit may be far more expensive than the cost of alternate financing such as a short-term bank loan.
- Consider the possibility of signing a note for each shipment, promising payment at a specific later date. Such a note, which may or may not be interest bearing, would give the supplier evidence of your intent to pay and increase the supplier's confidence in your business.

Ready Availability

Trade credit is often available to businesses on a relatively informal basis without the requirements for application, negotiation, auditing, and legal assistance often necessary with other capital sources.

Usage

Trade credit must be used judiciously. Its easy availability is particularly welcome in brief periods of limited needs. Used imprudently, however, it can lead to curtailment of relations with key suppliers and jeopardize your ability to locate other competitive suppliers who are willing to extend credit to your business.

Debt Capital

Debt capital is an amount of money borrowed from a creditor. The amount borrowed is usually evidenced by a note, signed by the borrower, agreeing to repay the principal amount borrowed plus interest on some predetermined basis.

Borrowing Term

The terms under which money is borrowed may vary widely. Short-term notes can be issued for periods as brief as 10 days to fill an immediate need. However, usually repayment is required within 60 to 90 days but can be up to 1 year. Notes are often renewed, in whole or in part, on the due date, provided that the borrower has lived up to the obligations of the original agreement and the business continues to be a favorable lending risk.

Commercial banks are the ordinary source of short-term loans for small businesses. When a business has established itself as being worthy of short-term credit, and the amount needed fluctuates from time to time, banks will often establish a line of credit with the business. The line of credit is the maximum amount that the business can borrow at any one time. The exact amount borrowed can vary according to the needs of the business but cannot exceed its established credit line.

These arrangements give the business access to its requirements up to the credit limit, or line limit. However, the business pays interest only on the actual amount borrowed, not the entire line of credit available to it.

This general classification includes "intermediate debt" which is borrowing for periods of 1 to 10 years. Long-term notes can be issued for a period of greater than 1 year.

Payment Schedule

When the terms of a debt are negotiated, a payment schedule is established for both interest obligations and principal repayment.

Discounted Notes

A *discounted note* is the total amount of interest due over the term of the note is deducted from the principal before the proceeds are issued to the borrower. This is particularly true in short-term borrowing.

Small Business Applications

For small businesses, borrowed capital for periods greater than 10 years is usually available only on real estate mortgages. Other long-term borrowing usually falls into the "intermediate" classification and is available for periods up to 10 years. Such loans are called "term loans."

Mortgage Payment Schedules

Principal and interest payments on mortgages usually involve uniform monthly payments that include both principal and interest.

Each successive monthly payment reduces the amount of principal outstanding. Therefore, the amount of interest owed decreases and the portion of the monthly payment applicable to principal increases. In the early years of a mortgage, the portion of the monthly payment applied against the principal is relatively small, but it grows with each payment.

Term Loan Payment Schedules

For term loans, payment of principal and interest is ordinarily scheduled on an annual, semiannual, or quarterly basis. For example, a 5-year, $50,000 term note bearing 10% interest might have the following payment schedule specified in the note agreement:

End of Year	Principal Repayment	Principal Outstanding	Interest Payment @ 10%
1	$10,000	$50,000	$5,000
2	10,000	40,000	4,000
3	10,000	30,000	3,000
4	10,000	20,000	2,000
5	10,000	10,000	1,000

Repayment Schedules

The dates on which principal and interest payments are due should be scheduled carefully. For example, a manufacturer with heavy sales just before Christmas and receivables collections through January would do best if repayments are scheduled in February. If a payment were due in October or November, when inventories were high and receivables were climbing, the payment could be crippling.

Collateral

Loans may be secured or unsecured. In a secured loan, the borrower pledges certain assets as collateral (security) to protect the lender in case of default on the loan or failure of the business. If the business defaults on the loan through failure to meet interest obligations or principal repayments, the noteholder (lender) assumes ownership of the collateral. If the business fails, the noteholder claims ownership of those specific assets pledged as collateral before the claims of other creditors are settled. In an unsecured loan the noteholder has no collateral.

Typical Collateral

In long-term borrowing, fixed assets such as real estate or equipment are usually pledged as collateral. For short-term borrowing, inventories or accounts receivable are the usual collateral.

Inventory Financing

Inventory financing is most commonly used in automobile and appliance retailing. As each unit is purchased by the retailer, the manufacturer is paid by the lender. The lender is repaid by the retailer when the unit is sold. Interest is determined separately for each unit, based on the actual amount originally paid by the lender and the period between the time the money is paid and the lender is reimbursed by the retailer.

Accounts Receivable Financing

Basically, accounts receivable financing falls into two categories as follows:

1. Assignments. The business pledges, or "assigns," its receivables as collateral for a loan.
2. Factoring. The borrower sells its accounts receivables to a lender ("factor").

Although these arrangements are not loans, in a pure sense, the effect is the same.

Receivable Assignments

When receivables are assigned, the amount of the loan varies according to the volume of receivables outstanding. Normally, the lender will advance some specified percentage of the outstanding accounts receivable up to a specific credit limit.

For example, if a company can borrow up to 80% of assigned receivables, with a maximum of $100,000 then its schedule would be:

Accounts Receivable	Amount Borrowed
$100,000	$ 80,000
125,000	100,000
150,000	100,000

On the first line, accounts receivable are $100,000 and the amount loaned is 80% of $100,000, or $80,000. The same formula can be used for the second line. However, on the third line, accounts receivable are $150,000. Eighty percent of this amount would be $120,000. This exceeds the established limit of $100,000. Therefore, borrowing is restricted to the $100,000 limit.

In many industries, accounts receivable financing is considered a sign of weakness. However, it is common in the garment industry and in personal finance companies.

Factoring Accounts Receivable

When accounts receivable are factored, they are sold to the factor and the borrower has no responsibility for collection. The borrower pays the factor a service charge based on the amount of each receivable sold. In addition, the borrower pays interest for the period between the sale of the receivable and the date the customer pays the factor.

Since the factor is responsible for collection, it will only purchase those receivables for which it has approved credit.

Unsecured Debt

The secured creditor's risk is reduced by the claim against specific assets of the business. In default or liquidation, the secured creditor can take possession of these assets to recover any unpaid amounts due from the business.

Holders of unsecured notes do not enjoy the same protection. If the company defaults on a payment, the unsecured creditor, under normal circumstances, can only negotiate the amount due, perhaps by seeking collateral, or force the company to liquidate. In liquidation, the holder of an unsecured note would normally have no rights that are superior to those of any other creditors.

Restriction on Business

When accepting an unsecured note, the lender will often place certain restrictions on the business. A typical restriction might be to prevent the company from incurring any debt with a prior claim on the assets of the business in the event of default or failure. For example, a term note agreement might prevent a company from financing its receivables or inventories since this would result in a prior claim against the assets of the business in liquidation.

Such restrictions may have no effect on the business' ability to operate. However, in other cases, such restrictions could be severe. For example, a business may have a chance to sell to a major new customer. The new customer may insist on 60-day credit terms which will require the business to seek additional external financing. Normally, this financing might be readily available on realistic terms from a factor. However, the restriction of the unsecured note could prevent the business from taking advantage of this significant opportunity for sales and profit improvement.

Personal Guarantees

The liability of a corporation's shareholders is generally limited to the assets of the business. Creditors have no normal claim against the personal assets of the stockholders if the business should fail. Therefore, many lenders, when issuing credit to small corporations, seek the added protection of a personal guarantee by the owner (or owners). This protects the creditors if the business fails, since they retain a claim against the personal assets of the owners to fulfill the debt obligation.

Interest Rates

The interest rates at which small businesses borrow are relatively high. Banks and other commercial lending institutions normally reserve their lowest available interest rate, the so-called prime rate, for those low-risk situations such as short-term loans for major corporations and public agencies where the chances of default are slim and the costs for collection, credit search, and other administrative tasks are minimal. Because of the higher risks involved in lending to small businesses, lenders often seek greater collateral while charging higher interest rates to offset their added costs of credit search and loan administration.

Equity Capital

Unlike debt capital, equity capital is permanently invested in the business. The business has no legal obligation for repayment of the amount invested or for payment of interest for the use of the funds.

Share of Ownership

The equity investor shares in the ownership of the business and is entitled to participate in any distribution of earnings through dividends, in the case of corporations, or drawings, in the case of partnerships.

The extent of the equity investor's participation in a corporation's distribution of earnings depends on the number of shares held. In a partnership, the equity investor's participation will depend on the ownership percentage specified in the partnership agreement.

Voting Rights

The equity investor's ownership interest also carries the right to participate in certain decisions affecting the business.

Legal Liability

The personal liability of equity investors for debts of the business depends on the legal form of the organization. Basically, the investor who acquires equity in a partnership could be personally liable for business debts if the business should fail. In a corporation, the liability of equity investors (shareholders) is limited to the amount of their investment.

In other words, if a partnership should fail, creditors could have a claim against the personal assets of the individual partners. If a corporation should fail, the only claims of creditors would be against any remaining assets of the corporation, not against any personal assets of the shareholders.

Equity Investor's Compensation

The purchaser of an equity interest in a business expects to be compensated for the investment in any of the three following ways:

1. Income from earnings distribution of the business, either as dividends paid to corporate shareholders or as drawings in a partnership.
2. Capital gain realized on the sale of the business.
3. Capital gain realized from selling his or her interest to other partner(s).

Capital Gains

Capital gain is the term used to describe any excess of the selling price of an investment over the initial purchase price. For example, if you purchased an equity interest in a business for $5000 and later sold it for $8000, you would realize a capital gain of $3000 ($8000 – $5000).

Tax Advantages

Long-term capital gains are those realized on investments held for a period longer than 6 months. These gains are, depending on the tax code of the day, subject to federal income tax at an effective rate less that of the investor's tax rate on ordinary income (salary). Therefore, income tax advantages can be a cause of the investor's desire to acquire equity interest.

Under current tax code provisions, capital gain is considered the same as ordinary income. Thus, there is no tax advantage, however, this can change easily.

Earnings Distribution

The equity investor in a partnership is entitled to a share of all drawings paid out to partners at a percentage established when the interest was purchased. For example, assume an investor acquired a 20% interest in a partnership. The distribution of earnings to all partners in a given year is $20,000. The holder of the 20% interest would receive $4,000 ($20,000 × 0.20).

The dividends received by the equity investor in a corporation depend on the number of shares held. For example, if a corporation voted a dividend of $1.50 per share in a given year, the owner of 1000 shares would receive a dividend of $1500 (1,000 × $1.50).

Sale (or Liquidation) of Business

If a business is sold or liquidated, the equity investor shares in the distribution of the proceeds. As with an earnings distribution, the share of the proceeds in a corporation sale depends on the number of shares held. In a partnership, each partner's share of the proceeds is based on the percentages specified in the partnership agreement.

If the proceeds received by the equity investor exceed the original purchase price, this excess is considered a capital gain and taxed accordingly at effective rates more favorable than those for ordinary income.

If the business were liquidated, the assets would be sold and the proceeds would first be used to discharge any outstanding obligations to creditors. The balance of the proceeds, after these obligations had been fulfilled, would be distributed to the equity investors in accordance with their shareholdings or percentages of interest.

Sale of Equity Interest

As a business prospers and grows, the value of an equity interest grows with it. Therefore, the equity investor may be able to sell his or her interest at a price higher than the initial acquisition cost.

For example, an equity investor in a corporation may have purchased his or her interest at $10.00 per share. As the business grows, the investor is able to sell the share at $15.00 per share, realizing a capital gain of $500 ($15.00 – $10.00) on each share sold.

Capital Gains Versus Dividends

In many cases, the equity investor in a small business is primarily interested in capital gains. Aside from the possible tax advantages described earlier, the equity investor usually realizes that the earnings of the small business are better retained in the business than distributed as dividends or drawings. Retention of earnings permits the business to grow so that the value of the equity interest increases. The investor can realize a return on the investment through a capital gain derived from selling his or her shares or on the sale of the business.

Public Stock Offerings

When businesses are first organized, equity capital is usually secured from a combination of sources such as the original owners' personal savings and through solicitations from friends, relatives, or other persons known to have financial capability for such investments.

As the need for equity capital becomes greater, say $50,000 to $200,000, it is customary to seek capital through the services of professional finders, who receive a fee for securing the necessary capital. These finders normally have access to wealthy individuals, capital management companies, estates, trusts, and others with sufficient capital to make such an investment.

When large amounts of capital are needed, shares are sold through public offerings. The public offering seeks to attract a large number of investors to purchase stock, in large or small amounts. A market is then created for the stock. Shares purchased by the public, as well as the shares held by the original owners, and any subsequent equity investors, can also be sold at the going market price. These transactions do not have a direct effect on the business' capital position, since it does not receive the proceeds from the sale.

The equity investor can realize a capital gain by selling shares at prices higher than the original purchase price.

Risks of Equity Investment

The equity investor assumes substantial risk. Unlike the secured creditor, the equity investor has no specific claim against any assets of the business. In liquidation, all claims of all creditors must be satisfied before any remaining assets become available for distribution to the owners. Even then, the equity investor's participation in the proceeds is restricted to a share that is proportionate to the number of shares held or the partnership interest.

Since the risks of equity investment are substantial, particularly in the case of small businesses, equity investors expect a considerably higher return than the lender. A lender might be willing to lend money to a business at an interest rate of 10% or 12% since it has certain legal protections in the event of default or liquidation. The investor of equity capital in the same business might seek a far higher return, perhaps 20%, 50%, or a higher percentage in order to compensate for the added risk of equity investment.

FINDING A BANKER/LENDER

Banks and other lenders provide the financing for your business, without them many entrepreneurs could not get their businesses going. Good bankers can provide your company with three essential services: they manage efficient staffs so that your transactions are handled smoothly; they write lines of credit and term loans when your business needs working capital and equipment; and they can provide sound advice on business trends and expansion.

Bankers and entrepreneurs share the desire to make a profit in a highly competitive marketplace. However, that is where their similarities end and their differences begin:

- The entrepreneur is a risk-taker who sees a need in the marketplace and sets out to fill it with his or her product or service. Preservation of depositors' funds is the banker's first concern.
- The entrepreneur is an optimist, looking for success and the riches it will bring. "What can go wrong?" is the banker's first and last question.
- The entrepreneur is an independent decision-maker. Seeking a group consensus is the banker's concern.

- The entrepreneur operates with minimal regulations. The banker operates in a highly regulated industry.
- The entrepreneur is a leader in charge of a business. The banker is employed by a bureaucratic organization.
- Entrepreneurs act; bankers advise.

Understanding a banker's viewpoint is just one aspect of building a relationship with your banker. You must also understand the bureaucracy in which the banker works. The title on your banker's business card indicates his or her position in the bank's hierarchy, and with that position goes a specific dollar value of lending authority—the loan amount he or she can approve without consulting anyone at a higher level.

Typically a loan officer at a bank branch might have a lending authority of $10,000; the assistant manager of the branch might be able to approve loans of up to $25,000; while the branch manager's lending authority might be twice that, or $50,000. At a small branch, loans above $50,000 would have to go to the bank's main office where several vice presidents would be authorized to approve loans of, say, $75,000 to $1 million, according to their seniority. Loans of up to $2 million would need the approval of the executive vice president, and anything above that would have to be presented to a committee.

However, your loan application for $80,000 to finance new equipment will not go directly to the vice president authorized to approve loans up to that amount. Instead, you must present your application to your own banker, who will review it and make an initial decision based on how well he or she knows you, values your business, believes your business can repay the loan, and trusts your intention to do so. Your banker will either turn down your application or forward it to the next banker for a similar review. This process of independent determination by each loan officer in a hierarchy will continue until the loan application reaches an officer with the appropriate degree of authority.

To find a banker, ask your business associates—your attorney, your accountant, and the members of your trade association and chamber of commerce—for a referral to a good banker. Ask about the specific services they have used, how your associates' loan requests were handled, and how long it took to get specific loan amounts approved. Of course, just because one person is turned down by a particular banker, you should not eliminate that banker from consideration. Get the opinions of several people, since so much depends on the quality of the individual loan application.

If you don't have any recommendations to go with, start by meeting the bankers at your local banks—both small community banks and branches of statewide banks—that advertise that they want to serve business clients. Such banks are likely to have the business services you may need—secured after-hours cash deposits, international letters of credit for exporting, Small Business Administration loan guarantees, and so forth, unlike banks that focus their services on car loans and home mortgages.

Take the time to meet with several bankers to discuss your business and the bank's services. Evaluate each banker according to whether he or she:

- Has a sincere interest in you and your business.
- Has common sense and can see the overall concept of your business.
- Communicates well without using financial jargon.
- Recognizes that financial reports are valuable, but that they do not reflect everything that affects a business's success.

- Points out the trends your financial statements demonstrate about your company and how they may effect you.
- Returns your phone calls promptly.
- Visits your business personally to better understand your operation and your financial needs.
- Looks for creative ways to finance your business needs, and still provides adequate protection for the bank, rather than simply rejecting your loan request.
- Gives direct answers to questions about loan amounts, terms, and the like.

Look for the banker who does more than simply say that the bank's policy is to make loans of $50,000 and up. While this "minimum" figure is, regrettably, being quoted universally, the truth is that bankers who are looking for "growth" business accounts can and will make loans from $3000 to $5000 and up when that is what a business needs to continue to grow.

You may find that a banker in a small community bank best suits your needs because these banks are finding their niche with the small-business community. It seems the bigger banks are going after the bigger customers.

Generally, however, look for a banker, or lender, you can relate to, who has common sense, who will get to know you and your business and work with you to meet your needs.

A decade ago, a small company would have all its funding needs met by its local bank. Now there are so many lenders that a small company can spin its wheels seeking a loan and come up empty. One company couldn't get a $1 million-plus line of credit at four banks. So the truck-line services firm was led to a bank that makes asset-based loans. The bank later even bought 17½% of the company.

THE ZETA SCORING SYSTEM

If you want to gauge your chances of receiving a favorable reception at a bank in advance of placing an application, the Zeta scoring system can help. It is a proprietary computer model which is used by banks and other institutions to measure a company's vulnerability to financial difficulties. Even if your bank does not use the Zeta system, your Zeta score should give you some indication of how you stand according to traditional financing benchmarks.

The heart of the system is a group of financial ratios, each weighted according to its importance as an indicator of financial health. As with all numerical ratings systems, the model has its flaws. Nevertheless, the Zeta scoring system has become one of the more common methods of evaluating a company's financial underpinnings.

All the information you will need to obtain your score comes from your most recent financial statements. The following are the key elements and a hypothetical illustration of how they were used by XYZ Co.:

Working Capital First, divide working capital (current assets minus current liabilities) by total assets. Then, to obtain proper weight, multiply by 1.2. XYZ's assets total $120 million, and working capital stands at $24 million. Thus,

$24 million/$120 million = 0.20.
$0.20 \times 1.2 = 0.24$

XYZ's Zeta factor for working capital is 0.24.

Cumulative Profitability Divide retained earnings by total assets. This measurement is weighted a little heavier, so multiply the answer by 1.4. Retained earnings of XYZ amount to $54.4 million. The Zeta calculation for cumulative profitability becomes

$$\$54.5/\$120 = 0.45 \times 1.4 = 0.63$$

Return on Assets This measure of profitability is given the heaviest weight of all. Use pretax (gross) profits, divided by net assets. Multiply your answer by 3.3. With pretax profits of $28.4 million, XYZ's Zeta calculation for return on assets becomes

$$28.4/120 - 0.24 \times 3.3 = 0.79$$

Return on Sales The total sales dollars as generated by each dollar of assets is measured here. Divide sales by total assets. The weighting is neutral. Multiply by 1.0. Sales of $145 million of XYZ are divided by $120 million, producting a figure of 1.2. When multiplied by 1.0, the Zeta for return on sales remains 1.2.

Leverage This final ratio is a bit different in that it attempts to measure the volatility of your company's capital structure. First, add the total book value of your common stock (if your stock is publicly traded, use the market value) and the liquidating value of your preferred stock, if any. (With sole proprietorships or partnerships use owner's equity or net worth.) Then, divide by your total debt. This final component is negatively weighted, so multiply by 0.6.

XYZ's net worth of $90.6 million is divided by a total debt of $33.0 million yielding a ratio of 2.7. This is multiplied by 0.6 yielding a leverage Zeta of 1.62.

To arrive at your company's Zeta score, merely add the scores for each of the individual components. If your final score is 3 or more, you are in good financial shape, according to the Zeta system. A score of less than 2.0 indicates that some problems exist, and anything less than 1.80 places a firm in the high risk category. A negative score is supposed to foreshadow imminent bankruptcy. In XYZ's case, the five components, added together, yield a total Zeta score of 4.48, or more than enough to justify a loan.

Working capital	0.24
Cumulative profitability	0.63
Return on assets	0.79
Return on sales	1.20
Leverage	1.62
	======
Total Zeta	4.48

Zeta scores are seldom crucial to a banker's evaluation of your company. There are many other factors of at least equal importance, such as are the books up-to-date and in good condition? What is the condition of accounts payable? Of notes payable? What are the salaries of the company officers? Are all taxes being paid currently? What is the order backlog? What is the number of employees? What is the insurance coverage? Nevertheless, if you find that your Zeta score is on the low side, you can prepare arguments to refute the implications. If you find that your Zeta score is satisfactory, you can prepare to cite it as evidence of financial health.

When writing a business plan for the lending community the Zeta score is not necessarily mentioned. However, be sure you emphasize the ability to pay back the loan amount in a specific time period and at the current interest rate. This pay-back plan must be backed up with studied facts that make the projections look reasonable and possible.

VENTURE CAPITAL

The success of American entrepreneurship, especially in the "hi-tech" industries, has been due largely to a formalized investment structure known as venture capital. Although venture capital is often thought of as seed financing for the startup of new businesses, many venture capital firms specialize in financing expanding companies, companies preparing for a public offering, and even financing for leveraged buyouts or plant revitalization. Thus, a businessperson can seek venture capital at any growth stage of his or her business.

How is the investment made? Venture capital is in the form of equity participation via stock ownership, warrants, options, or other convertible securities.

Venture Capitalists

Generally, when we think of venture capitalists today, we are thinking about the professional venture capital fund managers who make the decisions about which companies a fund should invest in. Typically these people are looking for young, high-growth "operating" companies—companies that are ongoing rather than "one-shot deals"—or real estate development. Of course, the original venture capitalists, wealthy individuals or groups who are not directly associated with a formal fund, are still the biggest part of the venture funding community.

Investors will often give more intense scrutiny when looking at a potential entrepreneur's character than lenders will. Part of this is based on the fact that they do fewer deals and have more time to do background checks. Some investors with entrepreneurial background develop a "sixth sense" about entrepreneurial character.

Venture capital funds are usually set up as limited partnerships, with the professional manager being the general or controlling partner. A venture capitalist—or the management company—usually puts up a very small amount of the fund's capital, often as little as 1%. The rest of the fund is financed by limited partners, who put their money at risk and can get great rewards, but have no say in the fund's day-to-day management.

Most of these limited partners are financial institutions, pension funds, and corporations, although a few wealthy individual investors may be involved. Minimum participation is usually at least a few $100,000, and can be over $1 million, which is why we see few individuals as limited partners in such funds.

Venture capitalists are mainly looking for two things:

1. Rates of return of 25 to 50% or more compounded annually.
2. Investments that will become liquid within a relatively short period of time.

The economics of a venture capital fund, which are somewhat peculiar, demand these two things. Venture funds have a defined lifetime, usually between 8 and 13 years. Within the first couple of years, the fund managers are sorting through hundreds of businesses looking for investment opportunities. Depending on the size of the fund and the number of managers in the venture management company, each venture fund may invest in as few as 10 or as many as 50 companies during its lifetime. Since venture capitalists like to keep a close watch on their investments, and have even been known to step in and run troubled companies on a day-to-day basis, they try not to spread their money or management too thin.

In the past decade or so, the pool of venture capital has grown dramatically on a national and international scale, so much that some people believe there is now more money chasing the same number of quality business opportunities and that future returns will consequently decline. This puts venture capitalists in a quandary—they must try to become fully invested while being careful to maintain an acceptable return.

Venture capital often is an all-or-nothing game. In order for a fund to have a 25%- or even a 50%-compounded return for its lifetime (not unheard of at all) it must find one or two big successes in order to meet its return objectives after absorbing the impact of companies that either go bust or fail to achieve anticipated profitability.

Some of the qualities venture capitalists associate with companies that have the potential to generate exciting returns are:

- The Quality of the Individual Entrepreneur. They are most often looking for maturity and experience in the area of other businesses started, along with a track record of success. What defines a quality entrepreneur for a venture capitalist is subjective and the evaluation is often intuitive.
- Functionally Balanced Teams. Increasingly, venture capitalists are looking for entrepreneurial teams that meet the human resource needs of a new company. With more dollars chasing deals today than 10 years ago, venture capital managers have less time to devote to helping structure management teams and overseeing day-to-day operations. Today the "one-man" show is less attractive than the professional and aggressive team.
- Proprietary Characteristics. Venture capitalists are always looking for businesses that have an edge on the competition that cannot easily be copied. Proprietary characteristics are often marked by patents, licenses, trademarks, or other legal protections.

In addition, many venture capital funds have special preferences for the type of business they will fund or the size of the investment they desire. Some provide "seed" money for rank start-ups, while others like to make larger second- or third-round financings to participate with businesses that already have a track record, albeit a short one. Such sources as *Who's Who in Venture Capital*, (Wiley-Interscience) and the *Venture Capital Journal*, (Venture Economics) can help entrepreneurs find these people.

Venture capitalists are often less sensitive to the issue of collateral than lenders. Typically, venture capitalists will ask for at least one seat on the board of directors.

A smooth progression of a financing from a venture capitalist might look something like the following timetable, which would hold for a company that not only has a fully written business plan, but has a well-defined strategy, intact management team, and some easy-to-reach references.

For 4 to 6 weeks, an entrepreneur is developing a business plan, and, simultaneously, identifying the appropriate funding sources. Then:

Weeks 1–2	Initial contact with potential financing sources by letter or phone.
Week 3	Mailing of executive summary or complete plan.
Weeks 4–6	Initial meeting with one or more potential financing sources.

Weeks 7–17	Follow-up with one or more financing sources: meetings, phone calls, additional information, or addenda to business plan.
Week 18	Offer from a financing source received.
Weeks 19–26	Negotiation of the deal terms, drawing up of documents.
Week 26	Closing.

The Venture Capital Process

Venture capital organizations raise funds of investment money periodically, symbolically put it in the bank, although in some cases the investors keep it and the fund managers draw from it periodically. Then the core of their activity is to try to find new start-up companies, at various stages of development. If they can't find them, they start them themselves, which they call incubating it.

Venture capitalists work with those companies very closely over a period of from 2 to 10 years, and in the best of cases, take them public or secondarily, merge them—have them be acquired by another company. Or, if not, they disappear into the ozone, and the venture capitalist goes on. The return on investment is over the entire pool of money, rather than on any individual company.

What does the business plan have to do to be attractive to the venture capitalist? What are the performance benchmarks that venture capitalists are looking for? First, they look for a distinct product or service, a competitive product, a technical innovation. In the old phrase, a better mousetrap. Then they look to sell that into a large or rapidly growing market. Third, they look for good management. These are rarely, if ever, present in a given situation. The venture capitalist has to either strengthen the management team, or the market's a big question, or it is unclear that the innovation will work. However, it is how the venture capitalists assess their presence or absence; under some circumstances the presence of extraordinary innovation can compensate for an immature market, a market that is going to be slow to grow, or a management team that is inexperienced.

Venture capitalists look for an investment opportunity, then structure the way things are going the work so the biggest risk happens as early as possible. This can mean opting for technical risk over market risk. That is, to know as early as possible if this company can make a quality product, that will sell. The reason for this is that a technical concept can usually be proven quicker than a market can be proven. If all these other things are right a return on investment will occur.

The investment parameters are reasonably narrow. Things have changed in the last 10 years, a normal first round is now $3 million plus or minus a half-million. If this is the initial or start-up amount involving three people and their idea, the venture capitalist will probably not ask for less than 50% of the company or more than 65%. If the deal is really attractive, the venture capitalist's percentage will be on the lower end of the range.

In the second round, most typically the product will have been developed? the principle will have been proven or there is something that either is thought to work, or even better, has been in the hands of a customer who has been tinkering with it and can give the second-round investor some comfort.

If the first price was $1 a share, the second rounds are typically anywhere from $1.50 to $4—in fairly heady times, a triple was the goal, but between two and three times is fairly standard.

The third round is where the entrepreneur has what might be called expansion capital. The entrepreneur has already got some manufacturing and marketing, but now he or she is really rolling out, and a public offering can be seen out there in the distance somewhere.

A form of help provided by the venture capital firms is called "zaibatsu." This is a network of relationships between companies that the venture capital firm is invested in. This network provides well beyond normal vendor-supplier relationships, these companies help each other develop.

This process is also followed in attracting talent from established companies. The venture capital firm uses its resources to make a manager a "soft landing" commitment, for example, "If this doesn't work out, come in, work in our offices, work on another business plan. Work there until you have found another deal."

Ultimately the talent that correlates most highly with success is a market-oriented chief executive officer (CEO), because once you can make the product, the chances are overwhelming that you can manufacture it, and then the battle is won or lost in the marketplace. Marketing orientation on the part of the CEO probably parlays more strongly with success than any other thing.

In the end, particularly when products get to be commodities, it is how well the entrepreneur understands his or her customers needs. And, how well the customer's requirements are satisfied—This becomes an almost personal relationship that is established between vendors and customers.

The American market environment provides an entrepreneurial atmosphere that forgives mistakes? that is, if the customers really want a product, then they just forgive you if you have a product that initially doesn't perform perfectly.

In America, unfortunately, our methods of high tehnology product development are not like the Japanese. The Japanese design products for reliability and low-cost manufacture, and test extensively, and by the time they ship it it works. The more common pattern in the United States is that you get sort of a breadboarded pre-prototype pre-production, pre-everything, and you just kind of ship it out there, and then you move half your engineering resources to the customer's facility, and then together with the customer's staff, you tweak it down the assembly line.

In a better world, products would be really ready before they hit a customer, but there is such enormous competition to get to the customer fast, in these enormously short product life-cycle products. Products are obsolete almost before they ship. Or you're obsoleting your own product—once your product is in beta site, you ought to be obsoleting it in the lab.

Entrepreneurs, today and over the last 5 years, have become increasingly sophisticated about the sources of money they go to. Most knowledgeable entrepreneurs have a hit list of half a dozen venture capitalists that they are going to go to and that they think will improve their chances of success.

The second way the venture capital competition shows itself is not so much in the pricing but in the proliferation of new competitive start-ups. It is the normal policy of each venture capital firm not to fund direct competitors. Venture capital firms specialize in certain types of companies.

The best way to shop for venture capital is to call the National Venture Capital Association in Washington DC and ask for their directory. However, if you are located in San Francisco, Boston, or any large city go to a company that was started with venture capital and ask the CEO "What do I do?" Most will help with advice. The second thing to do is get incorporated—there is probably less than half a dozen law firms that totally dominate that sort of business. A bad venture capitalist firm commits primarily sins of omission. That is, not help the company to do things right, and maybe give them bad advice. There is a whole bell curve in the abilities of firms, and it is important to not only pick the right firm, but to pick the right partner within the firm. You might ask, "Who will be following this?" Or "Who'll be on the board seat?" and then the firm may ask who you want. This is somebody you're going to spend an excruciating amount of time with.

If you're shopping for venture capital and have a choice of several firms, go for the firm with the track record of successes and a full range of services.

What types of businesses are eligible for venture capital? High-technology, medical, and communications projects continue to top the list of venture capital recipients. However, many venture capital firms consider a wide variety of projects, from real estate to service industries. But, as economic conditions and atmospheres change, the investment activities of the venture capital funds change.

THE VENTURE CAPITALIST'S SHARE

A venture capitalist wants just enough control of your company to justify the risk of investment. Therefore, the more secure you can make an investor feel about your project, the more control of your company you can retain. There are several methods used by the venture capital community to determine (evaluate) the risk position of an opportunity. Two are: The Rich-Gumpert Risk/Return Evaluation (see Table 2.1) and the Present Value/Future Value Evaluation (see Table 2.2).

The Venture Capitalist's Expected Return

What return on investment (ROI) does a venture capitalist expect to make on his or her investment? Your business plan will have to demonstrate to the venture capitalist how 25 to 50% compounded annually over a 3- to 5- to 10-year period can be earned. This criterion alone will generally determine the amount of ownership surrendered. Table 2.2 is a typical evaluation formula used by the venture capitalists in determining the necessary ROI and percent of ownership.

The Chances for Start-Up Venture Capitalist Funding

Since the 1987 stock market crash venture capitalists have exercised an air of caution in their investment strategies. There remains much uncertainty and caution in the investment community. Many of the trade and debt problems that worried the financial markets preceding that crash are still with us. Despite these conditions, it is a good time for starting a new technology-based business.

With a significant increase in the pool of investable funds ($4.2 billion in 1987) venture capital managers have been required to focus on investment opportunities where large amounts of money can be put to work. However, start-up opportunities, by comparison, require smaller dollar investments and are time intensive. For this reason the start-up investment opportunity can easily slip to the bottom of the pile. Thus start-up entrepreneurs need to develop a strategy.

Table 2.1. Rich-Gumpert Risk/Return Evaluation Chart

Note: The quality of the product/service and the management team will increase or decrease the desirability of the investment.

Product/Service Status				
		Most Desirable →		
Level 4: Product/service fully developed. Many satisfied users. Market established.	4/1	4/2	4/3	4/4
Level 3: Product/service fully developed. Few (or no) users as yet. Market assumed.	3/1	3/2	3/3	3/4
Level 2: Product/service pilot operable. Not yet developed for production. Market assumed.	2/1	2/2	2/3	2/4
Level 1: A product or service idea, but not yet operable. Market assumed.	1/1	1/2	1/3	1/4
Management status	Level 1: A single, would be founder-entrepreneur.	Level 2: Two founders. Additional slots, personnel not identified.	Level 3: Partly staffed management team. Absent members identified, to join when firm is funded.	Level 4: Fully staffed, experienced management team.

Table 2.2. Present Value/Future Value Evaluation Example

Expected return on investment is 35% per year without inflation over 5 years.

Present value of earnings is $4.5 million.

Future value of earnings is $15 million in 5 years.

Equity share to the venture capitalist(s) is calculated: 4.5/15 = 30%

Typical maximum investment is 10 times the first years expected gross earnings.

The following are some of the basic rules to follow—and what to avoid—when going out to look for capital. First, a list of the don'ts.

- Don't prepare an extensively printed, fancily bound business plan full of glossy photographs and rosy projections. Such documents are useful for training new MBA graduates but quickly find their way to the circular file in venture offices.
- Don't allow a third party to represent you or to develop your business model. The venture investor wants to understand how *you* think and wants everyone involved in developing the business concept to be committed to its successful execution. A third party who is not committing his or her future to the business has no part to play in the process. Third-party involvement is frequently a reason for a project to lose the consideration it may deserve. However, the use of a management consultant familiar with writing venture capitalist proposals can be used with success. However, the plan must be yours and your management teams.
- Don't be insecure about your own position in the proposed new business. The best way not to get the funding for your project is to request guarantees in the event of failure.

Now that we have the don'ts in mind, some of the positive steps you can take to get the time, attention, and funding your project needs will be examined.

- Do develop a strategy for approaching the venture partners that you think can provide the greatest help in making your project successful. In venture capital, as in other fields, there are leaders and followers. Focus your efforts on potential venture partners who have a reputation for being decisive and who will commit time to your project.
- Do identify a complete management team that includes all the skills necessary to develop successful products and run a business. Every member of the management team should have a demonstrable history of success.
- Do think through your business concept enough so that you are able to articulate it concisely. Find and develop quantitative data that defines your market niche. Clearly define the advantage your team will have over the competition to develop and defend that niche.
- Do think through every risk in your proposed business and identify strategies that minimize those risks and maximize your probability of success. Be prepared

to discuss the risks and the potential competition in addition to stressing your chances for success.

- Do sell yourself and your team. With the right team you can generate interest on the part of the venture investor with just a short discussion. The venture partner will want to interact with you to fully develop your business concept and establish an operating plan for your business. This plan will not be a sales document created for the purpose of raising funds. It will be the operating plan for the crucial first few years of your business. It will be the plan to which you and your management team will sign up to and the one by which you will be judged.

In general, venture capitalists look for business ventures in which to invest their client's funds. Points of interest regarding their general feeling and position are:

- Anybody with a good idea and a good team can get funded.
- Venture funds generally raise funds and then commit them over 4 years. Of the $4.2 billion raised in 1987 approximately 25% was committed by the end of 1988.
- Venture capitalists are looking for a minimum of $50 million in sales in 5 years.
- You seldom find an entrepreneur with a team and a plan all ready to go. The skill set must be filled out. Quite often, a good technology team will come along but it will be missing marketing expertise or general business management skills.

To find a venture capitalist firm, the entrepreneur should look for a one with a good track record. Look at the public companies that the venture capitalist has funded that you want your company to be like and get their prospectuses. See who were the lead investors. Ask what other companies the venture capitalists have taken through the stages to the company's first public offering. Check them out with the management of those companies.

Financing Angels

Another source of business finance is a group of informal investors known as financial "angels." These people normally do not have as much as the venture capital funds but still like the risk of venture-type investments.

These people go through a review process, but it is often a limited review, and they usually make decisions much faster than professional venture capitalists—often in 2 or 3 months or less. The entrepreneur does not necessarily have to show angels the opportunity for the company to be a raging success, but he or she must show the investor that the money will return more than the investor could get with other less risky types of investments. This often means showing the possibility of the business giving at least a 20% or more compounded annual ROI.

Another nice thing about working with these angels is that the deal can be structured any way the entrepreneur, the investor, and their respective lawyers wish to structure it. There can be a combination of debt and equity in such deals.

Informal investors can be found in a number of ways. Many of them frequent venture capital clubs, often breakfast clubs that meet in major cities. Another good way to find them is through professionals—lawyers, accountants, consultants, and financial planners.

Alternative Early-Stage Funding

As the normal venture capital industry becomes increasingly competitive and selective about what meets its investment criteria, it is becoming harder for niche-oriented start-ups or entrepreneurs whose ideas are at relatively early stages to obtain funding.

One innovative response to this problem is a growing number of informal investment networks nationwide. Such networks usually consist of smaller investors and use a variety of approaches for matching investors with entrepreneurs.

Perhaps the longest established and best known of these networks is the Venture Capital Network (VCN), founded in 1984 by William E. Wetzel of the University of New Hampshire. It is a loose affiliation of smaller investors who directly invest in the enterprise themselves, and operates in a manner very similar to a computer dating service. Investors and entrepreneurs pay a registration fee, after which investors submit profiles describing their investment criteria and entrepreneurs submit profiles detailing their business plans and financial projections. Anonymity is preserved until matches are made.

Essentially, these smaller investors invest in a deal that interests them. The network has some visibility, so people know to go to it to raise money. They also know to go to it to get some kind of association where they can get to see a deal flow without being a limited partner in a venture capital network, and they will not be bothered by "crazy" people looking to finance perpetual motion machines.

Technology Strategy Incorporated of Cambridge, Massachusetts is attempting setting up such a network, still in the early planning stages at this writing, to link investors and entrepreneurs in California and Massachusetts. While the particular approach a network takes may vary from the anonymous dating service model to one involving much more personal screening and hands-on involvements, there are, he said, some important considerations to keep in mind in setting up such an organization. Most significantly, strict federal and state laws restrict who can act as investment advisors, and such networks must avoid giving recommendations or advice as to the merits of a particular investment. (VCN, for instance, terminates its role once an entrepreneur and investor meet, regardless of the ultimate outcome.)

For the small or early-stage company, this approach can offer more flexibility and timely support than the conventional venture capital option. These organizations are really not trying to compete with venture capitalists. Investments that are made by individual investors and networks come at the prototypical stage, which is usually a little earlier than when most formal venture capitalists want to get involved.

Once the project gets past the early initial stage, it may be a good candidate for venture capital, and then again it may not. The standards that the venture capitalists have to use are that they are looking to create a company of considerable size—the classic rule of thumb for the venture capitalist's interest is, "Is your idea, market, and so forth sufficient to support a $50 million a year company?"

Also the people who tend to invest in these things are not under the same gun of having to produce an internal rate of return (IRR) in excess of 25%, so they can basically invest the same amount of money, but, for instance, take a longer time.

Resources

Venture Capital Network, Inc.
P.O. Box 882
Durham, NH 03824-0882
(603)743-3993

Michael Levy
Technology Strategy Incorporated
6 Bigelow Street
Cambridge, MA 02139
(617)547-1200

FINANCING ALTERNATIVES

In reality, any person or institution with a dollar to invest or lend is a potential source of financing. The entrepreneur must be a good detective, to identify the appropriate financing source for a potential business.

Each potential financing source has an agenda for success and a criteria for investing. Capital markets are imperfect, and there is no guarantee that an appropriate deal and financing source can be matched. It takes determination, persistence, and a strategy planned in advance by the entrepreneur to find the right source. A discussion of a few of the less well-known sources of financing follows.

Corporate venture capitalists is a relatively new concept where a number of large companies have set up their own venture capital funds. General Electric's Gevenco is a notable example. Often, these funds are looking to help finance companies that can contribute technology to their company, or are in some other way compatible. Sometimes the corporate venture company is even looking for entrepreneurs to spawn companies the larger company will eventually acquire. Agreements with these companies are sometimes called "strategic alliances."

The Small Business Investment Corporation (SBIC) and Minority Enterprise Small Business Investment Corporation (MESBIC) are companies that have investment pools of private money that are leveraged with federal government funds via the Small Business Administration. These companies make equity investments in small businesses and are often less demanding in their expectations of returns than are traditional venture funds.

Economic development groups, sometimes called "economic development corporations" or "business development corporations," administered on a federal, state, or local level, may provide either favorably structured debt or equity. These organizations try to make responsible investment and lending decisions, but because they lack the profit motive they are more benevolent in structuring a deal than other funding sources.

There are also loans available through the federal Economic Development Agency (EDA) and the Urban Development Action Grant (UDAG) program, although some of these programs have been terminated beginning with the fiscal 1987 budget.

Some private foundations and universities put a small percentage of their endowment portfolios into small, risky ventures. In addition, some foundations even make cash grants for development projects, if the venture dovetails with their own goals.

There are a few mutual funds that invest in start-up and small, growth-oriented companies. In effect, these are, venture capital funds for small investors who want a little of their money invested in high-risk ventures.

An extreme example of benevolence is seen in the Small Business Innovation Research program. Under this federal program, grants are awarded on a competitive basis. There is no obligation to pay the grants back. They are awarded based on the appeal of the company's technology. First-round grants of up tp $50,000 and second-round grants of up to $500,000 are awarded by federally sponsored programs. A good source of information on this program is *Entrepreneur's Guide to Small Business Innovation Research Programs: Research and Development funding through the Federal Government* by Patrick D. O'Hara, (Probus, 1990).

All these financial sources, of course, require a written plan, a business plan, before they will consider discussing the investment possibility. The plan's detail requirements vary with each resource type but the general information desired is the same.

Bootstrap Financings

The founders, friends, and business associates may provide financing to a company in the form of equity investments, loans, or by way of guarantees of institutional loans made directly to the company.

Sources of Funds

Savings, mortgages, proceeds, and cash reserves of whole life insurance policies, as well as guarantees, security, business plans or strategy statements, and commitment letters from potential customers or later round investors may be helpful or required in connection with bank loans.

Circumstances

Bootstrap financing is often required in a company's early development phases. Most founders do not have the resources to finance a manufacturing company beyond the development or start-up phase. However, founders may be able to finance some software, service, or other noncapital intensive companies until they achieve profitability.

Benefits

By bootstrapping, a founder may operate the company free of unwarranted involvement of professional investors and restrictions imposed by institutional lenders. Bootstrapping may also permit the founder to retain more equity.

Drawbacks and Risks

The following should be considered when bootstrap financing is a possibility

- Personal financial needs and relationships.

  The amount of bootstrap financing provided to the company by the founders, friends, and business associates should be consistent with the competing financial needs of the individuals, such as provision for adequate family living expenses, emergencies, and anticipated educational expenses of children. The impact of using this alternative on the founder's personal relationships with his or her family, friends, and business associates should be given careful consideration.
- Potential for retarded growth, lower valuation, and absence of professional assistance.

  A financing program that only involves bootstrapping may retard the development and rate of growth that the company could otherwise achieve if additional third-party financing were obtained at timely points in the company's life cycle.

Accordingly, it may adversely affect the valuation that the founder's interest in the company might otherwise achieve, even after dilution from third-party investments. It may deprive the company of valuable assistance that might otherwise be provided by professional investors.

Equity Investments and Venture Capital Financing

- Here the capital seeker must focus on the investors investment objectives, criteria, and policies.

  Venture capital firms and other professional investors seek to realize above average returns on their investments. Most expect to realize those returns through a public offering or acquisition within 3 to 7 years after making the investment. Criteria and policies for selecting from among investment opportunities vary among different firms. Some focus on start-ups and first round investments while avoiding later round investments. Others may follow contrary policies. Some expect or insist on active involvement in the company while others may prefer to be passive investors. Some always co-invest with other firms and individuals while others may prefer to be the sole investor. Many focus on particular geographic locations, industries, and products to the exclusion of others. Some disavow any particular criteria or policies. Exhibit 1, on page 45, is an example of one venture capital firm's statement of its investment objectives, criteria, and policies.

- Investor profile.

  Most reputable venture capital firms will have many of the attributes of "blue ribbon investors" described earlier. The company may also wish to obtain additional information about the investor from industry contacts and other companies in which the investor has invested.

- Complexity of structure.

  As described in more detail in the next section, most venture investments are structured as purchases of convertible preferred stock, with associated grants or contractual rights, such as registration rights. Most negotiation of the deal occur at the term sheet stage (Exhibit 2, page 49). Although the operative documentation can appear voluminous, most of it will follow established patterns and does not normally involve extensive negotiation between legal counsel for the parties. The structure is usually easy to administer and accommodates future rounds of financing without extraordinary adjustments or expense.

- Costs.

  Legal and other fees associated with venture investments are normally less than those associated with research and development (R&D) partnership financings. In addition, unlike many R&D partnership transactions, substantial costs are not usually incurred until an agreement in principle (as set forth in a term sheet) has been reached with the investors.

- Financial statement, accounting, tax, and cash flow impact.

  Unusual impact on the company. Investment is secured at early (most risky) stage of company's existence. Therefore its payback will be high in relation to company assets which may make the sale of the company a necessity (probably planned before hand).

- Securities.
  Common stock, convertible preferred stock or convertible debt are the most common forms of securities sold in a venture capital financing. Some venture capital firms also invest in R&D partnerships. The most frequently used security in a venture financing is convertible preferred stock. The terms under which the convertible preferred stock is normally issued allow the company to justify a relatively lower valuation of the underlying common stock. The maintenance of a low valuation of the common stock enhances its use in employee incentive programs, such as incentive stock option plans.

Convertible Preferred Stock, Common Detractants

Convertible preferred stock has the following potentially unattractive features a viewed by either the investor or the entrepreneur.

- Convertible into common stock.
  Stock is convertible at agreed on ratios, subject to adjustment for stock splits, reverse stock splits, stock dividends, and so on.
- Voting power.
  Voting power equal to the voting power of the number of shares of common stock into which it can be converted is normally granted holders of preferred stock.
- Liquidation preference.
  Upon liquidation of the company, the holders of preferred stock are normally entitled to all proceeds of liquidation up to the amount of the original sales price of the preferred stock. Thereafter, the proceeds of liquidation are shared among holders of common and preferred stock on an agreed on basis.
- No mandatory sinking fund payments or dividend payments.
  These are generally considered to be an unnecessary drain on company resources and inconsistent with objectives of the investors and the company.
- Permissive, but not mandatory, redemption.

Other Financing Terms and Issues

Venture capitalists or other equity investors may, by terms of their investment, limit the company's future financial alternatives and the founders ownership control in the following manner.

- Valuation of the company, equity dilution resulting from the transaction, and dollar amount of investment.
- Control and board representation.
- Price-based antidilution protection.
  Occasionally investors will seek to increase the amount of equity they receive for their investment if the valuation of the company fails to achieve specified levels in subsequent rounds of financing. The adjustment is most frequently triggered by a later valuation at less than 100% of the earlier valuation, although

some adjustments are triggered at higher levels such as 120% or the earlier valuation. The less aggressive formulas call for a weighted average adjustment that takes into consideration both the valuation and amount of equity dilution involved. The most onerous formulas call for a "ratcheted" adjustment that takes into consideration valuation only. Price-based antidilution protection that extends to more than one subsequent round of financing may create undesirable equity dilution uncertainties for later investors, and therefore hinder subsequent financings. Many venture firms now seek varieties of weighted average protection. Some venture firms never seek any type of price-based antidilution protection and will not invest in companies where prior investors retain such protection on an ongoing basis.

- Registration rights.

  Registration rights are customarily granted subject to certain limitations on the ability and extent to which such rights may be exercised.

  Demand rights. The investor normally obtains the right to cause the company to make one or more public offerings of the investors' shares of the company's stock.

  Piggyback rights. The investor normally obtains the right to participate in public offerings of the company's stock initiated by the company or others.

- Pre-emptive rights.

  The investor normally obtains the right to purchase a pro rata portion of any securities to be sold in any subsequent offerings.

- Covenants and restrictions.

  Among other things, the investors may impose contractual restrictions on the salaries and outside business activities of the management and founders. Management and founders are also customarily required to enter into agreements whereby a portion of their stock is subject to repurchase if they terminate their employment with the company within a specified period of time (normally 2 to 5 years). The amount of stock subject to repurchase varies depending on duration of employment prior to termination.

- Representations and warranties.

  The company and its founders normally make certain representations and warranties to the investors in connection with the transaction. Areas covered include: the company's valid existence, due organization, good standing, and power and authority to enter into the financing transaction; the existence or nonexistence of litigation; disclosure of material agreements (and any defaults thereunder); compliance or the lack thereof with all applicable laws and ordinances; adequate trade secret, proprietary, and patent rights necessary for the operation of the company (and noninfringement of the rights of others); title to properties; accuracy of financial statements; and good faith preparation of the business plan.

- Term sheet.

  A term sheet setting forth the principal terms of the transaction is normally prepared prior to drafting the operative agreements. An example of a hypothetical term sheet is set forth in Exhibit 2.

Debt Financing

Most institutional debt financing will not be available for a company prior to its emerging growth phase. The feasibility of debt financing will depend on the company's historical and projected short- and long-term financial results, conditions, and other commitments. The following are terms and features of debt financing.

- Complexity of structure.
  Debt financing, like venture capital financing, can involve voluminous documentation. Much of the documentation constitutes nonnegotiable boilerplate from the lender's standpoint. However, loan conditions can be complex and normally are the subject of negotiation. The structure does not normally have any impact on subsequent nondebt financing, but may involve restrictions on all varieties of future debt financing until the debt incurred in the financing is paid down.
- Cost.
  Costs can vary depending on the size and complexity of the transaction and type and extent of the underlying security.
- Financial statement, accounting, tax, and cash flow impact.
  Normal adverse impact on balance sheet and cash flow for debt service.
- Type and features.
  1. Small lines of credit.
  2. Commitment (or facility) involves fee on unborrowed portion prior to draw down.
  3. Term loan usually involves fixed maturity date and fixed payment dates for principal and interest.
  4. Revolving loan funds are usually advanced to the borrower as needed, then repaid and reborrowed. It involves grid notes or short-term notes that are rolled over periodically. Associated with short-term or seasonal needs, revolving loans can be structured to convert to a term loan.
  5. Unsecured loan has documentation limited to loan agreement, note, borrowing resolutions, and legal opinion. Probably not available to an emerging technology company because sound financial condition usually involving an earnings history and forecast.
  6. Secured loan can be secured by equipment and other tangible and intangible personal property, real property, leases, and secured or unsecured guarantees or founders and investors.
- Terms.
  1. Principal amount or commitment.
  2 Interest rate has multiple formulas including fixed, floating prime, and base rate related. The uncertainty associated with floating interest rates can prove troublesome for financial planning.
  3. Maturity date or pay down schedule.
  4. Commitment fee.

5. Prepayments may be mandatory or permissible and may involve minimums and fees.
6. Representations and warranties are similar to those in venture financings, although more extensive as to financial condition.
7. Conditions to advances provide compliance with other covenants, continuing accuracy or representations and warranties, and special hurdles may also be involved.
8. Affirmative and negative covenants often relate to financial conditions, ratios, and restrictions on additional borrowings. Designed to give the lender a basis to accelerate before maturity.
9. Default provisions and remedy provides acceleration of outstanding principal and interest and termination of lending commitment. It allows for foreclosure on security and call on guarantees.

Joint Ventures and Contractual Collaborations

Joint ventures and contractual collaborations may obviate the need for other sources of financing. They may be appropriate where the parties have a reasonable potential to achieve an objective through shared resources at a lower cost, and perhaps at lower risk, than either party would incur pursuing objectives independently. In some cases, cost savings may not justify the opportunity loss of increased valuation that might result from independent achievement of objectives.

Beyond the foregoing observations, it is difficult to generalize about the impact of such relationships, since each tends to be unique. In each case, the parties to the transaction need to clarify and carefully evaluate their own, and the other party's, objectives, the appropriateness of the structure, the relative contributions of each party, the likelihood for success, and all other terms and impacts of the relationship. Before commencing the relationship, the parties should satisfy themselves that the relationship is indeed preferable to financing and pursuing their objectives independently.

The following should be reviewed and answered when joint ventures and contractual collaborations are being considered.

- Objectives.

  What does each party expect to achieve from the relationship and how?

  1. Product objectives.
  2. Technology objectives.
  3. Tax objectives.
  4. Accounting objectives.
  5. Other objectives (Access to distribution channels, create assured sources of supply, create customer relationship, etc.).
- Antitrust issues.
- Resources.

  To what extent will each party supply resources and on what basis?

  1. Tangible resources to be loaned or contributed to the venture.

2. Funding (How much required from each party? Is third-party financing contemplated and on what basis?)
3. Equipment.
4. Technology.
5. Management and personnel.
6. Space.
7. Overlap or duplication.

- Location.
  Where will the venture be physically located?
- Corporate culture fit.
  Any significant issues—mutual trust, communication, and compatible management and operating style—that would imperil successful collaboration?
- Form of relationship.
  1. General partnership may be the most flexible form and best suited to parties' objectives.
  2. Limited partnership.
  3. Contractual collaboration.
  4. Corporation not as flexible as a general partnership but partners may be more familiar with the corporate form and for that reason deem it more desirable.
- Control.
  How will voting and operational control be allocated? Mechanism for day-to-day decision making. Use of management committee. Does one party have practical management, product, technology, and so on control and does that create any potential problems? Protection for minority.
- Withdrawal.
- Termination and liquidation.
  On what events? How will proceeds and rights be distributed?
- Buy-sell.
- Liquidity vehicle.

Forms of Financing

Among the most common forms of financing, of which there are many variants in particular categories, for prepublic companies are:

- Private placements of corporate securities:
  1. Common stock.
  2. Convertible preferred stock.
  3. Convertible notes and debentures.
- Royalty, equity, and joint venture R&D partnerships. (R&D partnerships has lost its appeal due to recent changes in the tax law.)

- Debt:
    1. Small lines of credit.
    2. Notes and debentures.
    3. Term debt.
    4. Revolving debt.
- Factoring and commercial finance, including accounts receivable financing and inventory financing.
- Equipment lease financing, including leveraged leases.
- Special forms of financing, such as:
    1. Joint ventures and contractual collaborations (strategic alliances).
    2. Special licensing, distributing, and manufacturing arrangements.
    3. Customer and supplier advances.
    4. Warrants and options for the purchase of equity.
       (These are usually granted to lessors, service entities, lenders, customers, suppliers, and others doing business with the company to secure other favorable terms or to reduce costs or fees).
- Government programs:
    1. Small Business Administration loans and loan guarantees.
    2. Industrial development bond financing.
    3. Other loan and grant programs.

Sources of Financing

Among the common sources of financing, and the forms of financing commonly associated with each, are:

- Founders, management, and business associates.
  All forms of corporate securities, notes, and R&D partnership interests.
- Individual private investors.
  All forms of corporate securities, debts, and R&D partnership interests.
- Venture capital firms.
  All forms of corporate securities, but most often convertible preferred stock; certain firms also invest in R&D partnerships.
- Venture capital and investment arms of investment banks, industrial companies, and banks.
  All forms of corporate securities; certain firms also invest in R&D partnerships.
- Banks and lending institutions.
  Secured or guaranteed lines of credit, notes, term debt, occasionally with warrants.
- Nonbank finance companies.
  Accounts receivable financing and inventory financing, occasionally with warrants.
- Equipment leasing companies.
  Lease financing, occasionally with warrants.

- Industry business entities.
  All forms of corporate securities and special forms of financing.
- Financial deal packagers, brokers, and finders.
  Individuals and entities engaged in raising funds on behalf of the company from individuals and institutional sources for specific private placements of equity, convertible debt, and R&D partnership interests.
- Government.
  Loans or loan guarantees such as those made through the Small Business Administration, industrial development bond financing, and other financing programs.

Avoiding Pitfalls

Without the assistance of independent professional advice, a company will frequently spend considerable time, effort, and expense unsuccessfully pursuing sources and forms of financing inappropriate to the company's circumstances and objectives. Often a company may obtain financing under circumstances and terms not in keeping with its long-term objectives and best interests. Such financings may eliminate many future financing alternatives that might have otherwise been available. For example, venture capital firms and other professional investors may be unwilling to invest in an otherwise attractive company if:

- The company has a poorly conceived or executed capital structure. Some particular problems include:
  1. Prior equity financings with onerous price-based antidilutions provisions.
  2. Prior insurances of equity or convertible debt, or grants or warrants and options, or overly generous terms.
  3. A large group of unsophisticated outside individual investors.
  4. Prior financings that may involve securities law compliance problems.
- The company was originally organized under certain types of R&D structures or has entered into certain types of joint ventures or other special forms of financing that:
  1. Create uncertainties as to equity dilution.
  2. Involve the transfer of, or ownership uncertainties concerning, proprietary rights necessary for the company's business.
  3. Involve material cash flow drains or other drains on the company's resources or personnel.
- The company has allied itself with certain sources of financing or industrial partners that by disposition, reputation or industry position may limit or adversely affect acquisition alternatives or the prospects of a public offering.

Although in some cases, it may be possible to restructure relationships and cure defects arising in connection with prior financings, the process can often be time consuming and expensive. Through early and thoughtful long-term planning in conjunction with professional assistance, the company can avoid many of these pitfalls.

Professional Advice

In evaluating and selecting from various financing alternatives, the company should solicit the independent advice and assistance of accountants, and attorneys, as well as experienced business colleagues with broad financing experience and particular expertise in the desired area of financing. An experienced professional with a thorough understanding of, and developed contacts in, the financial community should be of particular value. Such a professional should be able to:

- Advise and assist the company in the formulation of reasonable short- and long-term strategies and objectives
- Save the company considerable time, effort, and expense in the financing process by introducing it to appropriate interested sources of financing.
- Provide the company with a realistic transactional perspective, including insight into the legitimate expectations of the other parties to the transactions and the customary negotiable and nonnegotiable terms.
- Work effectively with the parties to negotiate and document a reasonable deal without undue delay, friction, or expense.

Relying solely on other parties to the financing transaction, in the absence of other professional advice, may not produce optimal results. In particular, deal packagers, brokers, and finders may have biases toward particular types of transactions and sources of financing and may lack familiarity with other available alternatives. Acting alone, they may lack the expertise and familiarity with your company required to assist you in formulating and executing a financing that fits optimal short- and long-term objectives.

Considerations for the Company

Your company, in consultation with its professional advisers, should analyze its business profile, circumstances, desires, and constraints, and formulate a realistic set of objectives and strategies. Among the various considerations for the company are the following:

- Long-term financing strategy.
    1. Long-term objectives concerning equity split among founders, management, other company employees and investors.
    2. Effect of present financing on long-term objectives.
    3. Securities law compliance planning.
    4. Long-term liquidity objectives.
    5. Anticipated investor group.
    6. Anticipated number, timing, and size of the prepublic rounds of financing:
        a. In an effort to minimize founder dilution, some companies initially engage in frequent small financings. These financings usually involve noninstitutional and nonprofessional investors. Such a strategy may initially achieve its goal, but exposes the company to other problems. Aggregate transactional costs (including legal and other fees) can be high. The continuing financing process can absorb substantial management time and inhibit the company's timely development. The company may face ongoing cash crises, which not only hinder development but can

adversely affect employee morale and reduce bargaining leverage in subsequent financings. The resulting investor profile may not be in the long-term best interest of the company (see below, "Desired Investor Profile").

b. More risk averse founders, concerned more with job security than equity, may try to raise most prepublic financing in the initial round. If successful, this approach may result in more dilution than would otherwise occur in a reasonably staged financing program.

c. In most instances, venture capital firms and other professional investors prefer to stage investments, since it allows them to manage their risks and re-evaluate their investment periodically before committing additional funds. Many professional investors also attempt to limit their risks and enhance their returns by assisting the company in putting together relatively higher prices later rounds of financing with professional investors seeking lower returns. Most professional investors expect the company's financing program to involve two or three rounds of private financings prior to going public or being acquired. Each round is expected to coincide with the achievement of a technological milestone, transition into a new phase of the company's development, or the occurrence of other events evidencing a reduction of risk. Accordingly, each subsequent round would be associated with a higher company valuation.

- Short-term financing needs.
    1. Amount of financing required.
    2. Purpose of the financing.
- Desired investor profile.
    1. Does the investor share management's vision, philosophy, and objectives?
    2. Are the investor's liquidity objectives consistent with management's objectives?
    3. Is special assistance from investors desired? Does the investor have required expertise? What are the investor's other commitments? Does the investor have a reputation in the industry of following through on assistance commitments?
    4. Availability of additional financing if needed?
    5. Blue ribbon investors may give the company credibility within the business community and in connection with subsequent rounds of equity financing, debt financings, public offerings, or acquisition. In particular, they may provide business contacts, assist in developing relationships with customers, suppliers, licensors, licensees, and the financial community. They may also provide other valuable advice and assistance.
- Industrial relationships.

    Will the industrial investor or joint venture partner adversely affect potential customer or supplier relationships? Does it enhance prospects for other customer or supplier relationships? What is the industrial investor's objective? Does it view the company as an acquisition target? Will it thwart or discourage interest from other potential acquirers? Will it adversely affect the potential for a public offering?

- Low quality investors.
  Investors with poor industry reputations could reduce the company's credibility in the business community and discourage interest of potential future investors.
- Unsophisticated individual investors.
  Potential problems associated with unsophisticated individual investore include: unusual demands on management time (numerous separate inquiries for information, progress reports, etc.); interference in management; lack of "staying power" during difficult times; more risk averse than originally represented; may not be a source of additional financing; difficulty in obtaining consents and approvals, especially with respect to the terms of later rounds of financing; and source of potential litigation. A large group of unsophisticated investors may discourage professional investors. These problems are not typically associated with individuals that invest indirectly through professionally managed venture capital firms.
- Complexity of financing structure.
  1. Ease of administering.
  2. Flexibility to accommodate future financings.
- Costs of financing.
  1. Attorney's fees.
  2. Accounting fees.
  3. Consulting fees.
  4. Deal packager, broker, or finders fees and equity compensation.
  5. Other miscellaneous fees.
  6. Warrants and options.
- Financial statement and accounting impact of financing alternatives.
  Tax impact or financing alternatives: joint ventures and contractual collaborations may raise unusual questions.
- Cash flow impact of financing alternatives.
  Timing and amount of debt service payments, mandatory dividends, mandatory redemption or sinking fund payments, license fees, or royalty payments.
- Management time and resources required.
  1. Which management people to be involved.
  2. Time required of each.
- Financing deadline.
  1. Financing deadline goal is chosen. Financing alternative likely to close by deadline?
  2. Adjusting the timetable to maximize valuation and minimize dilution, the company may want to delay or accelerate the financing deadline or timetable to coincide with external factors affecting valuation, such as the performance of the initial public offering market, expected announcements, or developments of competitors, customers, or suppliers.
  3. Back up alternatives if deadline is not met.

- Company profile.
    1. Management team: quality and prior track record of management team, gaps in the team.
    2. Industry.
    3. Market niche.
    4. Present and anticipated products or service.
    5. Proprietary position.
    6. Perceived management, technological, and market risks.
    7. Financial projections.
    8. Projected return for investors.
    9. Present phase of development in company's life cycle.

        Many financing alternatives may not be available to a company in its early phases because of the level of risk involved. As shown in the schedule of alternative sources of venture capital in Appendix A, most professional investors that invest in early phases will seek higher rates of return, and accordingly more equity and lower valuations than sought in later phases.

EXHIBIT 1: A VENTURE CAPITAL FIRM'S OBJECTIVES

Sample Statement of the Investment Objectives, Criteria and Policies of One Venture Capital Firm as Set Forth in the Firm's Private Placement Memorandum Delivered to Its Investors

INVESTMENT OBJECTIVES

The objective of the Fund is to achieve a rate of return superior to that associated with diversified equity investments in publicly traded securities. The Fund expects to achieve these returns primarily through long-term capital appreciation of investments in early stage technology related businesses or other special situations that the fund manager believes have high-growth potential. The Fund will seek liquidity of its investments, either through development of the investments into marketable securities or the conversion of the investments into cash or other marketable securities in connection with an acquisition of portfolio companies by publicly traded companies. The Fund intends to use the expertise, experience, and reputation of the fund manager to attract a stream of business opportunities; to effectively and efficiently evaluate, select, and structure good investments and dispositions of investments; and to work productively with the management of its portfolio companies. It expects its advisory board members to be of assistance in attracting and evaluating a portion of such opportunities.

INVESTMENT CRITERIA

General. The fund manager intends to evaluate each venture investment in terms of management, products, market, financial considerations, maturity of the business, and other factors that are determined relevant to the particular investment. It is believed that, in general, the optimum technology-related business is characterized by a highly competent and motivated management group; a proprietary product or service that clearly meets a market need coupled with a favorable cost and price relationship; a market that combines a favorable mix of size, growth potential, and competitive factors; and the capacity to generate substantial sales. A more detailed discussion of each of these factors is set forth below. The fund manager also believes that many potentially successful investment opportunities may not satisfy all of the criteria and factors discussed, and that depending on the particular opportunity, it may be appropriate to give different weight to such factors and criteria and additional factors and criteria that it determines are relevant.

Management. The fund manager believes that, in general, people are the most important factor in the success of any venture. The optimal management team would be characterized by the following: A complete and balanced management team with superior management skills; a team leader with a proven track record of profits and responsibility with a leading company in the industry; the capacity to attract and retain talented key employees; an appreciation for planning and control; a willingness to delegate; an ability to make difficult decisions and to work productively with its professional advisors; in the case of start-ups, a willingness to accept assistance from the fund manager or other members of the investor group; a high level of commitment to the enterprise; a will to win and a desire for large personal financial gain; goals and attitudes that are consistent with the liquidity, rate of return, and other investment objectives of the fund; a willingness to share a portion of the equity of the business with other key employees; and, above all, personal integrity. The fund manager believes that the management team should have a large portion of the ownership of the entity to create the appropriate incentive for building a successful enterprise.

Product or Service. The fund manager expects that most of its portfolio companies will engage in technology-related business, although opportunities occur from time to time in all businesses and the Fund may invest in companies engaged in other businesses. Of interest in the technology area are businesses engaged in the development, manufacturing, and/or sale of semiconductor equipment and devices; computers and related peripherals; telecommunications; instrumentation; systems, subsystems, and components; computer aided design and manufacturing; energy systems; software products; and health care products, among others, and service organizations related to these product areas. The fund manager has not established fixed ratios of investment in any area or industry. Ideally, the product or service should have a competitive edge based on cost, quality, or performance; should have the potential to command premium prices and yield high profit margins; and should have the potential to dominate or control a significant share of the market.

Market. Ideally, the market should be one that is young, growing fast, and can provide opportunity for a range of products, developments, and services. The initial product or service plan should reflect the ability to capture a dominant market position within a defined market niche. The niche should be one that is too small to attract dedicated efforts of large companies and yet has potential for expansion. Products or services involving an economic need but for which a market does not yet exist will also be considered. The lack of an existing market adds substantially to the risk of the investment, but may also increase the potential rewards if the business is successful. Management should have a realistic marketing plan for selling into the market. Ideally, the plan should be based on experience with the prior company and the marketing person involved should have extensive industry contacts among direct-sales people, sales representatives, and distributors.

Financial Considerations. The business should be capable of generating sales in excess of $20 million and earnings in excess of 8% after taxes within 5 years and should have the potential to achieve above-average return on assets employed, in general greater than 20%. In general, the fund manager favors businesses that are not capital intensive and that project prices and profit margins that can help cushion early period reversals and facilitate reaching a break-even point within 2 years. Capital intensive enterprises should be capable of adding significant value in the early years and attracting later rounds of financing at increased prices.

In general, the fund manager seeks a 10 to 1 return on investment and liquidity within a 5-year period for start-ups. For later stage financings, it seeks a ROI of between 5 to 1 in 5 years to 3 to 1 in 3 years.

Maturity. Under present market conditions, the fund manager believes that the risk-reward relationship is more favorable for investments in early stage rather than in later stage ventures. While more factors are known about later stage ventures, they may still be subject to significant uncertainties. Any such uncertainties if coupled with the relatively high valuation often commanded by later round investments and reduced opportunity for investor assistance to the venture may, in general, make later round investment less attractive than early round. Often, an early round investment may be made at comparatively lower prices because they are more difficult to analyze and may require assistance from the investor group. Favorable opportunities for investment in later stage entities also occur. Developing companies often take many years to achieve their potential and may require additional rounds of financing from investors other than founding management or early round investors. Also, it is not unusual to encounter attractive situations where founding management and early investors require some liquidity. Although most later round investments are usually made directly with the company, purely secondary transactions with founding management may also be of substantial indirect benefit to the company.

Opportunities also periodically exist in the securities of publicly traded companies. Many smaller, high growth potential companies are publicly traded in the over-the-counter market. In most cases, they have relatively few shares outstanding and even fewer as part of the trading "float." Accordingly, less research attention may be focused on them by the major brokerage firms, and fewer investors know about them or are prepared to invest in their securities. The result is a less perfect market than for major public companies, and opportunities for knowledgeable investors who can evaluate these companies' growth and prospects and invest without disturbing the market for their securities. Such companies may possess the same size growth prospects, and better liquidity, as their private counterparts.

The Fund may also invest in established securities of publicly or privately held businesses or divisions spun off from such businesses, some of which may be experiencing financial difficulties but which, in the judgment of the fund manager, offer growth potential because of rejuvenated management, changes in products or markets, or some other development that might stimulate earnings growth.

The fund manager has not established fixed ratios for investment in companies at different stages of maturity, however, the fund manager expects that a majority of the funds contributed capital will be invested in early stage entities.

OPERATING POLICIES

General. The fund manager has established the following guidelines with respect to the Fund's initial operations. Of course, changes in prevailing economic and market conditions or other relevant factors may affect the advisability of adhering to such policies. Accordingly, the fund manager may change these policies from time to time as he or she deems appropriate in the exercise of discretion.

Location of Portfolio Companies. The Fund intends to pursue attractive investment opportunities regardless of geographic location. However, due to its location, it expects a majority of its portfolio companies will be located in the West and Southwest.

Monitoring Investments. The fund manager intends to monitor all of the Fund's investments and, subject to any legal prohibition, to seek free access to management and business data of the portfolio company. It does not intend to operate its portfolio companies and in general will not seek a majority ownership of such companies. The Fund may participate in the exploratory or start-up phase of a new business in which it invests. In some start-up situations, management and other key elements may not be in place and the investment risks may be high, but the potential investment rewards may appear to be great. In such circumstances, the fund manager may play a significant role in identifying and attracting appropriate management and developing the company's business plan. It believes that productive assistance to portfolio companies can have a substantial beneficial effect on their development and, indeed, may be vital to early stage entities. Accordingly, the Fund intends to make itself available to assist portfolio companies in developing their businesses, either through board representation or through consultation with the management. The approach and degree of involvement will vary from company to company, depending on the nature of the investment, the growth stage of the entity, and the contribution that the fund manager can make. The fund manager expects that portfolio companies in their early growth stage will require more assistance than more mature companies, however, he or she anticipates that all portfolio companies will from time to time require assistance with obtaining and retaining key employees, organizational and management matters, the development and maintenance of key customer and supplier relationships, joint ventures; financings, security offerings, acquisitions, and the sale of the business or other matters.

Participation in Investments. Some investments may be made wherein the Fund provides the total investment needed by the portfolio company. Many investments may be made in conjunction with other investors, and such opportunities may be originated either by the Fund or the other investors. Such participations may provide the Fund with access to more investment opportunities and with additional resources of the co-investors to analyze the potential investment. The fund manager may manage other venture funds which may participate in investments made by the Fund. In the exercise of the fund manager's sole discretion, it may permit partners of the Fund or other partners in other funds, or other individuals, entities, associates, or affiliates to participate in investments made by the Fund, however it shall have no legal obligation to offer any such investment opportunities to any of such persons, or entities.

Follow-on Investments. The Fund may attempt to maintain sufficient capital resources to make follow-on investments where necessary. Such investments will be made when funds are available and when the fund manager determines that the investment is appropriate to sustain, enhance, or protect an investment.

Dispositions. Voluntary dispositions of investments will be undertaken when it is deemed to be in the best interest of the Fund. Dispositions may be affected through a sale or merger of the portfolio company, registered public offerings, secondary sale of the securities and private transactions, or in sales made pursuant to Rule 144*.

*Securities and Exchange Commissions Rule 144 governing such sales.

EXHIBIT 2: Sample Term Sheet

XYZ Technology, Inc.
Preferred Stock, Series A, Purchase Agreement

Offering	100,000 shares of voting convertible preferred stock, Series A, (representing 45% of the voting power of the Company after the offering).
Price per share	\$10 per share, aggregate proceeds \$1 million.
Terms of preferred stock voting	One vote for each share of common into which preferred is convertible on all matters submitted to shareholders of the Company (except (1) matters which by law are subject to class vote and (2) election of directors discussed below).
Liquidation preference	\$10 per share preference over common on liquidation.
Conversion	Initially each share of preferred convertible into one share of common subject to antidilution adjustments discussed below.
Antidilution	Normal antidilution protection for stock splits, stock dividends, and so forth, and weighted average price based antidilution protection for subsequent issuances of common stock or equivalents at a price below the conversion price (initial conversion price is \$10, the offering price per share of this issue).
Fixed dividend payments	None.
Redemption	No mandatory redemption; Company may call beginning on the earlier of (1) an acquisition of the Company, (2) first firm commitment underwritten public offering at a price in excess of redemption price, or (3) on the fourth anniversary of this issue, at the following prices:

Year	Call price
4 and before	110% of conversion price
5	107% of conversion price
6	103% of conversion price
7	Conversion price

Registration rights	Demand Registration. Two demand registrations at Company's expense for the Series A preferred. The exercise of demand rights is subject to the following conditions: 1. The first demand is exercisable after the earlier of the Company's first underwritten public offering, or third anniversary date of this issue, 2. A demand cannot be exercised prior to 12 months following the effective date of an underwritten public offering, 3. The share of common stock which the holders of the preferred propose to sell must have an aggregate proposed offering price of at least $3,000.00. Piggyback Registration Rights. Piggyback registration at the Company's expense on registrations initiated by the Company other than initial registration, or on demand of later round investors, subject to cutback at the underwriter's discretion. The Company will not be required to offer the opportunity to participate in a Company initiated registration more than once except to those holders whose individual holdings of record are at least 1% of the outstanding common stock of the Company at the time of the notice of registration.
Representations and warranties	Standard representations and warranties as to Company's valid existence, due organization, good standing, and power and authority to enter into agreement; no litigation; no default under other agreements, governmental compliance, no infringement on patent or proprietary rights of others; clear title to properties; disclosure of material agreements; accuracy of financial statements; etc.
Financial information and inspection rights	Audited annual, and unaudited quarterly and monthly, financial statements prepared on a consolidated basis. Copies of all SEC filings and all mailings to stockholders. Notice of revisions to business plan. Right to visit the Company upon advance notice, inspect the properties and obtain nonproprietary and nonclassified information concerning the Company's affairs.
Board representation	Five member Board to be elected by class voting. Preferred to elect three directors and common to elect two directors. After conversion of preferred, all five directors to be elected by common voting as a single class.
Pre-emptive rights	Right to purchase portion (based on percentage ownership of fully diluted outstanding common stock) of any subsequent issuance of the Company common stock or equivalents.

EXHIBIT 3: TYPICAL VENTURE CAPITAL DUE DILIGENCE INFORMATION REQUIREMENT LIST

1. Prospectus offering memorandum
2. Escrow agreement
3. Dealer manager agreement
4. Broker/dealer agreement
5. Legal opinion(s)
    a. Regarding federal income tax aspects
    b. Regarding the validity of the securities being issued
    c. Regarding federal securities registration:
        i. Exempt
        ii. Nonexempt
    d. Regarding Employee Retirement Income Act of 1974 matters
6. Blue sky memorandum or letter from counsel
7. SEC
    a. Registration statement (if applicable)
    b. Notice of effectiveness (if applicable)
8. National Association of Security Dealers, Inc. nonobjection letter (if applicable)
9. Appraisal(s)
    a. Of property
    b. Market study
    c. Financial feasibility
    d. Of business and/or business opportunity
10. Form 8264 (tax shelter registration)
11. Financial statement of general partner, sponsor, syndicator
12. Accountant's "management letter" (if applicable)
13. Sponsor's track record:
    a. List of past projects (offerings, etc.)
    b. Disbursement schedule
    c. "Books" of account on other partnerships
    d. Limited list of names of investors whom we may contact
    e. Limited list of other broker/dealers whom we may contact

3

EVALUATING MONEY SOURCES

When is 10% less than 7%? A 10% interest charge can cost less than a 7% interest charge if the time of the 10% loan is shorter than the time for the 7% loan. Financing is tricky and an important decision is selection of the right source of financing. The source affects the future of your business and the likelihood for success in your financing efforts.

As you learned in earlier chapters, there are several sources of funds available to you. Frequently, the key decision is to determine which is most appropriate for your current needs. Selection of the right source to meet this need can often have a pronounced effect on the future of your business as well as the likelihood for success in your financing efforts.

The short-term bank loan, when a longer-term loan is required, can soon create a crisis. Selling part of the business to raise capital that could have been borrowed can be extremely costly. Overextending trade creditors can be both costly and restrictive.

There are many opportunities for mistakes in the selection of the capital source. However, the correct selection can provide you with the capital you need while freeing you from unnecessary costs, risks, or the possibility of losing control of your business.

EVALUATION FACTORS

Five Primary Factors

To determine the most feasible source of raising needed capital in a particular situation, you should consider five primary factors. These are as follows:

1. Cost. How will each source affect the earnings of the present owners?
2. Risk. Which source exposes your business to the lowest degree of risk?
3. Flexibility. Will conditions imposed by any source reduce your flexibility in seeking further capital or in using capital generated through operations according to your best judgment?
4. Control. Could the present owners' control of the business be adversely affected? Could the loss of control prevent you from making operating decisions that you consider to be in the best interests of the business?
5. Availability. Which sources are, in fact, available to your business?

Cost

The cost of a capital source is usually measured by its impact on the earnings of the present owners, not simply the increased expenses incurred by the business. To understand the significance of this distinction, consider a company that needs $20,000. It can borrow the amount at 10% interest or selling 25% of the shares in the business. The business expects to pay interest on the loan of $2000 per year, which would reduce the business' net income by $2000 before taxes. If the business expects to earn $30,000, interest expense would reduce it to $28,000. In the equity alternative, the business' net income would be $30,000, since there would be no interest expense. However, only $22,500 would be applicable to the present owners since $7500 ($30,000 × 0.25) would represent the participation of new shareholders. Therefore, the business' income under the equity alternative would be higher, but the participation of the present owners would be less.

Each capital source has its own cost. Internal sources, such as the sale or liquidation of assets, could lead to loss of revenue following inventory disposal or added operating costs if machinery were sold to generate cash. Use of trade credit could cause discount forfeiture. In reaching a decision, it is important to consider all relevant costs for each source.

Risk

There are several types of risk involved in raising capital. Use of trade credit could lead to supplier dissatisfaction and possible damage to your credit standing.

Since borrowed money must be repaid with interest, debt capital imposes obligations on the cash flow of the business that must be met on a specified schedule to avoid default. A default could cause a number of actions as specified in the note agreement, such as forfeiture of collateral or forced bankruptcy.

The only money source that involves no risk to the business is equity capital since the equity investor, not the business, is the risk taker.

Flexibility

Total reliance on asset management to meet capital needs could cause a business to be overly cautious in credit extensions or inventory purchases, leading to lost sales.

The use of trade credit as a major capital source can make a business overly dependent on a few suppliers and unable to take advantage of better merchandise prices available from others.

Loans often carry stipulations that prevent the business from securing additional debt with a prior claim against assets. For example, a term loan agreement might prevent you from pledging receivables or inventories as collateral for additional borrowing.

Control

The use of internal financing and trade credit is unlikely to have any impact on the control of the business exercised by the present owners.

Equity investors are normally entitled to some degree of control in the company's operations. Shares issued to new investors normally carry voting rights in proportion to the number of shares held.

Lenders do not ordinarily participate in the affairs of the business, nor are they legally entitled to a vote in corporate matters, as are common shareholders. However, major loans from banks, insurance companies, or others may require that the lender be given some representation on the board of directors. This representation, usually taken only to protect the lender's interest in keeping abreast of corporate affairs, could affect the present owners' control of the business.

Availability

Frequently, a business may be restricted in its ability to raise capital by the lack of availability of preferred sources. Regardless of the source considered most feasible, the business has access only to whatever is available.

For example, a business may have retained all earnings and managed its assets prudently so that no significant additional capital can be raised internally. Trade credit may be exhausted and the company may be so burdened with interest and debt repayments that the only realistic alternative is equity, despite unfavorable cost and loss of control.

Weighing Evaluation Factors

Every capital source considered should be evaluated in terms of cost, risk, flexibility, control, and availability. Which of these is most important? Which is least important? The answer will depend on the application of your judgment to the particular situation. In many cases, availability may be all-important. In others, cost may be the deciding factor. The decision can only be made by the owners' prudent judgment after assembling and analyzing all the relevant facts.

GENERATING CAPITAL INTERNALLY

Prime Internal Sources

The three primary sources of internal capital are:

1. Increasing retained earnings through profit improvement and reduction or elimination of the earnings distributions to owners through dividends or drawings.
2. Prudent asset management including the disposal of non-productive assets and close control over receivables, inventories, and fixed assets.
3. Cost control, taking advantage of the most favorable prices available from suppliers and eliminating all unnecessary elements of cost.

Cost

A business can take advantage of internal capital sources without necessarily incurring any additional cost. However, there can be cases where additional costs are incurred. For example, fixed assets may be sold at a loss, customers may be lost through the establishment of overly rigorous credit controls, inventory reductions could cause the business to be out of stock on items needed immediately for sales or production, or the sale of certain fixed assets could force the business to resort to uneconomical alternate sources of supply.

As a general rule, a business that retains all, or most, of its earnings so that the business can grow and prosper will benefit from this decision. However, this policy could adversely affect any business that is also forced to seek equity capital from outside investors. The only available resources of equity capital might be interested in the income potential of dividends and drawings as well as potential capital gains. Such investors could easily be discouraged by a policy of retaining all earnings rather than distributing some portion to owners.

Flexibility

In general, the business would incur no loss of flexibility through internal generation of capital.

Control

Since no outside parties are involved when capital is generated internally, the present owners would retain all control over the conduct of the business affairs.

Availability

In many cases, the availability of capital from internal sources can be sharply limited. Retained earnings can be increased no faster than profit is realized, even if all income is retained in the business. Capital generation from the disposal of nonproductive assets might not produce significant amounts, particularly if prudent policies and procedures have historically minimized the accumulation of nonproductive assets.

First Source

In general, businesses should utilize all internal sources of capital that can readily be made available without the danger of lost sales revenue or forced recourse to other, more costly capital sources. Even if the amount of capital that can be generated internally is insufficient to meet the entire need, the need can be reduced through the internal sources. As a result, the company's exposure to the disadvantages of other capital sources is reduced. At the same time, the business will build the confidence of potential lenders and investors who may be more willing to risk their own capital in a business that has proven it can manage its own internal affairs.

Trade Credit

Trade credit is often the most easily accessible external capital source for small businesses. Unlike debt and equity, it seldom involves complex and often time-consuming negotiations. Thus it is treated here as akin to an internal capital source. An intelligent approach to the utilization of trade credit can help the business meet short-term needs with few complications.

Cost

The cost of trade credit can often be high, depending on the normal trade terms available from industry suppliers. For example, assume that a company purchases from suppliers who offer terms of a 2% cash discount within 10 days and a net date of 30 days. By forfeiting the cash discount of 2%, the business realizes use of its money for an additional 20 days at a cost of 2%. On an annualized basis, this is equivalent to a 36% interest rate. Similarly, late payments or delinquency penalties can often prove costly.

These usually run about 1 to 1½% monthly. On an annualized basis, this is equivalent to 12% (1% per month) or 18% (1½% per month).

Risk

Excessive reliance on trade credit as a capital source can invite risk. For example, suppliers might refuse to deliver or might put the company on a C.O.D. basis at a time when a company's cash shortage makes it unable to accept delivery if an immediate cash payment is required.

Flexibility

Even with a planned approach to maximizing available trade credit, a business may find itself heavily committed to those suppliers who accept extended payment terms. As a result, the business may no longer have ready access to other, more competitive suppliers who might offer lower prices, a superior product, or more reliable deliveries.

Control

In general, business owners would suffer no loss of control through the full utilization of available trade credit. Loss of control could only occur if trade credit were overextended to a point where suppliers take legal action, attaching property owned by the business or forcing the business into receivership.

Availability

The availability of trade credit is somewhat limited. Even the most liberal suppliers will seldom be receptive to terms that involve payment in more than 60 to 90 days.

Best Use

Trade credit is best used as a source of capital to meet relatively small, short-term needs. Effective use of trade credit requires intelligent planning to avoid unnecessary cost through forfeiture of cash discounts or the incurrence of delinquency penalties.

Every business should take full advantage of trade credit that is available without additional cost in order to reduce its need for capital from other sources.

AVAILABILITY OF DEBT

Debt capital may not be available for several reasons. Some of these are subjective judgments on the part of the lender. The lender may have doubts about the business; the future of its product, service, or market; or the managerial skill of its owners and officers.

Money Supply

While the business may be able to present arguments that counter objections for a loan, reasons beyond their control may make debt capital unavailable to them. The "money market" may be tight. The banking community's supply of funds available will be lent to borrowers of long-standing and proven capability with whom the bank has sustained a continuing, profitable relationship at little or no risk.

Financial Condition

The lender may feel that the business' financial condition is not strong enough to carry additional debt. In this respect, lenders often apply specific tests to determine whether the business has sufficient stability and liquidity to carry the proposed debt burden.

Stability

Stability is the capacity of the business to withstand periods of losses or low earnings without the threat of default on debt repayment obligations.

Liquidity

Liquidity is a measure of the company's ability to meet its current obligations. It is tested by comparing its cash and other assets that could soon be converted to cash (such as receivables and inventories) with its short-term demands for cash.

MEASURING STABILITY

The stability of a business' capital structure is also an indicator of its ability to carry more debt. If it is already so debt heavy that a lender would question its stability, the addition of more debt would make a bad situation even worse.

The ability to carry debt can be expressed statistically through ratios. Lenders, particularly banks, frequently rely on these ratios as guidelines to judge the feasibility of lending money which would increase a business' debt burden.

Debt-Equity Ratio

One common measure of stability is the "debt to equity ratio," which is calculated as follows:

Debt – equity ratio = Total liabilities/total equity

For example, a business has total liabilities of $75,000 and total net worth (equity) of $100,000. Its debt-equity ratio would be calculated as follows:

$75,000/$100,000 = 0.75

Its debt-equity ratio is expressed as 0.75.

Comparisons

The lender's judgment as to whether the ratio in the example is low, reasonable, or excessive would depend largely on a comparison with industry averages. A debt-equity ratio that is perfectly acceptable for a wholesaler may be excessive for a small manufacturer. If the business' debt-equity ratio is above the industry average, most prospective lenders would encourage the company to secure additional equity capital so that its capacity to carry added debt would be increased.

For example, assume that a company had $100,000 in net worth and $200,000 in total liabilities. Its debt-equity ratio would be calculated as follows:

$$\$200{,}000/\$100{,}000 = 2.0$$

If the industry average is 2.0, the potential lender might feel that the current position is relatively stable but that the addition of more debt would increase this ratio to an unacceptable level. If the business assumed $50,000 in debt, its total liabilities would then be $250,000 and its debt-equity ratio would be calculated as follows:

$$\$250{,}000/\$100{,}000 = 2.50$$

Debt Capacity

The debt-equity ratio can also be used to estimate the amount of debt that the business can carry based on its equity. This is estimated as follows:

$$\text{Debt capacity} = \text{Acceptable debt-equity ratio} \times \text{equity}$$

For example, consider a company with equity of $100,000. In its industry, a debt-equity ratio of 1.5 is considered acceptable. Its debt capacity would be estimated as follows:

$$1.5 \times \$100{,}000 = \$150{,}000$$

If the company's liabilities were already $150,000, a lender would hesitate to lend additional funds. If the liabilities were only $125,000, the lender might agree to a loan of $25,000, raising total debt to the full capacity of $150,000.

GUIDELINES

Ratios are only guidelines, they are not absolutes. The application of ratios to financial decisions must often be tempered by consideration of collateral, local conditions, temporary economic situations, asset turnover, confidence in the owners of a business, and the like.

Acceptable debt-equity ratios vary widely among industries. Economically stable industries with relatively high investments in fixed assets generally have relatively high debt-equity ratios. Industries with relatively low fixed-asset requirements that are highly susceptible to economic fluctuations generally have lower debt-equity ratios.

MEASURING LIQUIDITY

The debt-equity ratio is a measure of stability. However, it does not provide any indication of the business' liquidity—its ability to meet short-term obligations.

Even financially stable businesses can have liquidity problems. This usually occurs when commitments to fixed assets, inventories, or miscellaneous assets tie up the business' capital so that it is not available to meet short-term needs.

Measures of liquidity compare current assets with current liabilities.

Current Assets

Current assets are cash and any other assets that will be converted to cash within the coming fiscal year. They normally include accounts receivable, inventories, and any marketable securities owned by the business.

Current Liabilities

Current liabilities are those obligations that must be paid within the coming fiscal year. These obligations normally include amounts owed to trade creditors, employees, tax authorities, loan interest, loan principal repayments due within 12 months, and any short-term debt.

Relationship

Since current assets represent the cash that will be available to the business within the year and current liabilities represent the cash that will be needed, the relationship between the two is an indicator of liquidity. This relationship gives the potential lender a quick indication of the company's ability to meet its obligations in the forthcoming months.

Working Capital

The first common measure of a business' liquidity is its working capital. Working capital is the excess of current assets over current liabilities and is calculated as follows:

Working capital = Current assets – current liabilities

If a business has $50,000 in current assets and $25,000 in current liabilities, its working capital would be calculated as follows:

$50,000 – $25,000 = $25,000

Current Ratio

Working capital measures the dollar difference between current assets and current liabilities. A second indicator, the current ratio, expresses the current assets as a multiple of current liabilities. For example, a current ratio of 2.0 means that the business has $2.00 in current assets for every $1.00 in current liabilities. The current ratio is calculated as follows:

Current ratio = Current assets/current liabilities

If a company has $50,000 in current assets and $25,000 in current liabilities, its current ratio would be calculated as follows:

$50,000/$25,000 = 2.0

Acid Test Ratio

A third indicator of liquidity, which more specifically describes the adequacy of the business' short-term cash position, is called the acid test ratio.

To calculate the acid test ratio, determine the "quick" assets, those that will probably be converted to cash within 30 days. Ordinarily, this would include only cash and receivables. In addition, if a business has marketable securities, their value should be added. The acid test ratio is then calculated as follows:

Acid test ratio = Quick assets/current liabilities

For example, if a company had cash of $30,000 and receivables of $50,000, its quick assets would be $80,000 ($30,000 + $50,000). With current liabilities of $40,000, its acid test ratio would then be calculated as follows:

$80,000/$40,000 = 2.0

LONG- VERSUS SHORT-TERM DEBT

The debt-equity ratio, which measures stability, makes no distinction between short- and long-term debt. However, short- and long-term debt sharply influence indicators of liquidity. Current liabilities include only debt that must be repaid within 1 year, not debt due at later dates. Therefore, liquidity tests can often indicate whether a business should seek short- or long-term debt. With a short-term loan, the entire amount would be a current liability and would ordinarily reduce the current ratio. With a long-term loan, only the portion due in the first year would be considered a current liability and the current ratio would normally improve.

Consider a business with current assets of $100,000 and current liabilities of $50,000. Its current ratio is 2.0 ($100,000/$50,000). If it borrowed $50,000 on a short-term note, its current assets would increase to $150,000 and its current liabilities would increase to $100,000. Its current ratio would then be calculated as follows:

$150,000/$100,000 = 1.50

Before the loan, the current ratio was 2.00. However, if the business borrowed $50,000 on a 5-year loan payable in five equal annual installments, only the first year's principal repayment of $10,000 would be added to its current liabilities. Current assets would then be $150,000 ($100,000 + $50,000) and current liabilities would be $60,000 ($50,000 + $10,000). Its current ratio would then be calculated as follows:

$150,000/$60,000 = 2.50

Therefore, the addition of long-term debt has raised the current ratio from 2.00 to 2.50, indicating an improvement in the business' liquidity.

COLLATERAL

Frequently, the availability of a loan will depend on the collateral that the business can pledge as security for the amount borrowed. The lender, in valuing the collateral, will be concerned not only with the amount of collateral, but also the quality. Assigned receivables will be judged on the following:

- Aging.
- Credit-worthiness of customers.
- Bad debts experience.

Inventories will be judged on the following:

- Current market value.
- Sales history.
- Turnover.

Loans secured by fixed assets, such as real estate and equipment, will be based on the business' ability to repay, the current market value of the assets if the business defaults on the loan, and the ease with which the lender could dispose of the assets.

LEVERAGE, OR TRADING ON EQUITY

The lower cost of debt capital is the basis of a business financing technique called "leveraging the investment" or "trading on equity." In effect, the business borrows at a low rate of interest and invests the proceeds at a higher rate of return.

Consider the case of two identical apartment buildings called Bedrock and Swampside Heights. Each was purchased for $500,000 and each has the same monthly rents. The only difference is that Bedrock is debt-free, while Swampside Heights has a $400,000 mortgage at 9%. The owners of Bedrock have a 100% equity investment, while the owners of Swampside Heights put up only $100,000, 20% of the purchase price. Operating expenses (maintenance, utilities, advertising, depreciation, and property taxes) for each building are $75,000. At annual rentals of $125,000, the condensed income statements for both properties would appear as:

	Swampside Heights	Bedrock
Revenues	$125,000	$125,000
Less: Operating expenses	– 75,000	– 75,000
Earnings before interest and income taxes	$ 50,000	$ 50,000
Less: Interest	– 36,000	– —
Earnings before income taxes	$ 14,000	$ 50,000

While Swampside Heights' income is lower, the owners' equity investment was only $100,000. Therefore, the return on the owners' equity would be calculated as follows:

Return on Equity = Earnings/equity

$14,000/$100,000 = 14%

For Bedrock, with an equity investment of $500,000 and no debt, the return on the owners' equity would be calculated as follows:

$50,000/$500,000 = 10%

At this point, Swampside Heights appears to be well ahead. In fact, if they had $500,000 to invest originally, instead of just $100,000, they might have bought five buildings, not just one. With five buildings, they might have earned $70,000, well more than the $50,000 that Bedrock earned on the same investment!

CAPITAL GAINS

When Bedrock and Swampside Heights are eventually sold, the advantages of Swampside Heights' financing become even more dramatic. If each building sells for $750,000, the capital gain would be calculated as follows:

	Swampside Heights	Bedrock
Sales price	$750,000	$750,000
Less: Mortgage payout	– 400,000	– —
Proceeds from sale	$350,000	$750,000
Less: Equity investment	– 100,000	– 500,000
Capital gain	$250,000	$250,000

Swampside Heights' capital gain is 250% ($250,000/$100,000) while Bedrock's is only 50% ($250,000/$500,000). Swampside Heights certainly appears far ahead. This approach has been the foundation of many business success stories.

This same approach has also been the cause of many failures. If the local economy suffered, or a glut of other buildings caused revenues of both buildings to fall by 20%, from $125,000 to $100,000, the condensed income statements would look like this:

	Swampside Heights	Bedrock
Revenues	$100,000	$100,000
Less: Operating expenses	– 75,000	– 75,000
Earnings before interest and income taxes	$ 25,000	$ 25,000
Less: Interest	– 36,000	– —
Earnings before income taxes	<$ 11,000>	$ 25,000

Swampside Heights is now losing 11% of its equity investment annually while Bedrock is still earning 5% ($25,000/$500,000) on its investment. Further revenue declines make the comparison even worse. At $75,000, Swampside Heights would lose $36,000 per year while Bedrock would still break even. This is not a desirable situation, however, it is one that would permit them to stay in business until the local economy picks up or the demand for apartments in the area is more in line with the supply.

Leveraging is a way of supplementing equity capital with debt. As business improves, it permits dramatic returns. However, as business declines, it can cause rapid failure.

SOURCES OF MAJOR REQUIREMENTS

Despite the advantages of full utilization of internal capital sources and trade credit, major capital requirements ordinarily force businesses to borrow or locate equity investors to realize the capital they need.

COST OF DEBT CAPITAL

To determine the cost of debt capital, consider the case of a company that borrows at 10%. It is paying $10 interest for each $100 borrowed. However, the $10 interest expense is deductible in determining the income tax liability. At an effective tax rate of 25%, the amount of net income sacrificed to pay the interest would be calculated as follows:

Interest before taxes	$10.00
Less: Tax deduction	– 2.50
Net cost	$ 7.50

Since each $100 borrowed reduces net income by $7.50, the effective interest cost is 7.5%.

The cost of debt capital is calculated according to the following formula:

Cost of debt = Interest rate x (1.00 - effective income tax rate)

For example, you would calculate the cost of a 12% loan as follows, assuming an effective income tax rate of 25%:

$$0.12 \times (1.00 - 0.25) = 0.09$$

Or, stated as a percentage, the cost of debt would be 9%.

COST OF EQUITY CAPITAL

Earlier, you saw that the cost of capital is based on the cost to the present owners. Debt financing does not change the ownership structure. Therefore, the cost to the business is the cost to the present owners.

Equity financing gives the new owners a portion of the business' earnings. Therefore, the cost of equity capital is usually determined by dividing the portion of expected earnings that will accrue to the new owner(s) by the amount of interest that they pay.

For example, a partnership sells a 25% interest for $10,000. If the partnership's expected earnings are $12,000, the new owner's participation would be $3,000 ($12,000 × 0.25). Therefore, the cost would be calculated as follows:

Cost = Earnings participation/investment

$3,000/$10,000 = 0.30

Therefore the cost is 30%.

For a corporation, the cost is calculated by dividing the expected earnings per share by the selling price of each new share. For example, a business sells stock for $20.00 per share. It expects to earn $4.00 per share. The cost would be calculated as follows:

Cost = Earnings per share/selling price per share

$400/$20.00 = 0.20

The cost is, therefore, 20%.

COST COMPARISON

The cost of equity capital is almost always higher than the cost of borrowed capital. The equity investor is exposed to far more risks than the lender and, to justify this risk, expects a substantially higher return. The risks assumed by the equity investor can be summarized briefly as follows:

- Interest paid by lenders is deducted from operating income before determining the earnings available for equity investors.
- The business is legally obligated to repay amounts borrowed. There is no such obligation with respect to equity investment.
- Unlike many lenders, the equity investor does not have the protection of collateral. If the business should fail, the equity investor would have no claim against any specific assets of the business, nor against the personal assets of other owners.
- If the business should fail, the legitimate claims of all creditors, including lenders, must be satisfied in full before any proceeds are available to equity investors.

The equity investor is an owner of the business, sharing all the risks and, as well as, the rewards that all owners anticipate. If the business fails, the equity investment fails with it. In return for the added risks of equity investment, the investor expects to reap much higher rewards than the relatively secure lender. The result is a substantial increase in the cost of equity capital to the business.

RISK COMPARISON

Equity capital involves no risk to the business. All of the risk lies with the investor(s). By contrast, the risks involved with debt capital are substantial. Interest and repayment obligations could fall due at times that are inconvenient for the business, forcing default on the note. Depending on the conditions stated in the note agreement, this could give the lenders immediate ownership of collateral, drive the business into bankruptcy, or give the creditors ownership of the business. If the owners personally guaranteed the original note, the creditors would also have access to the personal assets of the owners.

Frequently, businesses attempt to refinance these obligations if they are unable to meet them when due. If all other indicators of the business' success are favorable, such as sales and net income, refinancing is often possible. However, the terms on which refinancing is available will invariably be more costly and more restrictive than the terms of the original note.

FLEXIBILITY COMPARISON

In general, securing needed capital from equity investors would have no negative impact on the business' flexibility in conducting its operations.

However, debt financing can often sharply restrict the business' flexibility in pursuing other financing or expansion opportunities. In some cases, specific provisions of the original agreement may prevent the business from securing additional debt, incurring expenses beyond a limit established by the lender, or investing in certain assets.

Even in those cases where no specific provisions of the note restrict the company's flexibility, the presence of substantial debt obligations will often discourage other creditors or lenders from providing extra financing that the business might sorely need.

CONTROL COMPARISON

Equity investors are owners of the business and are therefore ordinarily entitled to a voice in the conduct of the business' affairs. The extent of their control would depend on the number of shares held in a corporation or the percentage interest specified in a partnership agreement.

Lenders do not normally participate in the affairs of the business. In some cases, lenders may require some limited voice in the business' affairs such as representation on the board of directors or the option to approve officers' compensation.

DEADLOCK

Two votes for debt. Two votes for equity. However, as was maintained earlier, not all four factors are equally important. In fact, when things are going well the problems of risk and flexibility are not always important. Therefore, most small businesses are inclined to seek debt capital to meet their major financing needs.

Besides the sharply lower cost, borrowing is often more convenient than raising equity capital. A potential lender is no further away than your nearest commercial bank. However, the nearest equity investor may be hard to find.

Money can be borrowed on relatively short notice with minimal legal and accounting costs. Equity capital exposes the small business to a host of legal intricacies and audit requirements that may prove to be cumbersome, time consuming, and expensive.

WHY NOT ALWAYS BORROW?

At this point, you could conclude that borrowing is the only answer. Confident of your business' future and its ability to repay its obligations, why worry about risks and flexibility? Why not settle for the lower cost and easier accessibility of the lender rather than pursue the more elusive and expensive equity investor? The answer lies in availability, a subject that will be explained in detail in the next section.

NO SINGLE SOURCE IS ALWAYS BEST

Each of the capital sources discussed here offers certain advantages and disadvantages. No single source is best for all situations. In any given situation, the owners must evaluate those factors—cost, risk, flexibility, control, and availability—that will determine the source, or sources, best suited to their needs.

Combination

Frequently, a combination of capital sources will present the best solution. When a total need has been established, the amount that must be generated from lenders or equity investors can be reduced sharply through internal sources and trade credit. As a result, the owners can minimize exposure to the negative factors associated with borrowed capital or increased equity investment while inspiring the confidence of lenders and investors.

Typical Combination Program

A typical combination of capital sources for a small business might be as follows:

- Utilizing available internal sources through maximum retention of earnings, prudent asset management, and conscientious cost control.
- Taking full advantage of available trade credit without incurring unnecessary costs through forfeiture of cash discounts or delinquency penalties.
- Utilizing short-term debt capital to meet short-term needs, avoiding the higher interest expense and more restrictive conditions of longer-term borrowing. The availability of short-term debt is likely to be increased substantially if the business has quality collateral as security of the loan.
- Combining debt and equity as needed to meet the longer term capital requirements of the business.

Debt-Equity Combinations

As discussed earlier, the ability of the business to secure debt capital will often depend on the amount of equity in the business. A business with insufficient equity to permit borrowing needed capital can often resort to a combination, since increasing its equity will also increase its debt capacity. For example, a business with $50,000 in debt and $50,000 in equity wants to borrow $40,000. A lender feels that an acceptable debt-equity ratio for the business is 1.00. Consider the effect of the additional $40,000 debt on the business' debt-equity ratio.

$$\text{Total debt} = \$50{,}000 + \$40{,}000 = \$90{,}000$$

$$\$90{,}000/\$50{,}000 = 1.80$$

The addition of $40,000 in debt would increase the business' debt-equity ratio to 1.80, far above the acceptable 1.00 ratio. However, if the business chose to raise $20,000 in equity capital, its debt capacity would be calculated as follows:

$$\text{Debt capacity} = \text{Acceptable debt-equity ratio} \times \text{equity}$$

$$1.00 \times \$70{,}000 = \$70{,}000$$

With its debt capacity now increased to $70,000, the business could probably borrow an additional $20,000 ($70,000 debt capacity – $50,000 present debt).

SHORT- VERSUS LONG-TERM DEBT

Frequently, a company must decide whether its borrowing needs are best met through short- or long-term debt. The availability of short- or long-term debt may often depend on analysis of the current ratio of the business before and after the proposed loan. For example, a business may have $70,000 in current assets and $35,000 in current liabilities. Its current ratio would then be calculated as follows:

$$\$70{,}000/\$35{,}000 = 2.00$$

If the owners want to borrow $20,000 in short-term debt and a current ratio of 2.00 is considered acceptable for the industry, the additional $20,000 would lower the current ratio to an acceptable level. Current assets would increase by $20,000 to $90,000. Current liabilities would increase from $35,000 to $55,000. The current ratio would then be calculated as follows:

$90,000/$55,000 = 1.64

The current ratio is an unacceptably low level.

However, if the company chose to borrow $10,000 in short-term debt and $10,000 in long-term debt, its current assets would increase from $70,000 to $90,000. However, current liabilities would only increase from $35,000 to $45,000. Therefore, its current ratio would be calculated as follows:

$90,000/$45,000 = 2.00

Since this level is acceptable, the company could meet its needs through an additional $20,000 in long-term debt. Only $10,000 would be due in the current year and therefore be considered a current liability.

THE NEED FOR COMMUNICATION

Small business owners have often been frustrated in their attempts to borrow from commercial banks or to secure capital from equity investors. Frequently, the basic problem is one of communication. The small business owner, enthusiastic about the future of the business, does not understand why the banker or investor fails to share this enthusiasm.

Facts and Figures

Bankers or investors, accustomed to dealing in facts and figures, do not understand how a business owner could approach them in search of capital without a well-developed plan that they can use as a basis for making their decision.

Bridging the Gap

The small business owner is in a position to bridge this gap by preparing a plan that will help the financier make an analytic judgment about the future of the business and its worthiness as a credit risk or attractive investment.

Plan Elements

The basic elements of such a plan should consist of the following:

- Forecast of Capital Requirements. The forecast should state not only the amount of capital needed, but also the reasons for the need. It should detail such factors as amounts needed for fixed assets; the amount needed for receivables or inventories, and how these amounts were determined; how much cash will be generated from operations; how the owner plans to use internal financing sources; and when the capital will be needed.
- A Profit Plan. This should project sales and profit for a period at least equal to the term of any loan. In the case of an equity investment, a minimum period is 5

years. The profit plan should detail sales revenue, cost of sales, and expenses so that the banker or investor can make comparisons with other businesses in the same industry to determine whether or not the projections are realistic.

- A Marketing Plan. This plan specifies how the business intends to achieve its sales projections, describing specific marketing steps such as the addition of new locations, new products, or new services; increases in the sales force; and advertising budget; and promotional efforts.
- A Cash Flow Statement. This statement should indicate how much cash will be available from operations and how it will be used to acquire assets, reduce liabilities, compensate investors, and the like. The cash flow statement permits the banker to determine how the loan will be repaid and the equity investor to determine the compensation that can be expected from the investment.

BUILDING CONFIDENCE

The analysis, effort, and logic that go into the formation of such a plan will not only make it easier for bankers or investors to evaluate your business, but will also enhance their confidence in your business and your skill as a manager.

AVOIDING PROBLEMS

The selection of the proper source to meet a particular capital need can free you from potential problems. These problems include: unnecessary costs, possibility of debt repayments which cannot be met, curtailment of credit from suppliers, inventory maintenance needed for sales, and possible large loss of control to equity investors.

PRESENTING YOUR CASE

In particular, it is important that, as a small business owner you know how to present the best case for your business to potential lenders or equity investors. In effect, you must sell these people on the merits of your business and your management skills. To do this effectively, you must know what they are thinking, how they will evaluate your business, and how they will appraise you as a competent, skillful manager.

HUMAN FACTORS

Lenders and investors are human. After analysis of all the facts, their decision will often rest on their subjective judgment about the capability of the person who is managing their money. By applying the knowledge you have derived in the previous sections to your requests for capital, you will be able to present an intelligent case that will represent your business and yourself in the best possible light.

The following chapters develop the process of building the business plan. This process starts with market research and writing the marketing plan.

4

PLANNING

If you don't know where you're going, you will end up somewhere else. Think about that! Suppose you lived in New York City and decide to drive to Los Angeles, would you use a map? Of course you would. What would happen if you didn't? It would be a very long, hard trip. And, if you didn't know your geography, you probably would not make it to California, never mind Los Angeles.

Starting or running a business without proper planning is like driving from New York to Los Angeles without a map. Planning will show you your destination and the best road to get you there.

WHY PLANNING IS CRITICAL

The following is an overview of planning and discusses how and why to prepare a business plan.

- Planning gives you a path to follow. It makes your future what you want it to be.
- It is the most important guide to starting, building and managing a successful business.
- It is the best tool available to help a small business raise money.

A business plan must be a communications tool for investors, suppliers, employees, and others interested in understanding the operations and goals of your business. If you don't plan for the success of your business, you will fail.

PLANNING CAN BE DIFFICULT

Although planning is critical to your success, it is often overlooked in favor of intuition or "gut feeling." There are other obstacles that hinder planning, including:

- *Lack of Know-How.* It is sometimes difficult to know how to plan and what to plan for.
- *Fear of the Unknown.* It is hard enough dealing with today's problems without worrying about what's going to happen in the future.
- *Inexactness.* The best set plans often do not work out exactly the way they are supposed to.

These obstacles are very real. However, they must be overcome if you are to be successful. While it may be difficult to face the future, heading into it without any direction is much worse.

THE BUSINESS PLAN

The business plan is a written document that clearly defines the goals of a business and outlines the methods for achieving them. A business plan describes what a business does, how it will be accomplished, who has to do it, where it will be done, why it's being done, and when it has to be completed.

Dreams and ambitions are great and important. However, what really counts in the business world are results. Therefore, it is important to establish realistic goals with a sound methodology for achieving them. A business plan:

- Is the management and financial "blueprint" for a business start-up and profitable operation.
- Is written by the business owner(s) with outside help as needed.
- Explains how the business will function and depicts its operational characteristics.
- Details how the business will be capitalized and managed.

Elements of a Business Plan

Business Description

A business description should include business name, address, and owner identification. It identifies the business' goals and objectives and clarifies why you are or why you want to be in business.

Products and Services

This section is a very descriptive explanation of all products and services. It describes what you are selling and why.

Sales and Marketing

Sales and marketing are the core of your business rationale. Your plan should address several basic questions:

- Who and how large is your market?
- What pricing and sales terms are you planning?
- How will you market your products and services?

Operating Requirements

The plan should identify and describe the equipment, facilities, and people necessary to generate your products and/or services. How will they be produced and made available to the customer?

Financial Management

The financial management description is the most critical part of your business plan. You will establish vital schedules that will guide the financial health of your business.

If you are starting a business, your financial management plan should include:

- Projected (pro forma) "start-up costs".

- Expected profit or return on investment (ROI) for the first year.
- Projected income statement and balance sheet for 2 years.
- Projected monthly cash flow statement for 12 months.

If you are a young (5 years or less) or established business, your plan should include:

- Income statement and balance sheet for the last 2 years.
- Projected income statement and balance sheet for the next 2 years.
- Projected monthly cash flow statement for 12 months.

In all cases, your plan should include an explanation (narrative) of all projections. If you feel that your finance or accounting knowledge is not sufficient to prepare these statements, seek professional assistance.

The final and most important question to be answered is: Will, or does your company make a profit?

Concluding Narrative

This segment of your plan should summarize your business goals and objectives and send a message that you are committed to the success of your business.

PUT YOUR BEST FOOT FORWARD

Your business plan should be concise, complete, clear, neat, and accurate. It does not have to be fancily bound. It will be an extension of you and your business.

The length of a good plan will vary from a few pages to well over 100 pages. (30 to 50 pages is a good page count to aim for. In some cases a plan of more than 30 pages will be automatically rejected from further consideration.) The plan should provide a sound blueprint for your business and entice any reader to want to know more.

A Final Word On Planning

Planning is the most important part of starting and running a successful business. It is a fact—if you don't know where you are going, you will end up somewhere else.

In the following portion of this chapter we will explore the core of business planning—market planning. All other activities of a business are in some way dependent on a workable, successful product marketing strategy and methodology. In some situations the marketing effort is less pronounced than others but, if your business does not attract customers your business will not exist for long. By developing a solid marketing plan you can develop the other sections of your business plan with little difficulty.

MARKET PLANNING

Prior to developing the business plan some study must be accomplished which will help derive the information needed to determine the feasibility of converting the product or service into cash—which is what all business is about. The result of this study is a marketing plan which is a statement of who the product or service is going to be sold to, and the strategy of how it is intended to make the customer aware of and willing to buy the product or service.

Thus marketing is the act of defining your potential customer and a way to attract that customer as opposed to sales which is the act of convincing the attracted customer to buy.

Issues addressed by market strategy are: what can be sold, to whom, in what quantities, at what prices, and with what level of effort in regard to promotion, sales, and distribution.

Marketing is something that must pervade the entire company. It's the entire company's responsibility. Everyone employed by the company should be taught about the product or service their company sells. Product designers, business owners and managers need to go out and meet customers face-to-face.

Marketing studies make us feel secure about the marketplace. Studies tend to circumscribe our imagination. They limit the fact that we create market opportunity. For example, in the 1970s Mr. William Hewlett of Hewlett-Packard Co. was advised, after a 6-month market study, that the pocket calculator market was limited and not large enough to be sufficiently profitable to warrant the company's interest. Mr. Hewlett elected to go ahead with the project. Based on the success of the market created and its profitability a new company division was formed. The market has since been found to be large enough to not only support that division but other competing companies who later entered the market, on an on-going basis.

Studies give you one answer. However, they don't help you understand what is going on beneath the surface to create opportunity and change.

Marketing in its very fundamental sense means building relationships with customers, not with a statistic. Today the entrepreneur has the advantage. It's easier for a small business to service today's smaller market niches and to be close to the customer than it is for large corporations. Big firms have been set up to service mass markets. Changing over is a difficult task.

In an entrepreneurial company, decisions are made and implemented by a small team of people. By finding a market segment (niche) and dominating it, you can create your reputation and identity. Then you can expand. Today, the way to get big is to think small.

Qualitative marketing research must be performed in order to get in touch with your customer. What keeps the customer coming back to buy the same product requires some fundamental rethinking about how to maintain consumer loyalty.

One key to that process is to look at analogies. Consider lawyers and doctors. We don't change our doctors and lawyers very often. That's because we have a certain relationship with those people and it encourages loyalty. We have to learn how to create that feeling as part of a product relationship.

Another technique is looking at the infrastructure of a marketplace, isolating 50 to 100 important people, talking to them, getting their endorsement. This core of people forms your reference system. Through word of mouth, they'll establish your reputation.

If you were selling a new drug to treat heart ailments, you might want to start by pinpointing certain leading cardiologists, people known as gurus in the business. Those people tend to work in certain teaching hospitals. Try to get a few of these eminent specialists on your advisory board. Then you might determine the most influential older drug companies, and try to build distribution alliances with them.

Don't start out by spending a lot on advertising. Begin with a narrow reference structure and educate the people in it about your product.

Market driven companies need to incorporate the customer into product design. That means getting more and more members of an organization in contact with the customer—manufacturing and design people, as well as sales and marketing staff. You can, for example, have customers sitting in on your internal committee meetings. Or have your manufacturing, R&D, and marketing people call on customers as a team on a regular basis, and then write reports on their findings together. These changes must become a part of the culture of the company, so they're not an event but a regular process.

Do a lot of internal training. You don't want to bring in outside people, because you need to develop more of a mentoring process. And everyone must be involved.

The goal is to train people to think differently. You have to train them to react quickly and to be willing to make mistakes. That could involve special projects where, for example, you divide different employees into groups. Then tell each group to develop a marketing plan, and bring them back to debate their findings.

Today you must establish market relations: to build relationships in defined marketplaces, extending beyond the media to all influential players.

About a century ago, society underwent a transformation when we converted to mass-market manufacturing: Everything was done on a uniform basis. Eventually, that erupted into the societal movements of the 1960s and 1970s, in which individuals, pitted against institutions, cried out for an end to uniformity.

Technology has created tools of diversity that allow you to produce a solution for ever-narrower segments of society. This ability to reach increasingly defined targeted groups is feeding into larger societal pressure for less uniformity and more choice.

Issues addressed by production strategy today are: the processes and technology that will be issued, the requirements for materials, equipment, facilities, and staff; where facilities will be located, and, the cost of achieving sales goals.

We have to recognize that the future is uncertain, that we'll need to do more creative planning to deal with an unpredictable world.

DYNAMIC MARKETING PLANNING

At the heart of your marketing strategy must be a positioning strategy. Your company must develop a style of marketing compatible with this new era of rapid change—you must start with a new approach which has been called "dynamic positioning."

With this approach, positioning evolves gradually, like a person's personality. It has three interlocking stages: product positioning, market positioning, and corporate positioning. These stages create a whole that is much bigger than their individual parts.

Stage One. You must determine how you want your product or service to fit in the market. Should you build a reputation for low cost? Or for high quality? Will you try to sell to all companies?

Stage Two. Your product must gain recognition in the market. It has to win credibility with customers. You need to understand the network of retailers, distributors, analysts, and journalists who control opinion. If you can win the hearts and minds of the most important 10 percent of the people in an industry, your company's market positioning is assured.

Stage Three. You must not position your products but your company. This is done primarily through financial success. If the company's profits slip, its image becomes tarnished. Then the company must start over at product positioning and rebuild its place in the market.

Stage one may necessitate a formal R&D strategy. A formal R&D strategy is needed when a firm is in an environment characterized by rapid, frequent technological advances; when a firm is in a highly competitive environment in which a new or refined product introduction is a major determinant of market success; when new product development is expensive and requires long lead times.

THE MARKETING PLAN

A marketing plan is your program for selling your goods and services. The best marketing plans are written descriptions of your market; your customers' wants, needs, and preferences; your objectives (short and long term); and your strategies for attaining your objectives. To be most effective, your marketing plan should include the following elements:

- Marketing scope and distribution
- Market segmentation
- Market demand changes and Trends
- Major Customers and Concentration
- Sales tactics
- Market share and sales
- Objectives
- Strategy
- Media mix
- Budget

Marketing Scope and Distribution

Market scope may be local, regional, national, or international. Distribution may be direct to consumers or retailers or it may require a wholesaler, distributor, or broker. Describe your company's market scope and your channels of distribution. To what degree do you depend on middlemen?

Market Segmentation

A market segment is a group of customers who share common characteristics that distinguish them from other customers. Market segments are described in terms of geography (region, county size, city size, density, climate), demographics (age, sex, family size and status, income, occupation, education, religion or culture, social class), and phsychographics (life style, personality, purchase occasion, benefits sought, usage rate, degree of loyalty, sensitivity factor). Different market segments may require different products or services. Or they may require different distribution channels, promotion methods or sales terms.

Market Demand Changes and Trends

Describe any significant changes that have occurred in the market in the fast few years. Has market demand increased, decreased or remained steady? Has the market shifted its geographic location? Are new market segments emerging? Old ones disappearing? Pay special attention to any trends that point to future changes.

Major Customers and Concentration

Who are your principal customers? What are their key characteristics? What do they want and need from your products and services? List some actual and potential customers for your product or service. List your major purchasers and rank them by the percentage of sales each represents.

Sales Tactics

Describe the method you use or intend to use to sell your products or services. Will you use your own sales force, sales representatives, distributors, or retailers? What role will advertising, promotion, and public relations play? Compare your established margins and commissions to those of your competitors. Describe any special policies regarding discounts and exclusive distribution rights. Indicate the company's normal sales terms. What percentage of sales are made for cash or credit? What discounts are offered for rapid payment?

Market Share and Sales

What share of the total industry market does your company hold? Translate this market share to forecast market sales. Market sales are the estimated sales to a specified customer based in a specified geographical area within a specified period of time. Estimate in units and dollars the market sales that your company can achieve. Base this estimate on your assessment of your customers and their acceptance of your product or service, the size of your market, trends in the market and the competition. Market sales estimates should be monthly for the next fiscal year and yearly for the next 3 years.

Objectives

Based on the information gathered in the preceding sections, what must your marketing campaign accomplish? Increase profits? Stop a sales decline? Respond to competition? Take advantage of the competition's weakness? Maintain business as usual? Successfully introduce a new product or service? Expand market share? Reposition a product or service? Increase customer satisfaction? Your objective should go beyond these simple statements, however. It should include details. If your goal is to reach new customers, what new customers? Where can they be found? What will your appeal be? How will you reach them? What are your expected results?

Strategy

Your strategy should include the eight Ps of the modern market mix: package, product, price, premiums, promotion, physical distribution, personal selling, and publicity. Describe the combination of these factors that appeals most to your customers and potential customers.

Media Mix

A broad range of media is available to today's marketer, including local, regional, and national newspapers, trade journals, magazines, radio and TV stations, direct mail, outdoor displays, special events, community relations, and personal selling. Choose the media that will reach and persuade the most customers at the lowest cost. This can either be a complicated or simple procedure, depending on the scope of your business, the accessibility of your customers, and the types of products and services you offer. If your media mix is complex, you may want to enlist the help of an agency that can provide media analysis and buying services.

Budget

Budgeting is one of the most difficult decisions you must make. There is no infallible formula for setting marketing budgets. Methods that have been, and continue to be, used include spending whatever you can afford, keeping up with the competition, allocating a percentage of gross sales, using cost and objective (setting aside a total dollar amount for marketing, then breaking the total down into smaller amounts for specific objectives), establishing a per unit expense assignment, and marketing as an investment in the future (allocating a set amount based on a growth guess). Each method has advantages and disadvantages. For example, allocating a percentage of gross sales is easy to work with and effortless to figure out, but it leaves little room for mistakes and it can lock you into a no-growth pattern. Keeping up with the competition means you won't be pouring excessive amounts of money into marketing, but it also keeps you in a constant reactive position just when you need to establish an active direction. Spending whatever you can afford may seem sensible but this system leaves out the most important ingredient for success—flexible long-range planning.

Keep in mind that once you have developed a marketing plan, it shouldn't be carved in stone. Your company will change, and your customers will change. To keep pace with these changes you should re-evaluate and refine your plan at least yearly. In today's increasingly competitive marketplace. Remember your marketing plan is your blueprint for success or failure.

MARKETING PLAN FORMAT

With marketing plans, as with business plans, there are many different ways of presenting the information. It can be a brief verbal presentation to an informal gathering or a formally presented written document. It is suggested for reasons of reference and continuity of marketing activities toward a defined goal that the plan should be written. The plan should contain as much of the following material as is applicable:

- Major strategies
- Marketing objectives
- P & L (profit and loss)
- Communications plans
- Marketing research plan
- Sales management plan

Major Strategies

In two or three paragraphs the major strategies for the brand or service should be stated. This should specify such actions as improving, maintaining, or relinquishing market share; vertical integration; depth of product line; and market regulations.

Marketing Objectives

In five or six sentences, state the measurable marketing objectives that enforce the major strategies. These objectives should be concerned with what can be accomplished through sales, communications, and marketing research.

P&L Effect of the Recommendation(s)

A P&L statement indicating the effects of the recommendation should be included in the marketing plan. This statement will be a general indication of whether the marketing plan will be a success or not. A model P&L for XYZ, Inc. can be seen in Table 4.1.

Table 4.1 Model P&L Statement for XYZ, Inc.

	Actual	Estimated	Proposed
Volume			
Value			
Cases			
Percent increase			
Share			
Cost of Goods			
Sales and Distribution			
Advertising/Promotion			
Miscellaneous Costs			
Pretax Profits			

Communications Plan

There are three major sections to the communications plan: objectives, strategies, and specific plans. The objectives section encompasses two or three sentences on what you want to accomplish to help meet your overall objectives. Included here are specific goals, such as to increase brand recognition from 25 to 32 percent in 1 year.

"How are you going to accomplish your goals?" is a question that is answered within the four major strategies.

1. Creative strategy. Two or three sentences on the targeted audience, main message, positioning, and type of execution.
2. Media strategy. Two or three sentences on how advertising dollars are to be spent: on what media, at what rate, and in what parts of the country? Also included here are the reach and frequency figures.

3. Sales Promotion Strategy. Two or three sentences describing the type of promotional activities, the targeted audience, and what the promotion should accomplish.
4. Specific Plans. This sections details how each of the communication strategies will be implemented. For example will a creative plan utilize layouts and copy, storyboards, radio scripts, or some other plan.

Marketing Research Plan

There are two parts to the marketing research plan: strategy and plans. The strategy includes how research will provide information to assist in preparing and executing the marketing plan. This section also includes communications research. Plans contains the specific plans necessary to execute the strategies evolving from marketing research strategy.

Sales Management Plan

The sales management plan is the responsibility of the sales manager. The following items are discussed under this plan: where are sales coming from (by market, territory, size, price, and so forth), planning, communications, and training of the sales force.

PRICING

The primary goal of any business is to make a profit. Many small businesses fail to do so because they do not know how to effectively price their products or services. Pricing is the critical element in achieving a profit, and is a factor that all firms can control.

Before setting prices, you must understand your product's market, distribution costs, and competition. The marketplace responds rapidly to technological advances and international competition. You must keep abreast of the factors that affect pricing, and be ready to adjust.

Retail Cost and Pricing

A common pricing practice among small businesses is to follow the manufacturer's suggested retail prices. This price is easy to use, but it can cause problems. It may create an undesirable price image, and it doesn't consider the competition.

Competitive Position

Another approach to pricing is a strategy in which a firm bases its price on those of its competitors. A small retailer should compare prices with similar stores. Do not try to compete with a large store's prices, because they can buy in larger volumes and their cost per unit will be less. Instead, highlight other factors, such as customer service. Customers will often pay more for merchandise if they get courteous service.

Pricing Below the Competition

Many vendors have been very successful using a pricing below the competition strategy. Since this strategy reduces the profit margin per sale, a firm needs to reduce its costs and:

- Obtain the best prices possible for the merchandise.
- Locate the business in an inexpensive location or facility.
- Control inventory closely.
- Limit product lines to fast moving items.
- Design advertising to concentrate on price specials.
- Offer no or limited services.

This pricing structure can be difficult to maintain. Because every cost component must be constantly monitored and adjusted. In addition, it exposes a business to pricing wars. Competitors can match the lower price, leaving both parties out in the cold.

Pricing Above the Competition

The pricing above the competition strategy is possible when price is not the customer's greatest concern. Nonprice considerations important enough for customers to justify higher prices include:

- Service considerations: delivery, speed of service, satisfaction in handling customer complaints, knowledge of product or service, helpful and friendly employees.
- A convenient or exclusive location.
- Exclusive merchandise.

Price Lining

A price lining strategy targets a specific segment of the buying public by carrying products only in a specific price range. For example, a store may wish to attract customers willing to pay over $50 for a purse. Advantages of this pricing structure include:

- Reduced errors by sales personnel.
- Ease of selection for customers.
- Reduced inventory.
- Reduced storage costs, due to smaller inventory.

Multiple Pricing

Selling a number of units for a single price is the strategy used under multiple pricing. For example, two items for $1.98. This is useful for low cost, consumable products, such as shampoo or toothpaste. Many businesses find this a desirable pricing strategy for sales and year-end clearances.

Service Costs and Pricing

Every service has different costs. Many small service firms fail to analyze their services' total costs, and therefore, fail to price them profitably. By analyzing the cost of each service, prices can be set to maximize profits and eliminate unprofitable services.

Service Cost Components

Material, labor, and overhead make up the total cost of any product or service. Material costs are the cost of materials found in the final product. For example, the wood and other materials used in the manufacturing of a chair are direct materials.

This is the cost of the work that goes into the manufacturing of a product are labor costs. An example is the wages of all production line workers. The direct labor costs are derived by multiplying the cost of labor per hour by the number of manhours needed to complete the job. Remember to use not only the hourly wage, but also include the fringe benefits. These include: social security, workers compensation, unemployment compensation, insurance and retirement benefits.

Any cost not readily identifiable with a particular product are considered overhead costs. These include indirect materials and indirect labor, such as maintenance, supplies, repairs, heat and light, depreciation, and insurance. These are not charged to direct labor, but must be included as a cost. Examples are: clerical, legal, and janitorial services, supplies, insurance, taxes, rent, advertising, and transportation.

Part of the overhead costs must be allocated to each service performed. The overhead rate can be expressed as a percentage or an hourly rate.

Adjust your overhead costs annually. Charges must be revised to reflect inflation and higher benefit rates. It is best to project the costs semiannually, including increased executive salaries and other projected costs.

A cost list must always be used in preparing a bid or quoting a job. Include shipping, handling, or storage in the total material cost.

Figuring Costs and Profits for a Consultant Service

Pricing services where your own labor or expertise is used is different from pricing services that use materials and other labor. For instance, most consultants price their services by the hour. Senior consultants charge more for their time than do their less experienced counterparts.

Remember to charge for an adequate number of hours. Travel time is usually listed as an extra charge.

It is unlikely that all of your time will be billed to clients. Therefore, hourly or contract fees must be set high enough to cover expenses during slow periods. That is why one-half of the total normal working hours for a given year are used in figuring overhead rates. Try to obtain long-term, monthly, or contract assignments when possible.

MARKETING STRATEGY

This section is designed to help you understand and use the broader concepts of marketing and their application to the act of selling. The section contains information on:

1. Meeting market needs.

2. Specific market identification.
3. Pricing.
4. Marketing channels.
5. Advertising media.
6. Principles of selling.

It is hoped that the information presented here will help pinpoint possible weak items in a product line using available sales data. Decide what, if any, changes should be made in the product line or prices, using available information from a subject industry and projected changes in the market. Evaluate a competitor's strengths and weaknesses. Use demographic data from various local publications and broadcasting stations to establish a rational marketing plan. Use information pertaining to the target audience to develop an appropriate advertising message.

Marketing

In 2 years 20 million people visited the National Air and Space Museum in Washington, DC. Sidewalk vendors do very well around the museum. With the enormous traffic, glittery trailers, and hawkers' shouts of "Hot dogs here!" "Fresh Pizza!" "Cold Ice Cream" and "Hey, Souvenir!" the vendors have combined locations, products, and customers for steady profits. This shows the simplest and the ultimate in marketing. All the elements of marketing are here: a plan, survey, product selection, pricing, location, advertising and it is still the basic transaction, person to person, often with hectic bargaining. Marketing is an all inclusive concept.

As the operator of a small business, you can control some elements of marketing more closely than others. Obviously, if you are already in business, you have made basic decisions about what your product will be; you have established basic prices for your goods or services; and you probably have some ideas about how to promote your business. Marketing involves not only making the initial decisions about each of these elements, but also reviewing those decisions periodically to be sure that your business is operating as profitably as you had planned.

What Is Your Product?

If you are now operating a business, you already have a basic idea of what your product is. Your selection of a business was based on some prior experience with it—either an idea you had or a skill you possessed. You wanted to go into business for yourself so that you could put your ideas into practice and take advantage of the potential income that results from operating your own business.

Defining Your Product

When defining precisely what your product will be, whether goods or services, you must first evaluate the potential market in the area where your business will be located and then tailor your line of products to the needs of that area. For example, if you were planning to open a record shop in a predominantly student-populated neighborhood, you would want to find out whether those particular students listened to classical, jazz, hard rock, or other types of music. You would also want to know if most students preferred records, cassettes, or CDs. Would they need accessories such as blank tapes or record and CD cleaners?

Reevaluation and Change

Once the decision about your product or service line has been made, it must be constantly reevaluated. Use your sales and inventory records to determine which items sold quickly and returned a good profit. These same records can help you spot slow-moving or unpopular items so that you can remove them from your inventory and replace them with more profitable items.

You must also be able to anticipate changes in either your market or your product so that you can react to the change to ensure your continued success. Changes can come in many forms: Your basic market can shift in character; for example, the neighborhood constituting the market area for a record shop can become older (or younger), causing the demand for certain types of music to change.

Your product itself can change due to technological advances, changes in fashion or taste, or changes in general economic conditions.

Know Your Customer

"Beauty is in the eye of the beholder." This old adage can be applied to any characteristic of the product or service that you sell. The dress you sell is only beautiful if your customers think it is. The shoes you sell are comfortable only if your customers think they are. The storm windows you sell are economical only if your customers think they are.

Your own opinions, the opinions of experts, or sometimes even the facts are of secondary importance in selling your product or service. What the customer thinks is of primary importance. Certainly, facts or expert opinions can and should be used to influence your customers' thinking. However, in the final analysis, only your customers' thinking will determine what they buy.

Customer-Oriented Product Decisions

The easiest and most profitable products or services to sell are the ones your customers want to buy. Although their buying habits can be influenced through a manufacturer's advertising effort or your own persuasiveness, the surest path to marketing success is to identify your customers' needs and desires and shape your line of products or services accordingly.

Competition

No aspect of marketing can ignore competition. Just as competition affects the price you charge for your product or service and the methods you choose to market it, competition also influences the line you will offer.

Competition can frequently alter your marketing decisions. To market any product or service effectively, you must know your competition and the advantages that they offer, as well as the advantages that you offer or the steps you must take to gain a competitive edge. Too often, people tend to look on competition solely as a question of price. Yet a competitive edge can often be gained in other ways such as offering better customer service, a superior location, or more effective advertising. Marketing support activities, such as credit availability, product service, warranty, customer advice, or a more attractive buying atmosphere, can also help you gain a competitive edge.

To protect yourself from competitors, you must stay a step ahead in every respect of your marketing operation, including the selection of your product or service line. Frequently, this requires a further definition or review of what you are selling.

The record shop mentioned earlier must realize that it is in the recorded music business, not just the record business. The recorded music business includes cassettes, tapes, and CDs. The "record" shop that failed to offer these items would soon lose business to competition.

Furthermore, the record shop must assess its competition in other areas. Perhaps some are offering stereo equipment or car stereo equipment which the shop might also consider offering its customers. Or perhaps competitors offer customers the opportunity to preview records before buying them. Some competitors may offer more personal service. And, of course, some competitors may simply offer lower prices.

Granted, competition cannot always be met in every way in which it is possible to compete, but the small business person must continually be aware of the competition and what it is doing so that lines can be tailored to provide a uniqueness which will appeal to the market you are trying to reach, whether or not that uniqueness is in product selection, service, price, location, or some other quality.

New Products or Services

There are times when, based on your analysis of previous performance, industry trends, or market conditions, you will want to consider adding to or modifying the products or services you offer.

Since the ultimate test of the value of any new product or service is your market's reaction to it, you are usually well-advised to make some sort of market test before committing to any major change in your line. For example, a women's dress shop may be interested in adding a higher priced designer group, a sporting goods store might be considering the addition of camping equipment, or a restaurant might be considering supplementing its basic "meat-and-potatoes" menu with quiche or crepes. In each case, a tryout for a predetermined period of time can give you an idea of the likely success of a major commitment.

One factor must be borne in mind, however, when conducting a market test of a new product or service. This is whether or not you expect the added line to create additional sales with your present customers or to attract new customers.

For example, if a fast-food shop added salads to its basic hamburger menu, there may be little gain if this simply makes salad customers out of hamburger customers. In fact, it might even reduce the average check, resulting in a loss. However, if it causes hamburger customers to buy a salad also, or attracts new customers to the shop, it will probably prove to be a profitable addition.

Promotional Support

If the change in your product line is expected to increase sales among present customers, these customers must be aware that you are offering the additional product. In other words, your sales force must make the effort to suggest the new items to present customers as they purchase your current offerings. Also, announcements must be made, perhaps in the form of in-store signs, window displays, or even advertisements.

If a product innovation is expected to attract new customers, some form of promotional effort must accompany the introduction. Otherwise, the "new customers" will have no way of knowing that you are offering them the product and your effort will be wasted. While the cost of the promotional effort may exceed the profit potential of the market test, the knowledge gained can be rewarding in the long run. It will alert you to potentially profitable products while deterring you from investing in those that offer little hope of marketing success.

Pricing

As part of the marketing strategy pricing plays a major role. Establishing prices involves three primary considerations. These are:

- Your cost.
- Your competition.
- Your customer.

In normal circumstances, cost can be considered a minimum price. Certainly, when closing out a product line or reducing a surplus in inventory, you may temporarily sell below cost. But neither pricing below cost nor selling at your cost can be expected to make you prosperous.

If you cannot sell below cost, then how far above cost can you sell? This will be influenced by your competition. Perhaps your product has certain advantages that justify a higher price. Perhaps you plan to sell below competition to capture the largest possible share of the market. But there is a delicate balance involved in selling below competition. Will the increased number of units sold result in enough additional profit to warrant cutting prices? And, will a lower price give your products an unfavorable image?

Customer reaction is extremely important regarding prices. How will your customers react to prices higher than your competition? Will they recognize the advantages of your product and pay the premium? Can they be persuaded by salespeople that your product is worth a little more?

However, if your product is no better than that offered by competition, or if you can't point to any significant advantages in the product support that you offer such as service, delivery, or credit terms, then how large a discount will be necessary to attract customers away from your competition? How much will it cost to tell the market that you sell for less?

Establishing a Price Floor

The first step in pricing is to determine your product cost, the floor below which prices cannot fall.

All costs can be classified as variable or fixed (overhead). Variable costs are the out-of-pocket costs or costs of doing business that you incur with each unit of your product that you sell. They include the purchase price of goods acquired for resale, sales commissions, and any product preparation charges, such as alterations or delivery costs.

Fixed costs are the costs of being in business. These costs include such items as rent, administrative salaries, equipment depreciation, and office expenses. They go on from month to month with little variation due to sales.

Consider a product that sells for $1.00. You buy it for $0.50, pay a $0.06 commission on every sale, and incur delivery costs of $0.04 on every sale. Each time you sell one unit you realize $1.00 in revenue and incur $0.60 ($0.50 + $0.06 + $0.04) in out-of-pocket costs.

Each $1.00 sale provides $0.60 to pay your variable costs. The balance of $0.40 ($1.00 – $0.60) contributes to covering your overhead and, once your overhead is covered, producing a profit.

The difference between the selling price and the variable cost can be called the unit contribution.

Unit contribution = Unit selling price – unit variable cost

A product with a variable cost of $0.60 per unit and a selling price of $1.00 has a unit contribution of $0.40 ($1.00 – $0.60). If fixed expenses are $1000 per month, you can determine the number of units that must be sold to cover the fixed expenses. This sales volume is called the breakeven point, and is calculated as follows:

Breakeven = Fixed expenses/unit contribution

$1000/$0.40 = 2500 units

If sales are less than 2500 units, you will show a loss for the month. For every sale above 2500 units, you will show a profit of $0.40.

Effect of Discounting

Suppose you find that your product is not selling at $1.00. Therefore, you want to consider the possibility of discounting it to see if the lower price will encourage sales and produce an operating profit.

Consider the effect of various discounts. First, assume that you decide to discount your price by 20%, to $0.80 per unit. At this price, your average unit contribution would be $0.20 per unit ($0.80 – $0.60). To break even, you would then need to achieve units sales as follows:

$1000/$0.20 = 5000 units

Therefore, you must double your sales to 5000 units in order to offset the effect of a 20% discount.

Now try a 30% discount, of $0.70 selling price. At this price, your unit contribution is $0.10. Your new breakeven point would be calculated as follows:

$1000/$0.10 = 10000 units

As you can see, successive discounts of 10% have greatly increased the number of units that must be sold in order to break even. Whenever you discount to promote sales volume, you should be aware of the added volume required to break even and be reasonably confident that the additional sales volume can be generated by the lower price.

Promotion

Promotion of your products or services involves two elements, both of which relate your selling effort to your market.

1. What is your product message? Describe your product or service so that your customers will recognize the benefits they can expect from purchasing it.
2. How will you deliver the message? Select marketing channels that will reach your audience. Advertise to a large audience through radio, television, or newspapers. Use merchandising activities such as displays and product support activities.

Utilize direct face-to-face selling. Or do you consider your location alone sufficient to attract all the customers that you need?

Frequently, a combination of efforts is necessary for success. Through advertising, you attract a certain number of potential customers to your business. Once there, displays and merchandising aids heighten the customer's interest in buying. Finally, a salesperson takes the time to present and demonstrate your product to close the sale.

All marketing, from large-scale advertising to direct person-to-person contact, must be aimed at satisfying the purchaser's buying motives. Therefore, the buying motives of the audience you are trying to reach must be understood before you can select the product message and media channel which will best serve your needs.

Buying Motives

Why do people buy? Not so much for the sake of owning specific things, but to satisfy certain basic needs or wants. Some of these basic needs include clothing to keep warm, food to avoid hunger, or medicine to relieve pain.

People's buying motives are also determined by wants. A desire for comfort or an interest in styling will often dictate people's preference in furniture, cars, and clothing.

As a marketer, you must convince potential customers that your product or service meets their needs and wants and that it satisfies one or more of their buying motives. You can do this only by relating your product to their needs and wants, and by proving how it will satisfy their buying motives.

The product or service that you sell may have any number of features that appeal to your market. A feature is usually a specific product characteristic. Features should be explained especially if the product is sold at a premium price. A temperature control could be a feature of a clothes washer. A remote channel selector could be a feature of a television set.

But what do these features mean to the buyer? How do they satisfy buying motives? With relatively simple products, the buyer is often familiar with the advantages that the features offer. In many other cases, you may have to explain how the features of your product satisfy the customer's buying motives.

Any description of features must be related to the prospect's buying motives. The temperature control of the washer provides protection for the owner's fabrics. The remote TV channel selector offers the convenience of channel changing without leaving your seat. The key words are protection and convenience—basic buying motives or benefits that people look for when they buy a wide variety of products or services, not just washers or television sets.

Suppose you sell insulated windows with flexible vinyl glazing. Mr. and Mrs. Wilson enter your store to look at insulated windows. They already know that insulated windows reduce heating costs because they have talked with other suppliers. Why should they buy yours instead of theirs? If you said, "Mr. and Mrs. Wilson, these windows have flexible vinyl glazing," their answer would probably be, "So what?," a shrug of the shoulder, or "What is the price?" Flexible vinyl glazing means nothing to the average customer.

As a seller, you must explain the advantages of the flexible vinyl glazing in terms that show Mr. and Mrs. Wilson the benefits that they would realize. If you explain, "Flexible vinyl glazing won't chip and will not require painting," the Wilsons will recognize how this will preserve the appearance of their windows and eliminate the cost and inconvenience of maintenance.

In today's world, products are becoming increasingly complicated: to prompt a customer to buy, technical features must be explained in terms of the increased satisfaction that they will bring to the owner. If customers do not understand how advanced, sophisticated features provide them with specific benefits, the technology and cost of these features are wasted.

THE SELLING PROCESS

Direct Selling and Your Product Message

Although not all products or services are sold person-to-person, an understanding of the direct selling process is often useful in explaining the key elements of any marketing message.

Customizing Your Marketing Message

Direct selling is the ideal marketing situation. When you are face-to-face with a customer, you have an opportunity to find out which specific benefits are most important to that particular customer. Then you can explain how your product or service provides those benefits.

Not all prospects will be interested in all the benefits that your product offers. For example, your product may offer superior styling, quality, and convenience. If you know that a prospect doesn't care about styling, you would stress the quality and convenience features of your product.

Detailed Presentation

A direct selling situation lets you present your product or service in more detail than an advertisement. You have the prospect's attention and the time needed to explain your product thoroughly.

Naturally, direct selling does not apply to many products and services. Perhaps the price is too low to justify the time or the audience is too scattered and too numerous to permit talking with each individual customer. These customers can only be reached through advertising.

The selling principles of a successful direct selling effort are equally valid in shaping a message to larger audiences. Therefore, to understand the basics of the sales message, we will begin by analyzing the direct selling situation. Later we will relate these principles to developing the message for other marketing channels.

Major Steps

A direct selling situation usually consists of three major steps.

1. *Qualifying the Prospect.* Determining the prospect's needs and wants so that you can then explain your product or service in terms that will show how its features provide those benefits.
2. *Presenting the Product.* Describing your product and its features in terms of the benefits that the prospect seeks.
3. *Closing the Sale.* Securing the prospect's commitment to buy your product or service.

In the first step, qualifying the prospect, you want to learn why the prospect needs or wants your product or service. Perhaps you sell sewing machines. A prospect has seen your ad for a low-priced model and has arrived at your shop. Naturally, you have a variety of models and you want to find out which model is best suited to the customer's needs. By simply taking the order for the lowest price model, you might be doing a disservice to both yourself and the customer. If the customer simply wants a machine to hem dresses or patch jeans, perhaps the lowest priced model is entirely adequate. If the customer plans to make clothing for a family, a higher priced machine might be better suited to the customer and more profitable for you.

Qualifying questions should be indirect questions, usually beginning with words such as Why, What, When, and How. These questions usually cannot be answered with a simple "Yes" or "No." They require complete answers that reveal buying motives.

Sample questions from the sewing machine model include:

- "How do you plan to use the machine?"
- "How often do you sew?"
- "What type of sewing do you do?"

You can learn about your customer by asking about the competition. This is particularly helpful when selling high-ticket consumer goods or when selling to commercial and industrial customers.

If a person is buying a replacement for something already owned, you can ask questions about the product now owned. "What kind of refrigerator do you now own, Ms. Baker?" When Ms. Baker tells you that she now owns an Electromat X99, you might ask other questions such as:

- "Is that the 12 or 15 cubic foot model?"
- "Is it equipped with automatic defrost?"
- "Does it have automatic ice-making?"

The answers to these questions will help you lead into such features of your more expensive refrigerators as larger capacity, automatic defrost, and an automatic ice-maker.

The second step in direct selling is presenting the product. An effective presentation often depends on the information received in the first stage, qualifying the prospect. This permits you to explain the features of your product, and its advantages, so that your prospect clearly understands its benefits. Qualifying information lets you direct your explanation to those specific benefits in which the particular prospect has expressed an interest.

The presentation is followed by the primary objective—closing the sale. This is most effective if introduced as a smooth transition from the presentation. Sometimes it's easy. The prospect, absolutely convinced of the advantages of the product and the benefits that it offers, will come right out and buy it. More frequently, it's up to the salesperson to bring up the closing question.

An easy way to do this is through trial closes. A trial close is a question that is asked to determine the prospect's readiness to buy. For example: "Are you satisfied that our product will help you reduce your maintenance costs?"

If the answer is negative, you can reemphasize how your product reduces maintenance costs or you can ask the prospect to be more specific about the cause of his or her doubt.

If the prospect agrees with the salesperson on a series of points, it becomes difficult to say no when the salesperson asks for the order. However, the prospect who disagrees on a number of points will probably defend this position by also saying no when the salesperson asks for the order.

The salesperson should seek agreement on a number of points such as:

- "Don't you think the self-defrosting feature of this refrigerator is a real convenience, Ms. Baker?"
- "You probably need a larger refrigerator than your present one, don't you?"

The salesperson probably knows the points to which the prospect will agree. The idea is to summarize them and ask them consecutively to establish a pattern of agreement, one that will make it difficult for the prospect to say no when the salesperson asks for the order.

Another effective transition is a statement that summarizes product benefits, such as "Mr. Andrews, I think you'll find that the Brand X washer has everything you're looking for. A partial load cycle saves you water, energy, and money. Temperature controls protect your fabrics. And Brand X's reputation for quality assures you that this machine will operate dependably for a long time with little or no maintenance."

Finally let us look at the most vital factor in the selling process step three—closing the sale. All previous steps have been taken with one purpose in mind—to close the sale, to get the prospect to buy.

Unfortunately, many salespeople fall apart at this stage. The salesperson is afraid that a negative response will end communication with the prospect forever. Having maintained a sociable communications level up to this point, the salesperson resists the possibility of rejection. This is a perfectly natural reaction for many people.

A variety of techniques can be used to close the sale. The best approach often depends on the salesperson's individual selling style, the prospect, the product or service that is offered, and the salesperson's earlier success in convincing the prospect of the advantages of the product and the benefits that it offers.

One technique is the direct close technique. This approach assumes that the prospect is ready to buy. In closing, the salesperson asks a direct question such as:

- "We can deliver your sofa next week. What address should we ship it to?"
- "You want this in green, don't you?"
- "Will this be cash or a charge?"
- "Would you like to put this on a budget plan?"

The assumptive close technique is a modification of the direct close. The salesperson assumes that the prospect is ready to buy, but asks less direct questions, such as:

- "Which color do you prefer, red or green?"
- "Which model do you prefer, the standard or the deluxe?"
- "Shall I call an electrician to arrange the installation?"

In the open-ended close technique, the salesperson asks open-ended questions that imply readiness to buy, such as:

- "How soon will you need the sofa?"
- "When should I arrange for installation?"

The prospect's answer to these questions leads to an easy close. If the prospect needs the sofa in 3 weeks, the salesperson can respond, "Then I'll need an order right away, to assure you of delivery on time."

In the action close technique, the salesperson takes some positive step toward clinching the order, such as:

- "I'll write up the order right now and as soon as you sign it, we can deliver."
- "I'll call the warehouse and see if they can ship immediately."

The urgency close technique is when the salesperson advises the prospect of some compelling reason for ordering immediately. Examples are:

- "That's a pretty tight schedule. I'll have to get an answer from you very quickly if we are to be able to meet it."
- "That item has been very popular and our inventory is running pretty low."
- "Our special price on this product ends the 15th of the month."

Not all closing attempts are immediately successful. The prospect may delay, unable to make a decision. If so, the salesperson should ask the reason for the delay. The reason will often help the salesperson plan the next course of action in reestablishing the presentation of the product or service.

For example, the prospect might say: "I think I'll stick with my present machine a while longer." If you properly qualified the prospect earlier, you might respond: "But didn't you say that repair costs were running awfully high? Isn't it worth a few dollars to know that you will save on maintenance costs, and not have to worry about a breakdown at a critical time?"

A prospect may express some objection, real or imaginary, to your product. An objection should never be considered a barrier to a sale. Once you know about it, it is no longer a barrier, simply a hurdle that must be cleared.

A prospect may say, "Your price is too high." Try to discover how high. Perhaps it can be reduced. Or, the objection might be a signal to reemphasize more features of the product that offset any apparent price disadvantage.

Developing Selling Skills

Some people seem to be born with natural powers of persuasion. At an early age, they can easily convince a person of the value of some product or service. However, not all people have these inherent skills.

These skills must be developed, and the way to develop them is through the use of a logical, well-considered, planned selling system of qualifying, presenting, and closing. Through planning, practice, and diligent pursuit, almost anyone can learn these selling skills.

The ability to sell is particularly critical in small businesses where the owner is often called on to conduct the entire selling effort personally. Even if the owner does not sell personally, the sales force must be trained, supervised, and directed.

Selling Skills and Other Marketing Techniques

Any marketing technique that you use must incorporate many of the same selling concepts that were explained in the direct selling situation. Consider how the basic principles of qualifying and product presentation apply to the development of an advertising message. You cannot qualify the prospect directly by asking questions—unless you can afford a costly marketing research effort. Instead, you must make certain qualifying assumptions about your prospects. What are their needs and wants? What benefits do they seek?

These answers then determine the benefits that you will stress in your product message. The message must explain your product in terms of these benefits.

- "Our insulation will save you money."
- "Won-Kote latex paint is easy to apply and lasts longer."
- "Our trained technicians will repair your television set and back it up with a 12-month warranty to put an end to your maintenance worries."

Closing

An advertising message seldom has a specific "close," but it should have an objective. This objective should be expressed in terms that incorporate the concepts of the closing techniques of a direct selling situation.

- "Don't you owe it to yourself to look at our new line of washers before your present one fails?"
- "Buy now while the special price offer lasts."
- "Call today for a free estimate, before winter sets in. Our estimator will show you how much you can save with all-weather insulation protection."

Media Selection

The principles of direct selling can guide your development of a marketing message. The selection of a suitable channel, or medium, for the message depends on the nature of your market and the complexity of your message.

The Table 4.2 describes some of the key features of the various marketing channels that could be available for your product or service. Advertising has been broken down into two categories.

1. *Media Advertising:* Radio, TV, newspapers, and magazines
2. *Direct Advertising:* Mailings, handbills, and telephone solicitation

The third promotional channel, direct selling, has been included as a basis for comparison.

Table 4.2 Key Features of Marketing Channels

	Audience	Message	Cost per 1000	Expected Sales Return
Media advertising	Large, scattered	Brief, universal	\$2 – \$15	1%
Direct advertising	Medium, selective	Intermediate	\$100 – \$1000	1% – 10%
Direct selling	Small	Detailed	Product dependent	10% – 90%

Compare the three approaches in Table 4.2. The first column compares the audience. Media advertising, where the audience is scattered, is ordinarily most useful for products and services that are sold to the general public.

In direct advertising, the advertiser has relatively limited control over a specific audience. For example, the audience for a radio commercial is limited to the show's listeners. With a direct mail or telephone campaign, the advertiser has greater selectivity. The mailer can be addressed to particular persons whose income, occupation, or special interests indicate a desire for the product or service.

Finally, in the case of direct selling, the audience is usually known. The seller's only contact is with parties who have a known need or desire for the product or service.

The second column compares the message capability of each of the three types. Media advertising messages must be brief—perhaps 30 seconds of broadcast time or a few inches of print. Even if more space and time are available, there is a limit to how much the audience is willing to hear or read.

In a direct mail or telephone campaign, the selected audience is usually more interested in the particular product or service and has time available to digest a more detailed message.

Finally, in direct selling, the seller has the advantage of being able to make a detailed presentation of the product or service and address it specifically to the needs of a particular customer.

The third column describes the cost per thousand persons reached, generally referred to as the "CPM." For example, a newspaper advertisement that cost $50 and reached 10,000 persons would have a CPM as follows:

$$\text{CPM} = \text{Cost/thousands of persons}$$
$$\$50/10 = \$5.00$$

A direct mail campaign, with its more selective audience, would have a somewhat higher cost, perhaps $100 to $1000 per thousand, as shown on the table. This would include the cost of mailer preparation, envelopes, postage, purchased mailing lists, and so on.

In direct selling, costs can vary widely. In fact, the sky is the limit! Perhaps a delivery driver is the salesperson. At each delivery point, the driver makes a quick sales presentation. The cost is virtually nothing. At the opposite extreme, when selling is a high-priced service or product to industrial or commercial accounts, transportation costs, living expenses, commissions, and salaries must all be considered. For a salesperson in New York to make a single call in Los Angeles, the cost could be $500 to $1000 or more.

The final column shows the expected sales return. For media advertising, less than 1% of the entire audience can be expected to buy. Frequently, even a small fraction of 1% will more than justify the cost of the advertisement. In a direct mail or telephone solicitation, a somewhat higher return is expected, perhaps 1 to 10%. In direct selling, where the cost of each call is higher, a somewhat higher rate of return must be expected, usually 10% or more.

Advertising Media

A wide variety of advertising media is available. Each has specific applications to various businesses. We will examine some and see how they apply to small businesses.

- Television. The biggest and most expensive. A single network television spot can cost tens or even hundreds of thousands of dollars. Yet brief (10 – 30 seconds) spots on local television channels can often be a wise buy for certain small businesses.
- Magazines. While the national news magazines are usually far outside the budget of small businesses, local magazines, regional editions of national magazines, and special interest magazines with relatively small circulations often fall within the budget capability of small businesses.

Evaluating Advertising Media

In evaluating any individual advertising medium, you will normally want to know three factors that are closely interrelated.

1. Cost.
2. Audience demographics.
3. Audience quality.

To a seller, a quality audience consists of those people who are most likely to buy the product. It does not mean rich versus poor or educated versus uneducated. To the seller of janitorial supplies, a magazine with a high percentage of janitors among its readers is a quality magazine. Why bother with magazines that reach polo players, yachtspersons, or gourmets? Conversely, the furrier would have little interest in advertising in a janitors' magazine.

The question to ask in evaluating the quality of a particular medium is whether or not its audience is representative of your market. The local suburban weekly may have a higher cost per thousand readers than the metropolitan daily, yet offer a higher quality audience for the local retailer. The suburb, not the entire metropolitan area, is the retailer's primary market.

To the seller of blue jeans, the local rock station offers a higher quality audience than the adult-oriented radio news show, regardless of relative audience size or audience income.

In selecting an advertising medium, it is frequently wise to examine the demographics of the audience. The demographics are an analysis of the audience according to social and economic factors. For example, Table 4.3 shows the demographics for two radio stations serving the same geographic area.

The audience of station A is considerably younger, has a lower income, less education, and fewer job skills than audience B. Nevertheless, the more youthful audience A might be a higher quality audience for certain products such as records, contemporary clothing, or fastfoods.

To the seller of higher priced items, such as expensive automobiles, home furnishings, or real estate, audience B would be far more interesting.

In measuring the cost per thousand of a particular advertising medium, you are usually better advised to determine an effective CPM,—that is the cost per thousand people reached who are representative of your target population.

To determine an effective CPM, you would divide the cost of the advertising by the effective audience—that portion of the total audience that is likely to be interested in your product—not the entire audience.

Table 4.3 Audience Demographics

	Station A	Station B
Age		
Under 18	43 %	6 %
18 – 25	27	7
26 – 35	13	23
36 – 50	8	42
Over 50	9	22
Income		
0 – 5000	64 %	5 %
5001 – 10000	16	8
10001 – 20000	11	27
Over 20000	9	60
Education		
High school graduate	42 %	12 %
College graduate	12	65
Graduate school	3	23
Occupation		
Student	51 %	5 %
Unemployed (nonstudent)	10	1
Clerical	7	8
Skilled	8	7
Unskilled	6	7
Technical	7	27
Managerial	6	26
Professional	5	19
Sex		
Male	46 %	73 %
Female	54	27

Effective CPM = Cost/effective audience (in thousands)

For example, assume that you have defined your market as persons with incomes over $25000. You are considering advertising in one of two magazines, whose audience demographics (by income) are described in Table 4.4.

Table 4.4 Audience Demographics by Income

Cost	$ 100	$ 150
Total readers	10000	15000
CPM	10	10
Reader income		
0 – $10000	25%	5%
10000 – 25000	45%	15%
Over $25000	30%	80%

Each magazine has the same CPM, based on total number of readers:

X: $100/10000 = $10 CPM

Y: $150/15000 = $10 CPM

However, you are only interested in readers with incomes over $25000. Therefore, the number of potential buyers you would reach through each magazine must be calculated as follows:

$$X: 10000 \times .30 = 3000$$

$$Y: 15000 \times .80 = 12000$$

You can now calculate an effective CPM based on the number of readers of each magazine that fall within your market.

Magazine	Cost	Effective Readers	Effective CPM
X	$100	3000	$33.33
Y	$150	12000	$12.50

Although both magazines have the same CPM based on total readership, the effective CPM of magazine Y, based on the total number of readers within the market, is far less expensive.

The expected sales generated from media advertising is generally small, usually less than 1%. However, since audiences are large, even a small fraction of 1% often justifies the cost of the advertisement. Consider the example of a local radio advertisement with a $5.00 CPM. If one out of 100 listeners bought the product, the advertiser would realize 10 sales (1000 x ($5.00/10) per sale. While this would obviously be unsatisfactory for selling a $0.50 product, it could be a bargain when selling a higher priced product with sufficient gross profit margin to justify the expenditure.

Direct Promotion

In those businesses where media advertising is impractical, it is often economical to promote through direct mail, telephone solicitation, or some other medium. The first advantage of these promotions is the availability of a far more selective audience.

The CPM of direct mailers is generally higher than that of media advertising. Among the costs involved are:

- Preparation of copy.

- Photography, artwork, typesetting.
- Printing.
- Envelopes.
- Postage.
- Cost of purchased lists.

In some areas, there are businesses that will handle the entire job from start to finish at a fixed cost. Or it may be more economical to purchase mailing lists, hire printers or art services as needed, and do the rest of the job yourself.

The cost per thousand mailers is generally from $100 to $1000 per thousand persons reached. However, the return expected from a direct mailing is usually higher than that expected from advertising since the original audience should have a higher degree of interest. For example, a ski equipment advertisement in the local newspaper would be read by thousands of people who hate the snow and the cold! For less money, you might be able to make a direct mailing to all skiers in your area. The more selective your audience, the higher the rate of return you can expect.

The direct mail message may be brief or somewhat detailed. In the simplest case, with a mailer similar to a handbill, preparation costs may be no more than a few cents each. The piece could be self-sealing so that there is no need for an envelope. Addressing costs could be 3 or 4 cents each and postage, using lower mail classes, can be reduced to pennies.

YOUR PLAN

Your marketing plan, or overall marketing strategy, is a combination of the elements you have just studied:

- Your product.
- Your price.
- Your promotion.

Your product, whether it be goods or services, is the basic reason you are in business. Your product must be oriented to the audience, or market segment, you expect to attract. To that end, your product must be the items or services which that audience demands, and be offered at a competitive price which that audience can be expected to pay. And to get your message across to that audience, you must promote your product in terms which relate to that audience.

The three elements are closely interrelated, and a change in any one of them necessitates a review of how you are handling the other two. No one of the three can be considered independently. Your overall marketing strategy is a careful balance of all three.

Marketing: The Core Element

Of all the elements required to make a business successful, none is more central than marketing. The greatest product and service ideas are of little value unless their story is told in the marketplace. Your marketing effort is the foundation of all other aspects of your business. Marketing attracts the sales dollars which cover the costs of doing business while providing the profit on which to build the future of your business.

Consumer Orientation

Successful marketing strategies are based on knowledge of customer needs and wants. Your product or service line should be determined by the purchasing interests of your market. After all, it is easier to sell what people want to buy.

Establishment of the best price to charge for your product hinges on the determination of customer reaction to various possible prices. There is no one and only price to seek for most products or services. Instead, there is a range of possible prices. As the price becomes higher, you can expect sales to decline. Therefore, you must try to select that price which offers the most profitable combination of sales volume and unit contribution.

Similarly, your choice of a marketing message should stress the benefits that your product or service offers customers. And your choice of marketing channels to convey your message must consider which channels provide the most efficient and effective means of reaching your intended audience.

Application to Your Own Business

The principles of marketing, as presented here, applied to your business, can guide you in the development of a customer-oriented marketing strategy that can dramatically improve your business' chances of continuing success.

MARKET RESEARCH DATA SOURCES

Market research must be performed in order to gather the data necessary to back up your belief in your product or service. This means looking into and becoming aware and knowledgeable of both your potential customers and potential competition. You can be sure that if your product or service is successful there will be competition.

The first and most logical place to start is with a listing of your company's competitors. If you don't know who they are, then visit a major public library with an extensive business section, where you should be able to locate the pertinent information. For those who need help in using a business library, a book on this subject such as *How to Use the Business Library, with Sources of Business Information*[1] may help.

The major part of this book covers specific publications (handbooks, periodicals, business services, government publications), but there are also brief sections on the mechanics of locating information in libraries, writing reports, and using audiovisual aids, as well as on data processing.

Directories

Business directories are usually available through library services that provide information on products, manufacturers, potential buyers, and trade associations. A good place to start is the reference book *Guide to American Directories*.[2] Its information on directories, classified by industry, profession, and function, is useful for identifying specific directories to locating sources of supply (competitors) and new markets.

1. Webster, H. and S.W. McFarland. *How to Use the Business Library, with Sources of Business Information*, 4th ed. (Cincinnati, OH: Southwestern, 1957).
2. *Guide to American Directories*, 9th ed. (Rye, NY: B. Klein, 1975).

Library services can also provide manufacturers' directories, often by state and industry. The *United States Industrial Directory*,[3] in three volumes, lists manufacturers alphabetically and gives a description of each firm's product lines, number of employees, address, and telephone number(s). A classified section includes products with names and addresses of manufacturers (competitors). The directory also offers special sections with chemical and mechanical data and trademark and trade name identifications.

Another good annual directory is *Thomas Register of American Manufacturers*.[4] This 11 volume set is a purchasing guide, listing names of manufacturers (competitors), producers, and similar sources of supply in all lines.

Financial directories are an invaluable source of information. *The Dun & Bradstreet Reference Book*,[5] published six times a year, contains the names and ratings of nearly 3 million businesses of all types located throughout the United States and Canada.

An excellent annual financial reference source for the electronics industry is *Electronic News Financial Fact Book and Directory*.[6] It is an alphabetical listing of most publicly held electronics corporations, and includes company addresses, corporate officers, directors, areas of work, divisions, subsidiaries, and a 5-year financial history covering sales and earnings, revenues by line of business, common stock, common stock equity, income account, assets, liabilities, and a statistical summary.

A directory for studying competitive successes and failures is *World's Who's Who in Finance and Industry*.[7] It provides biographical information of men and women prominent in finance, industry, and trade.

Security Exchange Commission and Other Public Sources

A listing of your competitors and data on each can be compiled by researching privately published directories and other sources. If your competitor is a public corporation, the job is simplified. Extensive company data are found in the registration statements, prospectus, proxy statements, and other reports resulting from the full-disclosure requirements of:

Securities and Exchange Commission (SEC)
Interstate Commerce Commission (ICC)
Federal Power Commission (FPC)
Federal Communications Commission (FCC)
Civil Aeronautics Board (CAB)
New York Stock Exchange (NYSE)

A registration statement is the basic disclosure document for a public distribution of securities registered under the Securities Exchange Act of 1934. It is made up of two parts. The first section, the prospectus, is the only part that is generally distributed to the public. It contains a wealth of information on company history, investment risk factors, use of stock proceeds, and capitalization; a financial statement of operations (usually covering several years); and a description of the business. It will include a general description of the products and their market, the percentage of sales for each, and how the products are marketed. Competition, product development, manufacturing facilities,

---

3. *United States Industrial Directory* (Boston: Cahners).
4. *Thomas Register of American Manufacturers* (New York: Thomas).
5. *Dun & Bradstreet Reference Book* (New York: Dun & Bradstreet).
6. *Electronic News Financial Fact Book and Directory* (New York: Fairchild).
7. *World's Who's Who in Finance and Industry* (Chicago: Who's Who).

number of employees, officers, remuneration of officers, stock option plans, principal and selling shareholders, balance sheets—all these are also discussed. The prospectus, in other words, offers everything you always wanted to know about your competitor but were afraid to ask.

The second section of the registration statement contains information of a more technical nature dealing with such matters as marketing arrangements, the expenses of distribution, relationships between the registrant and certain experts, sales of securities to special parties, recent sales of unregistered securities to subsidiaries, and the treatment of proceeds being registered.

The Securities Exchange Act of 1934 has four types of disclosure requirements relating to registration, periodic reporting, proxy solicitation, and insider trading. Listed (New York and American exchanges) and OTC (over the counter exchange) registered companies are required to file certain periodic reports. The most important of these reports are Forms 8K, 10K, and 10Q, of which 10K is the most useful for obtaining competitive information.

Form 10K is an annual report due 90 days after the end of the fiscal year. It contains certified financial statements, including a balance sheet, a profit and loss statement for each fiscal year covered by the report, an analysis of surplus, and supporting schedules. It includes a breakdown of both sales and earnings for each major line of business, although a company with sales greater than $50 million does not have to carry an individual breakdown unless a product line contributes 10 percent or more to total volume of pretax profits. Smaller companies must break out such product line data on their annual 10K reports to the SEC, they need not disclose the information in the annual report to their shareholders.

The 10K report must reveal the amount spent on R&D in the preceding year, the size of order backlogs, the availability of essential raw materials, competitive conditions in the industry, and the financial statements of unconsolidated majority-owned subsidiaries. It must also disclose any leasing and rental commitments and their dollar impact on both present and future earnings. Therefore because it provides an abundance of information the 10K report is a bonanza for evaluating a competitor's business.

Since not all of the information in a 10K report finds its way into the company's annual report to the shareholders, competitive research should be done with the 10K supplementing the annual report.

Large public libraries, large financial houses, and leading business school libraries have microfilm copies of 10K reports and up to 10 other reporting documents that are required by law. A company's 10K report can usually be obtained by requesting a copy in writing from the company's financial officer or marketing vice president.

If a competitor is a private corporation, then the data, though more difficult to obtain, are not out of reach for an aware and observant analyst. Data are often published in the newspapers, trade journals, and information bulletins reporting on new contract awards and their value, contract losers, personnel movements, litigation, new product announcements and prices, user-reported product problems and manufacturers' responsiveness in correcting them, and other pertinent data.

Information Sources within Your Industry

Trade shows offer a wealth of information. Visit your competitors' product booths and examine their products for the latest features, strengths, and weaknesses. Listen to their salespeople's stories, especially what they are telling other prospects. Many trade shows have seminars where competitors often present papers on their products and/or developments. This can be a rich source of information.

Another less-glamorous technique for gaining information on your competition is to interview their personnel for positions in your company. Much can be learned through intelligent questioning about your competitor's operations without compromising an employee's position.

If a competitor is local, a periodic inspection of its parking lot during working hours will reveal if its employee count is up or down, which has a direct relationship to its business activity.

Keep a current file on your competitors' product brochures and specifications. Often, changes in these indicate trends in a company or in the industry itself. Competitive information is available, if only you have the imagination, alertness, and determination to uncover it.

Evaluating the collected data to determine why a competitor is a success or a failure is the more difficult side of information gathering. With a public corporation, first examine the bottom line profit on its income statements for several years to determine if it is a success or a failure. Since one good year doesn't make a success and one bad year doesn't make a failure, look for trends. A consistent growth in net profit in actual dollars and percentages of sales over a period of years certainly indicates a successful operation. Conversely, a consistent decline would seem to indicate failure. If a business is sensitive to national economic expansion and recession, then national conditions figure into your calculation.

A further examination of a business's income statement will reveal how it has allocated its sales dollars among labor, material, overhead, engineering, marketing, and General and Administrative expenses. If its allocation has been a success, try to duplicate it. If not, compare the expenditures against those of a successful company and try to determine the cause of failure. Knowing why a company has failed is as valuable as knowing why it succeeded.

If labor costs are too high or low, question why. If labor costs are too high, perhaps the firm has priced itself out of the market. If too low, it may have caused high labor turnover and thus incurred increased training costs and inefficiencies. This liability may show up in other cost areas, such as increased overhead and scrap. If labor turnover is high, question why. Is it because of low wages, poor working conditions, poor management, or even a high turnover in management itself?

If overhead costs are too high, perhaps your competitor has a staff larger than is required to do the job. Or perhaps building rent and operating costs are more than they should be. If overhead costs are too low, it could mean there is inadequate supervision to maximize labor's efforts. The same logic holds true for engineering, marketing, and G&A. Not spending enough is just as bad and is sometimes worse, than spending too much. Striking the right balance is the key.

If it is possible, and oftentimes it is, visit and tour your competitor's facility. Be observant. Are its offices and manufacturing areas neat, clean, and well organized for a smooth logical flow of raw materials to completed and shipped products? Or are they unkempt and helter-skelter? It is often stated that the cleanliness and physical organization of a company is a direct reflection of its managment's thinking and a yardstick for measuring a product's quality.

The behavior of a firm's personnel is very revealing. If they are neat about themselves, it usually means that they take pride in their work. This point should not be taken lightly because it is people, not things, that make a company succeed or fail.

Observe the offices and how they are decorated. And the type of factory equipment employed. If a facility's furniture, floor and wall trappings, and manufacturing equipment are more expensive than required, it is also a reflection of management's thinking. Its priorities indicate whether the company will succeed or fail.

If financial statements are not available and facility tours are not possible, much can still be learned about a competitor's success or failure by examining its product—in detail! Buy one and have a manufacturing, purchasing, and engineering team dissect and examine it objectively.

A manufacturing expert can determine how it was put together and how much it cost to do so. The engineers can evaluate its performance, and estimate its design and manufacturing cost. The industrial engineers and purchasing department buyers can estimate piece parts and subassembly costs. Put all the pieces together, and the development and manufacturing costs will be known.

The marketing people will know its selling price, competitor's discount policies, facility size, manufacturing capability, sales force, and customer base. The marketing data provides the remaining puzzle pieces. Product costs, gross margins, expenses and profits (or losses) can be estimated.

Knowing your competitor's customer base even reveals the likelihood of it (your competition) being paid on time and discloses something about its financial condition. Added finance charges must either be absorbed (subtracted from profits) or passed on to the customer (higher prices).

Executive and first-level management stability is also an indicator of a successful or failing company. If the financial reports are available for several years, examine the names filling the executive management posts. If the same names appear year after year, it indicates stability. If not, it may mean that the company is still trying to find the right combination to make it work.

The same holds true for the first-level managers. Trade journals regularly report their comings and goings. Management changes are expensive. They cause morale problems, which foster inefficiency. This in turn is reflected in lower productivity, lower quality, higher costs, and the bottom line: lower profits.

There are many ways to be an effective industrial management detective and to evaluate competitive reasons for success or failure. It just requires imagination and common sense.

Other Market Research Sources

The following references sources are published by the Federal Government and are available through most public libraries and yield valuable marketing and competitive information.

U.S. Industrial Outlook (Dept. of Commerce)

Industry surveys (Dept. of Commerce)

Annual Statement Studies (Robert Morris Associates)

Industry Norms and Key Ratios (Dun and Bradstreet)

Standard Industrial Classification Manual (Dept. of Commerce, National Technical Information)—Gives the definitions of the classifications of industrial establishments by activity engaged in and by Standard Industrial Classification (SIC) codes which the government and the business information industry use to classify and track all segments of industry. The SIC classifies firms by the type of activity they're engaged in, and it is used to promote the uniformity and comparability of statistical data relating to market research.

Census of Business for 1982. Retail—U.S. Summary (U.S. government Printing office). Final figures from the 1982 Census of Retail Trade, includes statistical totals for each region, state, city, and standard metropolitan area—tabulated by type of establishment.

Census of Manufacturers for 1982 (Dept. of Commerce). Five volume report about manufacturing industries. Location of manufacturing plants tabulated by State and counties.

Census of Wholesale Trade of 1982 (Dept. of Commerce). Two volume report of wholesalers, including geographical breakdowns by state, cities over 5000 population, and standard metropolitan statistical areas.

Census of Selected Service Industries for 1982 (Dept. of Commerce). Two volume report of more that 150 types of service industries.

Census of Population for 1980 (Dept. of Commerce). Most complete source of population data in the United States. Census is taken every 10 years.

County Business Patterns, 1982 (Dept. of Commerce). A series of publications presenting first quarter employment and payroll statistics, by county and industry. Separate reports issued for each of the 50 states, the District of Columbia, Puerto Rico, and outlying areas of the United States.

County and City Data Book (Dept. of Commerce). Contains data for 50 states, 3141 counties, or county equivalents, 840 cities of 25,000 inhabitants or more, among others.

Statistical Abstracts of the United States (Dept. of Commerce). A general review of statistical data collected by the U. S. government and other public and private organizations. A good source of secondary data.

Survey of Current Business (Dept. of Commerce). The most current monthly and quarterly statistics on a number of general business and economic topics.

Business Statistics (Dept. of Commerce). A historical record of the statistics presented monthly in the *Survey of Current Business*.

Federal Reserve Bulletin (Dept. of Commerce). Current economic indicators and analysis of changing financial conditions.

Survey of Consumer Expenditures (Dept. of Commerce). Includes comprehensive information about consumer expenditures.

BUSINESS STRATEGY: DEVELOPING THE COMPETITIVE ADVANTAGE

Successful smaller companies either intuitively or explicitly have a business strategy; they make careful choices. Large companies, however, lumber along making mistakes. They have the financial momentum to survive.

The question, though, is not whether a company has a business strategy or not. Every company has one. It exists whether it's explicit or is something that just happened.

Perhaps it's inside the head of the CEO, and he or she has been acting it out. The real question is how to improve a strategy by developing it explicitly. You can leave strategy to chance. You can come up with one in the shower. Or a CEO can reap the important benefits of marrying analysis and creativity, the essence of a good strategy.

Most good companies have a strategy that has been well worked out. Many companies have been successful without doing so. These companies see a need and go after it to fill it. With intuition and luck, they have come upon a formula, an image, their positioning, and package. It adds up to an interesting strategy.

But, in a world where competition is getting tougher every day, there are benefits in having an explicit strategy. Unless you make a strategy explicit, it's very hard for everybody in the organization to know what they should be doing. One real benefit of a strategy is that it unites effort. Everybody in the company, from the salespeople to the plant worker, know what the fundamental advantage of the company is and can act it out in their daily behavior. The best strategists are usually those CEOs who can really institutionalize a strategic vision, talk it up, get the organization excited about it.

In companies with an explicit strategy, one should be able to ask any person what the company strategy is and some semblance of the company's strategy will be the reply. And because the employees all know what that strategy is, they can make decisions based on their understanding of it. That's the power of strategy: All the many daily decisions that get made reinforce a common theme.

Having an explicit strategy allows a company to cause change. Too many companies and too many CEOs don't cause change; they simply react to it. Most companies imitate or emulate their rivals. They are stuck doing what somebody's already doing. They're making incremental adjustments, not creating real competitive advantage. The most successful companies are ones that cause changes. They push the nature of competition in the right direction—their direction—because they're out in front of industry evolution.

A good example of this is Federal Express. Before there was a Federal Express, there was no small-parcel delivery industry as such. Fred Smith did not imitate anyone. He figured out a new buyer need and created an entire new method of serving that need with his Memphis hub and his fleet of airplanes.

One can create a strategy without having a planning staff or incurring any overhead. Almost any CEO or entrepreneur can—if the management team is gathered together and thoroughly thinks it through—follow a systematic process of developing a strategy.

The small-business person should know that having a strategy doesn't require a staff, overhead, or hiring a consultant. Simply get your management team together and pool your knowledge about the competitive environment. Strategic planning can be done at the CEO's house on a Saturday morning.

What is most needed is not overhead, but a framework to help managers take a systematic approach to analyzing their business. A framework helps organize the issues and makes sure you look at the relevant variables. It won't, though, give you the answer. The answer is a creative act, but it will ensure that you're looking at the right variables.

An example of a framework model is Michael Porter's[8] Five-Force Framework. The

8. Porter, M.E., Competitive Strategy (New York: Free Press, 1981)

forces noted affect an industry's profitability; its jockeying for position among current competitors:

1. *Threat of New Entrants.* High barriers to entry keep competitors out by making it costly to get in.
2. *Bargaining Power of Suppliers.* Suppliers that are too strong flatten industry profits.
3. *Bargaining Power of Buyers.* The leverage of buyers is a function of their alternatives, including doing it themselves and going elsewhere.
4. *Threat of Substitutes.* How easy is it for a buyer to substitute another product entirely?
5. *Rivalry among Existing Competitors.* Who has the competitive advantage.

You should look at the variables such as customers, suppliers, manufacturing costs, and so on. Much of the information you already know. But by conducting a systematic industry analysis, companies get a clearer sense of the dynamics in their industry. By being systematic in analyzing their sources of competitive advantage, they can better prioritize.

The best strategies are ones developed by the operating managers. Successful strategies are the work of people doing the work. Ten years ago, strategy became a fad; everybody had to have a strategic-planning process, a planning department, and consultants. Then came a general disillusionment with strategic planning. Many of the plans that resulted from these early efforts have proved to be total bull. They were not connected to reality. All the overhead of strategic planning didn't produce much in terms of actual behavior.

Today strategy and its implementation are much more connected. Line managers are being charged with the formulation of strategy, not planners—because they know the business, and they're the ones who have to make it work.

The strategic CEO develops strategy with the heads of the important functions—manufacturing, R&D, and marketing. The essence of strategy is to integrate the company's functions into one consistent position in the competitive environment.

In a successful company, such as Cray Research Inc., you see consistent behavior in every function. Its sales force is trained to find buyers who will need a supercomputer; it doesn't try to sell to everybody. Everything is consistent.

Eventually it is the CEO who makes the decision about which option a company will adopt. The leader exercises judgment and sets the vision. Functional managers have an input. Having them involved not only leads to better information, but helps in communication of the strategy. A strategy has to be communicated to be truly effective. Good CEOs are always finding ways to help the key people understand the company's strategy. There's no way a CEO can be on top of everything.

The framework model previously noted helps companies systematically analyze their competitive advantage. And it helps managers determine the long-term profit potential of the industry they're in.

One important component in selecting a business is industry structure. If you are an entrepreneur, or someone considering starting a new business or buying an existing one, the structure of the industry is vital.

Generally, entrepreneurs start companies when they discover a need not being met. But just meeting a need is not enough. The question is whether a company can make money at it. You won't make money if the customer is price sensitive, and the barriers to entry are so low that there will be 25 new companies in a year. The Five-Force Framework can help select which businesses will be attractive.

The most common error entrepreneurs make is to assume that high growth means profitability. Industries such as video games and personal computers had explosive growth. For a year or two, companies did well, then very few were successful because barriers to entry were too low. The lesson is: If the structure is not attractive, then the industry will crash.

One method of creating barriers to entry is heavy or focused advertising to create a brand image that is hard to overcome. Another is to innovate with some form of new technology that will increase the economies of scale. American wine producers increased advertising and product introductions in the 1960s—that raised the cost of entry. In the 1970s, California wine growers banded together to designate regions for certain varietals, such as Napa and Sonoma, which limited the area of land under cultivation—that's another barrier to entry.

Most successful smaller companies are focusers. They have found a particular kind of buyer. They've chosen a narrow market in which to compete. Now, the key to a good focus strategy is picking the right segment to focus on. For example, the La Quinta motel chain: It's a motel chain catering exclusively to the frequent business traveler. They dedicated their entire strategy to serving this traveler in ways that companies who were also serving other types of buyers had difficulty matching.

Ideally, using the framework analysis process, you can spot an industry in the process of evolution. That's how most successful companies get their start. They get in when it's not too hard, and enjoy the fact that entry barriers are going up. This can be called a state of competitive disequilibrium—when an industry's structure is changing. When that happens, it is time to look for a new competitive advantage. An example is in pharmaceuticals. For the last 80 years, competition was based on chemical technology. Now biotechnology is impacting the market, providing a new basis of advantage. It's a change in the rules of that industry.

Change is extremely important to competitive advantage. Generally, if you try to compete on the same basis as established companies, you'll lose. Competitive disequilibrium nullifies the advantages of established rivals. The entrepreneur of today must find sources of disequilibrium. How is technology changing? How are demographics changing? What are the bottlenecks, the problems in the industry?

Eastern Airlines is a classic case of a company that is "stuck in the middle." Eastern is not known for superior service, but it is also not low cost. Buffeted by low-cost Continental on the one hand and differentiators American and Delta on the other, Eastern has nowhere to go. American, however, stands out, because it made a very conscious choice to pursue a differentiation strategy (targeting service to the business traveler) that everybody in the company understood. American also illustrates another important point. Having a strategy can in itself be a source of competitive advantage. Most companies imitate the leading companies in their industry, almost ensuring mediocrity.

It takes years—3 to 5 years—for companies to make a fundamental shift in strategy. This is because its staff must be convinced of the new direction and retrained. New projects must be developed. Similarly, customers, distributors, and suppliers don't instantly grasp a new strategy—it takes a certain amount of time for them to understand that a company is really going to change.

If a company is shifting positions every year, it will never achieve any competitive advantage. This highlights the importance of taking a fundamental, long-term look at the industry, and not just reacting to day-to-day events and trends.

To innovate a company must become a moving target. There is no contradiction here. The company must constantly be raising the standards of the execution of a consistent strategy. If the strategy is to be the low-cost producer, there must be an ongoing cost-reduction program that marshals all the creativity a company can muster. There should be a goal of cutting costs 5, 7, or 8 percent a year. If the strategy is to be a differentiator, you must be constantly thinking of innovative new ways to enhance service or to provide new features.

There is no such thing as a short-term strategy. Strategy is a long-term construction. Its object is to place a company in a sustainable position in its industry and to improve that position over time.

There are times when a strategy must be changed. One of those is in a time of competitive disequilibrium—when the structure of the industry fundamentally shifts.

The real acid question that every CEO in a difficult environment must ask is: What's my competitive advantage going to be? Address that question first, and chances are the company will be on the right track.

Part of any good strategy is some consideration of how a company can defend itself from attack. If you are most vulnerable to a low-cost competitor, explicit steps should be taken to keep costs in line. However, there must be a clear offensive element: to constantly bolster competitive advantage. A focuser like Cray Research, for example, aggressively invests in software to defend its lead at the same time that it is working to increase performance.

An advantage of an articulated strategy is that it relieves the pressure of "short-term performance." If a company gives the analysts nothing else to go on, numbers will be the sole standard of measurement. However, a company that can clearly articulate a convincing strategy gets a lot more slack in the market.

Financial numbers are, in and of themselves, a very incomplete yardstick with which to gauge a company's health. Emerson Electric's Skil business unit is a case in point: While their numbers seemed to show that things were getting worse, things were actually getting better. They had greatly improved their defect levels, raised customer satisfaction, and lowered costs.

To keep tabs on the underlying health of the company a CEO needs sources of ongoing feedback, and ones that will deliver the bad news. This is one area where having an outside adviser can be very helpful, someone who will stand up to a CEO and tell the truth. One good way to get feedback is for the CEO to take the time to go visit a group of the company's leading customers. Tell them, "I'm not here to sell you anything. I'm here to listen. Tell me the top three or four things that we're doing as well as our competitors."

Companies must offer buyers a clear-cut choice in order to sustain a competitive advantage over rivals. Failure to make a choice means that a company is stuck in the middle, with no advantage. The result is poor performance. A company either offers lower costs or something unique (differentiation) at a premium.

But a company must also choose its scope—whether it will target a particular segment or go for a broad market. By analyzing its industry with the Five-Force Framework, then using the analysis to choose one of the four generic strategies shown in Table 4.5, a company can pursue its true competitive advantage.

Steering a business by financial controls alone is not enough. The small business owner needs more than a budget to manage the future direction of his or her company.

Table 4.5 Market Targeting

Strategic Target	Strategic Advantage	
Broad (industrywide)	Broad cost	Broad differentiation
Narrow (Particular Segment Only)	Focus cost	Focus differentiation
Specific Customer	Low cost	differentiation

Through strategic planning, you can get employees in all areas of your business pulling in the same direction and sharing the same vision that you have for the future of your business. At the same time, plans of this type enable you to act and react quickly to market opportunities and problems.

You can also use your plan to communicate with bankers who often do not understand the nature of your business. Bankers need to be convinced that your company is in control of its future before they will lay their money on the line. A comprehensive plan aimed at sustained growth in sales and earnings can be very convincing.

A plan is also very helpful in dealings with your suppliers, advertisers, attorney, accountant, auditor, investors, and/or business consultants.

What Is Strategic Planning?

Ask 10 people for a definition of strategic planning and you will probably receive 10 different answers. But, most will agree that it relates to the overall direction of the company.

Every company exists for a purpose. That purpose is its "mission," and everything it does is generally directed toward fulfilling that mission.

Strategic planning is a process by which key people in an organization can:

- Define or redefine the company's mission.
- Assess its current situation.
- Decide what they want the business to look like in say 3 to 5 years.
- Map out a course of action to bring the company from where it is now to where they want it to be, recognizing its strengths, weaknesses, opportunities, and threats.

When done properly, strategic planning is a simple, creative, and flexible process that works well for a small business, a way to replace separate marketing, operational, financial, and/or budgeting plans with one comprehensive plan.

The first step in the strategic planning process is the analysis of current external factors situation. The process begins with an assessment of the current situation in which the business finds itself. Those areas that predominantly relate to external factors impacting on the company are usually examined first. In most cases, it makes sense to divide your analysis into groupings. For example:

- National economic outlook.
- Local or regional economic outlook.
- Industry outlook.

This part of the analysis should begin early, at least a quarter or so before you begin the formal planning process. By making a folder for each of the preceding outlook areas, you can begin to collect information for later analysis. Among the common sources are:

- *The Wall Street Journal.*
- *The New York Times.*
- *Business Week.*
- Industry periodicals.
- U.S. Department of Commerce (especially for the 12 leading economic indicators).
- Federal Reserve banks.
- Local industry associations.
- Local chambers of commerce.
- Public library.

After data is collected, its present and future impact can be assessed. For example, slow housing starts, weak retail auto sales, reductions in real disposable personal income, and increasing levels of unemployment would signal reduced future demand for goods and services.

After preparing a written, concise assessment of the impact of these external factors and sharing it with key people in your organization, you are ready to begin the next phase of your planning effort.

The Planning Session

After preparing a concise, written assessment of the external environment, you are ready to gather together key people in your organization for a marathon planning session. These should include owners and key people in sales, service, finance, processing, manufacturing, and so forth.

It is essential that all effective areas of the company be represented. In that way, you will reveal the company's strengths, opportunities, weaknesses, and threats and all areas of the company will be more likely to "buy into" the goals eventually set. Strategic planning is most successful when it is a participative process.

For the process to be most effective, an energized environment must be created. One that is free of interruptions and distractions. To get the creative juices flowing, it is usually best to get away from the business premises. A hotel meeting room where coffee and lunches can be brought in is usually sufficient. For many businesses the process takes two full days, so you may want to accomplish it over a weekend.

The sessions will function best if they are structured. The following is a proven technique:

- Appoint someone to be the facilitator of the group. It should be someone impartial and not so locked into his or her own ideas that the potential merit in the ideas of others cannot be seen.
- Agree in advance that creativity is desirable so no idea brought up at the session will be immediately discarded as impractical or undesirable. (Sometimes impractical or impossible suggestions can "spark" other extremely positive ideas).

- Appoint someone who can capture the essence of what the group agrees to and write it down.
- Equip the room with a flip chart and bring a sufficient number of felt tip markers.
- Bring masking tape and/or thumbtacks for use in tacking up the flip chart pages around the walls of the room as needed and
- Follow an agenda. The one shown in Exhibit 1 on page 144, has proven very effective.

After the meeting's opening comments, review of the session's procedures, and report on the external environment, you are ready to begin what is perhaps the most important part of the process—Strengths, Weaknesses, Opportunities, and Threats (S.W.O.T.) analysis.

Here the facilitator divides the flip chart page into two sections by drawing a vertical line down the middle and heading the page as follows:

Strengths & Weaknesses
Opportunity & Threats

Then the facilitator asks anyone in the room to identify a strength, weakness, opportunity, or threat for any area of the company. He or she explains that eventually these areas will be addressed in the goal setting portion of the session.

Each SWOT is written concisely on the flip chart. Everyone is asked to identify any SWOTs they can think of. The process can be accomplished by starting with one person and going around the room in a clockwise fashion. By announcing this technique, you put everyone on guard that when their turn comes up, a response is expected. This rapidly creates a "charged" atmosphere. No one wants to feel foolish in front of a group, so they will listen carefully to what is said and think hard about a number of possible responses they may use when their turn comes up.

Most companies have several SWOTs designed to impact on their ability to:

- Increase revenues.
- Improve financial condition (profitability, liquidity, solvency, credit and collections policies, etc.).
- Keep pace with competition.
- Improve efficiency, productivity and service.
- Capitalize on emerging trends.
- Improve labor relations, human resource development and training (personnel issues: salary administration, job descriptions, benefits, personnel manuals, etc.)
- Improve internal communications.
- Improve distributor or supplier relationships.
- Improve public relations, advertising, promotions, and so on.
- Improve or enhance products and services.
- Capitalize on physical facilities (location, capacity, layout, parking, costs, etc.) improve or enhance insurance coverage.
- Function at peak efficiency within current organizational structure.
- Get the most out of their present legal structure.
- Arrange for the orderly retirement and transfer of ownership and control of senior owners to junior owners or potential owners.

The facilitator should be certain that all SWOTs are recorded on the chart. If someone's description of a SWOT is so complex that it cannot be recorded concisely, ask that person to describe it in no more than five words.

As pages of the flip chart become full, tack them up around the room where everyone can see them. They will be used again later on.

When the facilitator has gone around the room several times and every conceivable SWOT has been identified, the group is ready to attack the next phase of the planning session.

Development of the Mission Statement

An organization's mission statement (usually no more than one or two sentences) describes the purpose of the organization. It is aimed at enabling all members of the organization to share the same view of the company's goals and philosophy.

The mission statement describes the business you are in. It typically speaks to:

- Reason the organization exists.
- Products and services offered.
- Clientele served.
- Nature and geographic marketing territory of the business.
- Areas of specialization.

Every organization needs a mission statement and many require one for every business unit that is part of their organization.

The facilitator should lead the group in establishing (or redefining) its mission statement in view of the changes discussed earlier regarding their external environment, and the SWOTs they have discussed.

Some sample mission statements as stated in each company's annual report are:

- "The Johnson Corporation of Ohio is dedicated to maintaining its position as a leader in providing quality insurance and financial service products to businesses and individuals through a staff of highly trained people sharing a tradition of integrity and service to its clients."
- "Budget Travel provides economical vacation travel and related services to customers in the greater Chicago area, who expect efficient, problem-free travel arrangements at a low cost."
- "Our goal is simply stated. We want to be the best service organization in the world." IBM
- "Whitefield Markets' goal is to be the lowest cost provider of quality foods and groceries in the West Orange area."
- "Velvet Green Nurseries' goal is to provide a full range of high quality wholesale and retail nursery products to professional landscapers and discriminating homeowners."
- "Smith Packing Company's mission is to be the lowest cost producer of pork products in Delaware."

Identification and Analysis of Key Results Areas

The next phase of the planning session is to identify and analyze your company's key results areas (KRAs). Most companies have from 8 to 15 (KRAs) where the organization must achieve success for it to grow and prosper. The company's objective and tactics can be grouped into these key areas, making it easier to process, prioritize, allocate resources, and coordinate with other areas.

The facilitator should lead the group in identifying KRAs for their business. Many of the areas mentioned earlier in the SWOT analysis section (increase revenues, improve financial condition, etc.) will often become the KRAs for a company.

Establish Strategic Objectives

After each KRA is agreed on, the next phase of the session is to establish strategic objectives for each. Usually there will be one or two strategic objectives for each KRA, but occasionally there can be more. As with all objectives, it is important to make them as quantifiable as possible.

Example 1

Key Results Area: Increase Revenues

Strategic Statement: Increase revenues from new customers, expanded sales to existing customers, acquisition of other related businesses, opening new branches, marketing new products/services, investment income and inflation to achieve:

$_____________ in revenues by Dec. 31, 19__
$_____________ in revenues by Dec. 31, 19__
$_____________ in revenues by Dec. 31, 19__
$_____________ in revenues by Dec. 31, 19__
$_____________ in revenues by Dec. 31, 19__

Example 2

Key Results Area: Improve Financial Condition

Strategy Statement: Establish and maintain a financial condition sufficient to support planned growth through achieving liquidity, solvency, and profitability as follows:

	19__	19__	19__	19__	19__
Liquidity: Achieve a working capital position of					
Solvency: Achieve a net worth of					
Profitability: Achieve pretax profit margins as follows:					

Establish Tactical Objectives

After strategic objectives are established for each KRA, you are ready to establish tactical objectives to support each strategic objective. Eventually you will prioritize these tactical objectives, assign responsibilities, and agree to target dates for completion.

An easy way to do this is to review the ideas from the SWOT analysis (they should still be tacked up on the walls of the room) and use them to facilitate the process. Group each idea shown on the SWOT analysis into one of the KRA categories. For example, say the flip chart pages identified 12 SWOTs that could either positively or negatively impact on the first KRA, "Increase Revenues." Use those SWOTs to develop tactics for the increase revenues strategy. Strengths and opportunities can be capitalized on by establishing tactics to get the most from them. Weaknesses and threats can be reduced or eliminated by establishing tactics to deal with them.

Tactical objectives are specific objectives, usually of a short-term nature, aimed at supporting the strategic objective. For example, if your strategic objective is to increase revenues, some tactical objectives might be to:

- Produce and market a new product (take advantage of an opportunity).
- Develop and market a new service (take advantage of an opportunity).
- Identify a specific market you have been successful with and develop a target marketing plan to penetrate that market (capitalize on a strength).
- Retain sales staff or replace weak sales staff (correct a weakness).
- Revise traffic flow of store or change displays, signs, and so forth (correct a weakness or capitalize on a strength).
- Change marketing or advertising theme (take advantage of an opportunity).
- Establish a sales campaign with meaningful incentives (take advantage of an opportunity).
- Change salary program for salespeople from fixed salary to variable salary based on their sales (correct a weakness).

After you have established tactics to address each SWOT and have categorized all of the SWOTs, you are ready to proceed with the next phase of the process.

Integration of Budgeting into the Strategic Plan

The strategies and tactics agreed to will impact on revenue and expenses to differing degrees and at different times, depending on implementation dates. The group needs to consider the potential impact of each objective on both revenue and expenses so that they can eventually be prioritized and reflected in future budgets.

When this has been completed you are ready to prioritize your objectives.

Prioritizing Objectives, Assigning Responsibilities, and Establishing Target Dates

It is important that you resist the temptation to set extremely ambitious target dates for your objectives. In most cases, the tactics you have agreed on need to be accomplished by people who already have a full day's work with no time to spare. Each employee must be given sufficient time to achieve the specific objectives assigned to him or her, or the plan will quickly be viewed as impossible to accomplish and will relegate itself to uselessness.

When assigning a tactic, let the recipient tell the group how long it will take and accept that target date, if at all possible.

After prioritizing all the objectives, assigning responsibilities and agreeing to target dates for each, you are ready to discuss business plan coordinating and monitoring.

Business Plan Coordinating and Monitoring

For maximum sustained results, an overall coordinator for the business plan must be appointed. That person should be responsible for bringing together the various pieces of the business plan into one comprehensive plan and for monitoring the continuing process of following the plan.

Exhibit 2 on page 146, displays a suggested format for the business plan and Exhibits 3 and 4 are examples of the two primary forms used for recording strategic and tactical objectives.

Exhibit 3 on page 147, should be completed for each key strategy area. It displays the key strategic objectives and all the supporting tactical objectives. It also provides the name of the person responsible and the agreed on target date, with a section for comments on the status of each objective.

Exhibit 4 on page 148, is an Individual Objective/Summary Status report. This form enables the individual to keep track of the status of each objective he or she is responsible for and report monthly to the business plan coordinator.

The monitoring process should be made as simple as possible. Each month, the business plan coordinator collects the updated individual objective summary/status reports from employees and makes certain that all objectives in the plan have been accounted for. The coordinator makes note of shortfalls, needs for reforecasts, or meetings to be called, and documents progress in a brief memo to all business plan recipients. For example:

- "At the end of April, we are on target or ahead of plan in all but 2 tactical objectives. The attached individual objectives status reports describe the status of every objective."
- "Where a shortfall exists, I have highlighted the shortfall and made notation of the actions being taken."
- "Overall we are well on our way toward achieving our major objectives."

When this procedure has been discussed with the group, agreement should be reached on when the written business plan should be completed and ready for use. The method of communicating the content of the plan to all employees should also be discussed.

Why Business Plans Fail

No treatment of this subject would be complete without mention of the fact that some business plans fail—and for good reasons.

The major reasons some fail are:

- Plans are constructed around incorrectly defined strategies.

- Plans do not have detailed implementation strategies with tasks, schedules, and responsibilities.
- Plans do not state goals in quantifiable terms.
- Process used to develop the plan did not allow all individuals to share a common view of the organization's future and how to get there.

The process described here is aimed at avoiding these pitfalls and has been proven effective with small businesses.

BUILDING THE BUSINESS PLAN

This section has been prepared as a question/answer process to assist in the preparation of business plans for both internal management and financing purposes. It should be considered a guide in developing your plan. There are questions to assist in the collection of information useful in preparing your plan. It is designed to assist you in exploring the foundations of your business, its present needs and opportunities, and the requirements for writing your business plan.

As you go through this section, you will answer questions about many aspects of your business. Many of the questions are designed to stimulate your thinking and increase your understanding of the planning process. The questions may also be used to collect information from your planning assistants or management team (if one exists); consider having each assistant or team member respond to certain subsection(s) and compare the perspectives.

Your business plan, however, is not the sum of these questions; it is the final written product that results from the conclusions you draw while going through the questions. Once you have answered the questions (or as many as apply to your situation), you will have information to help you prepare your written business plan.

Company History

1. When was your company founded?
2. What is your form of organization?
   a. Sole Proprietorship
   b. Partnership
   c. Corporation
3. If a corporation, what is the date and state of incorporation?
4. If a corporation, identify the following:
   a. Class of stock
   b. Shares authorized
   c. Shares issued and outstanding
5. If a partnership, what are the partners' respective interests?
   a. Name
   b. Percentage interest

6. If a corporation, identify management's ownership interest.
   a. Name
   b. Class of stock
   c. Percentage of interest
   d. Amount paid
7. If the business' original name was different, what was it?
8. Who were the founders of the company? (Create 1/2 page summaries of their resumes or background information if they are still with the company or if this is a new business.)
9. How was you product or service developed?
10. Discuss any significant additions or changes in the company's products, purpose, management structure, and so forth.
11. Describe any major obstacles or problems the company has faced.
12. What have been the company's greatest accomplishments?

Definition of the Business

1. What business are you really in?
2. What need(s) do you satisfy?
3. Whose needs are these?
4. Are these the needs of the buyer? Or is the buyer just an intermediary?
5. Why are you in business? (Prioritize at least three reasons.)
   a. Profit, service, other (explain)
   b. Self-employment, Other (explain)
6. How is your business different from others in your industry?

Definition of the Market

1. What is the present status of your company, your industry, and your competition in life cycles? (Are you a new company, experiencing rapid growth, fairly stable, or experiencing a phasing out of operations?) Check one stage for each of the following items.

	New	Growing	Mature	Declining
Your industry				
Your competition				
Your company				
Your products or services (list and check)				
1.				
2.				
3.				

2. How do you sell and distribute your product or services?
3. What geographic areas are covered in the sale and distribution of your product or services?
4. Discuss the commissions and discount schedules given to retailers, wholesalers, and distributors. (How do they compare with those given by the competition?)
5. Describe any special policies regarding such items as exclusive distribution rights. How will these affect your sales and profits?
6. Describe any seasonal impacts on your sales efforts.
7. If you have distributors or sales force, how are they selected, trained, and compensated?
8. If your products or services are purchased or used by individuals, which of the following characteristics describe your customers? (Check the pertinent items, and give specifics.)
   a. A particular age group?
   b. A specific ethnic group?
   c. One gender?
   d. Within a geographic area?
   e. A particular income level?
   f. A particular occupational category?
   g. A particular educational level?
9. If your products or services are purchased or used by companies, which of the following describe your customers? (Check the pertinent items, and give specifics.)
   a. Merchandisers?
   b. Service organizations?
   c. Manufacturers?
   d. Industrial users who use your product or service in their own operations?
   e. Regulated users who have special constraints or rules influencing their buying decisions?
   f. Government users?
   g. O.E.M. (Original Equipment Manufacturer) users who buy to incorporate your product into their own for resale?
   h. Contractors who buy from you to include in their services?
   i. Industrial distributors who concentrate on industrial products and sell to O.E.M.s or industrial users?
10. What customer groups have you targeted for future penetration?
11. Identify any major customers who have made or are willing to make purchase commitments. Indicate the extent of those commitments.
12. List the advertising, public relations, and promotional tactics you use and will use to bring your product or service to the attention of potential customers.
13. How do you and will you utilize the media to announce your product or services?
    a. Newspapers?
    b. Television?
    c. Radio?
    d. Print literature?

14. What does your competition do in their advertising strategies?
15. What are your company's advantages in the market?
16. What are your company's disadvantages in the market?
17. What have been the historical sales trends with the company's major customers or classes or groups of customers over the last 4 years? (This question should be duplicated for as many customer classes or groups your company's product(s) addresses.)

Major Customer/Class or Group: ________________

	19__	19__	19__	19__
Number of units sold (billable hours)				
Increase or (decrease) (%)				
Total units (%)				
Revenue				
Increase or (decrease) (%)				
Total company (%)				
Revenue				
Gross Profit				
Increase of (decrease) (%)				
Total company (%)				
Gross profit				

18. What have been the historical sales trends in the company's major geographic market areas over the last 4 years? (This question should be duplicated for as many geographic market areas your company's product(s) addresses.)

Geographic Market Area: ________________

	19__	19__	19__	19__
Number of units sold (billable hours)				
Increase or (decrease) (%)				
Total units (%)				
Revenue				
Increase or (decrease) (%)				
Total company (%)				
Revenue				
Gross Profit				
Increase or (decrease) (%)				
Total Company (%)				
Gross Profit				

The following questions marked with an asterisk (*) can relate either to the entire company or can be subdivided by product class, service, or service class. Duplicates of the questions should be used if it is appropriate to assess each product or service separately. Each of the following questions relate to the product or service identified in question first following.

19.* What have been the historical sales trends of the company's major products (or product lines) or services (or service lines) over the past 4 years?

Product/Service: ______________________________

	19__	19__	19__	19__
Number of units sold (billable hours)				
Increase or (decrease) (%)				
Total Units (%)				
Revenue				
Increase or (decrease) (%)				
Total company (%)				
Revenue				
Gross Profit				
Increase or (decrease) (%)				
Total Company (%)				
Gross Profit				

20.* What are the total sales and marketing costs over the last 4 years?

	Cost Per Call	Cost Per Order	Cost Per Sales ($)
19__			
19__			
19__			
19__			

21.* Is demand for the products or services in your market greater than supply? What data support your estimate?

22.* How big is the market for your products or services?
a. Currently?
b. In 1 year?
c. In 2 years?
d. In 3 years?

23.* Anticipate the expernal changes that you think might take place over the next several years and which would impact most on your marketing strategies.
a. What are the two most important conditions which could change?
b. What two potential changes have the greatest likelihood for harming your market?
c. What two potential changes have the greatest likelihood of providing you an advantage in the marketplace?

24.* What can be done to prepare for the changes in questions 23a and 23b?

25.* Identify three chief competitors in your industry.
a.
b.
c.

26.* Rank the performance of your company and competitors identified in question 25 on a scale of 1 to 4 (1 = high, 4 = low) in each of the following areas. Also indicate by use of an arrow (^) next to each ranking whether it is going up or down in the near future.

	A	B	C	Us
Market Share				
Price (1 lower price, 4 = higher price)				
Profits				
Quality				
Research and development				
Reputation				
Sales				
Service				
Other				

27.* Evaluate your company and its three chief competitors in the area of aggressive competition. (Check the phrase in each column which best characterizes your competitors and your company.)

	A	B	C	Us
Aggressive, no holds barred, cut-throats				
Hold your own, maintain, react, price cut response				
Follow the leader, but nonaggressive				
No competitive action or responses				

28.* Evaluate your company and its three chief competitors in the area of risk taking. (Each column should have one check mark.)

	A	B	C	Us
High degree				
Moderate degree				
Low degree				
Almost never				

29.* How do you determine your pricing policies?

30.* Compare your prices with those of your three chief competitors. (Place a check mark for each competitor which answers the question, "Are our prices higher, lower, or the same as this company?")

	A	B	C
Higher			
Lower			
Same			

31.* If your product or service is priced lower than your competitors', explain why and how you can do this and maintain profitability.

32.* How will you justify any price increases over competitors' products or services? (Check one or more.)
  a. Newness
  b. Quality
  c. Warranty
  d. Service
  e. Delivery time
  f. Other (explain)

Evaluating Market Strategy

The focal point of market analysis is:

1. Who are and have been key customers?
2. What products/services have they purchased?
3. What has been the level of their purchases?
4. How has the level of purchases been affected by product/service prices and sales, promotion, and distribution policies and efforts?
5. What has been the net impact on revenue levels of changes in product/service prices?

These questions can be answered by using data from the firm's cost accounting system and sales records to complete a series of structured, historical trend formats. An analysis of key customer sales, a product revenue analysis, and a geographic sales analysis should be completed to support this overall evaluation.

Description of Products or Services

1. What is the nature and application of your product(s) or service(s)?
2. What patents, trademarks, copyrights, or other proprietary features does the company possess?
3. Describe any agreements with your employees and subcontractors regarding unauthorized use of trade secrets.
4. List key suppliers, including type, size, and location.
5. Are there any parts, supplies, or merchandise necessary for production or sale which are only available from one supplier, from overseas, or which might be subject to shortages? If yes, describe.
6. To what extent are you now dependent on outside vendors?
7. What are the backup sources for vendors?
8. What future research or new product developments are you planning?

9. Include in an appendix to the plan any photographs, engineering studies, and so on, as appropriate. List which items seem likely to be included in the appendix.

The following questions should be asked if your business is a merchandise organization.

10. List the breakdown of how your space is utilized (storage of inventory, merchandising display, office, support functions, other).
    a. Area
    b. Approximate square feet
    c. Total space (%)
    d. Allocated rental cost

11. Complete the following for each of your significant areas or departments.
    a. Area or Department
    b. Square footage Total space (%)
    c. Annual sales (or revenue) ($)
    d. Annual sales (units)
    e. Revenue/square foot
    f. Gross profit margin (%)
    g. Gross margin/square foot
    h. Inventory(s)
    i. Inventory turnover (days, weeks, etc.)
    j. Cost per square foot (rent, util., etc. divided by square footage)

12. Do you stress a special area of appeal? (Such as lower prices, better quality, wider selection, convenient location, or convenient hours?)

13. Identify your two fastest and slowest moving product lines. Also indicate next to them, by use of an arrow, whether they are speeding up or slowing down in sales.

Fast	Slow
a.	a.
b.	b.

14. What product draws customers best during sales?

15. Which product's rate of sale is least affected by markdowns and sales? Why?

16. Which products are bought largely "on impulse?" Which products are largely planned purchases with comparison shopping?

Impulse	Planned
a.	a.
b.	b.

17. What special customer services do you offer? (Check those applicable.)

Children's area	"Rain checks"
Credit terms	Returns & refunds
Delivery service	Special orders
Discounts or coupons	Waiting areas
Other	

The following questions pertain to manufacturing organizations.

18. What manufacturing processes are utilized to produce each of your products?

19. What are your quality control procedures?
20. How are your quality control procedures similar to or different than those used in other parts of your industry?
21. What inventory control procedures do you use?

Professional service organizations should ask these questions.

22. Service organizations have available hours for the delivery of services. How many staff members do you have? Multiply this by the average number of hours they are available to provide services per week.

    Available hours = Number of staff × average hours per week

23. How many hours, on the average, are "billable" weekly?
24. Divide the average number of billable hours by the total number of hours available. (This gives you a rough percentage of utilization figure and may indicate your first step in increasing revenue.)

    Utilization percentage = Average billable hours/available hours

25. What is the average billing rate?
26. Multiply the average number of billable hours per week times the average billing rate. (This represents an estimate of your weekly revenue.)

    Weekly revenue = Average billable hours × average billing rate

27. What is your average overhead cost? (Add monthly salaries, commissions, rent per month, utilities, office expenses, etc. Make this the weekly average by dividing by 4.33.)

    Average weekly overhead = Sum of monthly overhead expenses/4.33

28. Divide your average weekly overhead by the average number of billable hours per week. This will determine overhead per hour.

    Overhead per hour = Weekly overhead/average billable hours

If your company is involved with new products ask yourself the following questions.

29. Are there any critical processes or parts of the manufacturing process which are not completed and available at this time? If yes, describe them.
30. Discuss any Underwriters' Laboratory, regulatory (e.g., FCC or EPA), or other special approval or licensing requirements your processes require.
31. What type and extent of technical assistance are required to get your product to a marketable state? How will this be obtained?
32. What are the estimated costs and time required to achieve each step in your product's developmental process?

	Costs	Time
Engineering		
Research		
Tooling or startup		
Design		

Recruiting personnel
Training personnel
Packaging
Patent work
Other

Evaluating Research and Development Strategy

The primary basis for evaluating the R&D strategy are:

1. Have scheduled objectives been accomplished?
2. Have the results of R&D activities justified the level of investment made?
3. Are current R&D activities still appropriate in light of marketplace developments?
4. To what extent has the firm been able to bring responsive products/services to the market in a timely manner (i.e., with respect to customer needs and preferences)
5. How do the firm's current R&D capabilities and plans relate to trends and emerging developments in the external environment?
6. What is the firm's reputation for innovation? For useful, quality products/services?
7. To what extent has the firm been able to maintain or expand its market position by continually introducing new or improved products/services?

Evaluating Production Strategy

Focal points of the analysis:

1. What raw materials and supplied products/services does the firm use?
2. What are the labor costs in terms of both wages and fringe benefits? What are the productivity rates from labor?
3. What are the firm's space and equipment costs? What are the output/productivity rates of its equipment? What is the historical relationship among production volume, equipment productivity, and labor productivity?

A firm can answer these questions by using data from its cost accounting system.

In evaluating its production strategy, a firm should assess both the overall factors that are common to most products/services and the factors that are unique to specific products/services. A firm should recognize that an ultimate objective of this assessment is to develop standard production costs for each product/service. These costs are used to prepare the production operating plan.

Human Resources

We've all heard the saying "employees are our most valuable asset." Usually when we hear it, we snicker and say to ourselves, "Oh sure. Just more management propaganda."

But in today's competitive business environment, that propaganda has probably never been more true. Chances are, if your company doesn't have its share of competent, hard-working and committed employees, your balance sheets aren't as healthy as they could be.

Attracting competent employees—and keeping them happy and productive—is one of today's biggest business challenges. This often involves one or more of three areas: pay, benefits, and communication.

Balancing the financial realities of your business with employees' needs and expectations is an ongoing challenge. To ensure long-term effectiveness in managing human resource programs, it is recommended that you regularly assess its foundation. The following are some questions to guide you in your thought process:

1. With whom does your company compete for business and/or employees (what companies and where)?
2. How competitive does your company wish to be in the compensation and benefits it provides (average, above average, below average)?
3. Are your current pay scales and benefit levels competitive?
4. Are benefits viewed as compensation that is earned at your company or do employees view them as an entitlement?
5. Do employees understand their pay and benefits?
6. Should/can pay and benefits be used as an incentive to increase employee productivity?
7. How should the pay and benefits provided be linked to company financial results?

By asking these and other questions, you'll begin to clarify your company's basic beliefs about managing its most valuable asset.

The following questions should be asked regarding the management structure.

1. Who are your company's key managers? (Include short (no greater than 1/2 page) resumes and job descriptions, if available.)
   a. Name
   b. Responsibilities
2. What strengths do you have as a management team?
3. What is being done to overcome any management weaknesses?
4. What is the total cash compensation for members of management and their ownership in the business?
   a. Name
   b. Annual compensation
   c. Ownership (%)
5. Describe significant fringe benefits available to members of management (including stock options).
6. What are the terms of any outstanding loans between company and management?
   a. Borrower
   b. Amount Outstanding
   c. Terms
7. Complete the following for board members.
   a. Member
   b. Annual compensation

c. Ownership (%)
d. Stock options

8. What kind of additional expertise would strengthen the board?
9. Who are your consultants or advisers and their firms and associations?
10. Is there a current organization chart? Does it reflect the way the company actually functions? (Include the chart in an appendix if available.)

Nonmanagement personnel questions would include:

11. Consider the abilities or limitations of your nonmanagement staff with respect to the following activities or situations and indicate with a check those areas needing improvement.

	Production	Marketing	Administrative	Financial
Changing functions				
Varying volumes of work				
Changing priorities				
Technical abilities				
Innovation				
Attaining objectives				
Maintaining timetables				
Holding to budgets				

12. What was your employee turnover rate:
    a. 2 years ago?
    b. 1 year ago?
    c. Currently?
13. How does your turnover rate compare with others in your locality and your industry? If yours is significantly lower or higher, explain why.
14. What types of employees would be difficult to replace, if necessary, during the coming year?
15. What recruitment procedures have been used?
16. How successful have your recruitment procedures been?
17. What orientation or training programs do you provide?
18. How effective are your orientation or training programs?

The following questions relate to unionized employee groups.

19. Which personnel groups are unionized?
20. What are your relationships with the unions? (Describe work stoppages or significant grievances filed.)
21. When do union contracts come up for negotiation?
22. Are any other employees likely to be unionized? (If yes, explain.)

Evaluating Organization and Management Strategy

The primary basis for evaluating the organization and management strategy includes the assessment of environment:

1. Understanding and clarity of a firm's goals, performance objectives, and values.
2. Understanding of a firm's organizational structure, assignment of responsibilities, and reporting and accountability relationships.
3. Effectiveness of a firm's management and supervision.
4. Effectiveness of a firm's internal communications procedures.
5. Assessment of staff morale.
6. Effectiveness of a firm's personnel management policies and procedures.
7. Equity and fairness of a firm's compensation policies.
8. The match between the current skills profile and the skills required to effectively support a firm's operation.
9. The effectiveness of a firm's policies and procedures for training and developing existing staff.
10. The effectiveness of a firm's procedures for directing, evaluating, and improving performance.

Four key questions for organizational/management evaluation:

1. What are the areas of skills deficiency and poor or inadequate performance within the firm?
2. What actions have been taken to correct these deficiencies, and what have the results been?
3. To what extent have hired and promoted staff performed effectively in their positions?
4. What formal and informal training opportunities are provided to staff? What has been the impact of on job training performance?

Objective and Goals

1. What is the length of the planning period?
2. Generally speaking, where do you want to be during the planning period?
   a. Profits (dollar amount, percent net to gross, etc.)?

b. Markets (market share, new geographic areas, etc.)?
c. Services or products (sales, development of new ones, etc.)?
d. Personally (sale of business, go public, merge, etc.)?

3. What are the primary roadblocks to getting where you want to be, as indicated in Question 2?
   a.
   b.
   c.
   d.

4. What are your internal strengths that will have the greatest impact on getting where you want to be, as indicated in Question 3? How will you use these strengths?

	Strengths	Actions to Build on Strengths
Production		
Marketing		
Administrative		
Financial		

5. What are your internal weaknesses that will have the greatest impact on getting where you want to be? How will you correct these weaknesses?

	Weaknesses	Actions to Minimize Weaknesses
Production		
Marketing		
Administrative		
Financial		

6. Describe your present facilities, both plant and office space, whether leased or owned, and any significant amounts of equipment or furniture.

7. Name the limitations involved in your present facilities.

8. What are the advantages and disadvantages of being located in your area in terms of the following?

	Advantages	Disadvantages
Labor availability		
Proximity to primary customers		
Proximity to suppliers		
Transportation		

9. How do the advantages and disadvantages listed in Question 8 affect your ability to meet objectives?

10. What have been the effects of changing governmental actions (increased spending, tax cuts, tight money, etc.) on your company?

11. What has been the impact of inflation on your company?

12. How does current legislation in the following areas affect your operation?
    a. Regulation or deregulation?
    b. Health and safety issues?
    c. Product standards?
    d. Advertising and promotion?
13. What legislation is currently being considered or prepared which could affect your company?
14. What regulatory or governmental agencies have jurisdiction over your industry?
15. What are the likely changes in your industry? (For example, the extent of innovation within this planning period.)
16. How could the changes in Question 15 affect your company?
17. What kind of lag is your industry experiencing between R&D and application? (How long does it take to get a new idea into the marketplace?)
18. What results do you anticipate during the planning period if your company continues on its present course without change?

	Up Significantly	Up Moderately	Same	Down Moderately	Down Significantly
Sales					
Net income					
Product costs					
Margins					
Overhead					
Cash					
Collections					
Working capital					
Inventories investment					
Liquidity					
Quality					
Service					
Pricing					
Staff attitudes					

19. What are at least two changes in each area of operations which, if accomplished, would help your company make progress in this planning period? (You might solicit suggestions from departmental staff on this one.)
    a. Production
    b. Marketing
    c. Administration
    d. Financial
20. In the following list rank your most serious problems. (Rank them in order to importance, 1 = most important.)

    Cash flow
    Changing your markets

Competition: keeping up with it or ahead of it
Cost containment
Cost of product or service
Creativity
Distribution channels
Employee productivity
Employee turnover
Government regulation
Market acceptance of your products or services
Physical plant: space, machinery, and equipment
Pricing
Public opinion
Quality
Raising capital
Service
Systems: accounting and controls
Technology
Other (describe)

21. How will your company benefit from solving its top three problems as noted in Question 20?

22. Given all of the ideas you have explored in Question 21, list at least six tentative objectives which you would like to achieve.

23. For each of the six objectives listed in Question 22, list at least two different or alternative ways to get to each of the objectives.

24. What internal changes are needed to achieve the results you want with each of the objectives in Question 23. (Identify whether they are in the production, marketing, administrative, or financial area of operations using a "p", "m", "a", or "f.")

25. What will each objective require?
    a. Number of weeks
    b. Cost of personnel
    c. Other costs

26. List at least two risks associated with each objective?

27. What can be done to minimize or avoid the risks?

28. Which of these objectives, emphasize and use your strengths?

29. Which de-emphasize or are unaffected by your weaknesses or limitations?

30. Is each objective "doable," given your resources?

31. For the chosen objectives, complete Table 4.6. Below are explanations of the items to consider.
    - *Objectives.* Briefly list the objectives you have chosen to focus on during the coming planning period.
    - *Tactics.* List the specific steps or stages required to accomplish each objective.
    - *Due Dates.* List the expected dates of completion for each objective and for significant tactics used to meet that objective.

- *Person(s) Responsible.* The person(s) responsible for executing each objective or tactic should be designated in the space provided.
- *Reports Due.* Establish a reporting schedule for checking the progress of work on the objectives. These reports should be made at least quarterly.
- *Evacuation Routes.* Indicate what alternatives are available if there arises a need to alter your plan at a specific point, probably between stages of development. Tactics may need to be reevaluated.

Table 4.6 Planning Chart

Objectives	Tactics	Due Date	Person(s) Responsible	Reports Due	Evacuation Routes

32. With the objectives you have set for this planning period, where is your first bottleneck likely to be? The second? The third?
    a. Capitalization
    b. Outside processors
    c. Parts or supplies lead times
    d. Promotion and sales of products
    e. Specific types of equipment
    f. Trained workers
    g. Transportation of products
    h. Warehousing
    i. Other
33. For each identified potential bottleneck in Question 23, what can be done to minimize the negative effects on your operation?

Financial Data

1. Gather your historical financial statements together for the last 3 years and insert them here. List the statement years that are included.
2. If there are reports that management utilizes to plan, direct, and monitor the company's operations, gather samples or all these reports (by quarter if provided that way) and insert them here.

If you are financing externally answer these questions.

3. How much money do you need now?
4. How much will you need over the next 3 to 5 years? When?
5. Do your plans indicate sufficient liquidity at each check point (quarter, year-end)?
6. How will the initial and subsequent amounts of money be used?
7. What are your future plans for repayment of the money? (For example, will you go public? Merge?)
8. What assets are available to collateralize long-term loans (land, buildings, equipment, etc.)?
9. What collateral is available for short-term loans? (This is primarily inventory and receivables for the existing company. The new business must typically rely on other ways to support financing needs.)
10. Will the owners of the business personally co-sign the loans? If so, are their personal balance sheets current?
11. List the financial assumptions in your plan. These may include:
    a. Revenue:
    - Sales prices
    - Sales growth
    - Sales force
    - Sales promotion
    - Market share
    - Time period required to develop additional customers
    - Distribution methods
    - Product and mix
    - Supply and inventory
    - "Other income"
    - Technology
    - Substitute products
    - Geographic markets
    - Advertising and promotion

    b. Production:
    - Facilities
    - Payroll, including overtime
    - Fringe benefits
    - Overhead
    - Material costs
    - Production efficiency
    - Time period required to increase production capability and capacity to achieve the production requirements
    - Availability of factors needed to increase or maintain production

    c. Operating Expenses:
    - Payroll costs
    - Payroll tax and other related payroll costs

- Real estate taxes (including payments in lieu of taxes)
- Insurance
- Utility costs
- Repairs
- Sales commissions
- Professional fees
- Depreciation
- Interest
- Income taxes

d. Balance Sheet:
- Accounts receivable collection period
- Inventory turnover
- Accounts payable turnover
- Debt financing requirements
- Loans or loan commitments
- Capital expenditures
- Capital structure

e. General:
- General economic conditions (e.g., inflation, unemployment, growth/recession, interest rates) that may affect many key factors of the business.

12. Consider the assumptions you have listed. Several of these assumptions may be interdependent. Examples of interdependencies among assumptions include:
    - Sales commissions/sales revenues
    - Production costs/sales volume
    - Payroll taxes/salary expense
    - Equipment requirements/production capacity
    - Production volume/production capacity
    - Sales revenue/market potential
    - Sales salaries/sales volume
    - Interest expense/debt levels
13. Do you believe there are any internal inconsistencies in your assumptions? If yes, explain.

Evaluating Financial Strategy

The primary basis of financial strategy evaluation is ratio analysis. From that analysis a firm should be able to answer the following questions:

1. What is the firm's liquidity position in relation to its need to make short-term immediate use of funds?
2. To what extent is the firm making effective, productive use of its assets? Are assets underutilized? Overutilized? Is the level of investments in relation to production requirements too high? Too low?
3. What is the firm's debt position? To what extent is the debt position contributing to or detracting from the firm's overall profitability?

4. To what extent is the firm's investment strategy adding to or subtracting from profits?

5. To what extent are the firm's cash-flow management policies and procedures contributing to increased debt or diminished profitability?

Computerized Assistance

The material covered so far in this discussion of business plan development may seem complex and, in some cases, overwhelming. And, there was a time when that is exactly what building a business plan was. Because of this people who were required to build business plans dreaded it especially if the plan was required to be rewritten for any reason. But, today because of the availability of personal computers and attached printers the problem is not as great.

As you probably already know computers consist of two basic elements: hardware and software. And when attempting to establish a system, which consists of the hardware, software, and attached equipment, you should first determine what you want the system to do. Then determine the software (programs) that can do it. Finally, select the hardware that is required by the software.

We will now discuss the components of a computer system that can assist you in assembling a computer system that will make the writing of a business plan and all its related activities much easier than it has ever been in the past. First, a brief explanation of software, provided second, an explanation of various application type (productivity) software, and finally an example of one company's selection criteria of the computer based on the expressed needs of a variety of users and their applications.

Software

Software is the medium that generates your unique information needs through your microcomputing machine. There are two primary types of software: operating system software which controls the general operation of the computer (the most popular is DOS) and application or "productivity" software which you, the user, must select and deal with.

The selection of the most appropriate application software to achieve just the degree of uniqueness you want, is a difficult process. There are many similar software packages that purport to do essentially the same thing. You will want to look into the features each has and compare those features against such things as product cost, product performance, ease-of-use, the quality of documentation, error-handling, and support. Table 4.7 is a suggested software evaluation criteria form.

Table 4.7 Software Evaluation Criteria

	Poor	Fair	Good	Excellent
Performance				
Documentation				
Ease of Use				
Error Handling				

There are many types of applications software. Among them are:

- Spreadsheet software
- Word processing software
- Databases and file managers
- Graphics software
- Integrated software
- Business planning integrated software

Spreadsheet Software. Both spreadsheets and accounting software can help you run your business. Accounting packages keep track of real financial events that have already happened. The amount of analysis they allow is usually limited.

Spreadsheets are generic information tools; you can manipulate any data you want in a variety of ways. They are more flexible than accounting packages, but they're also more work.

Do you need both a spreadsheet, and an accounting package? How do you select the right product? We'll start with spreadsheets.

Lotus' 1-2-3™ is the de facto standard for spreadsheets. Lotus' package is the biggest seller, but that doesn't necessarily make it the best choice. There are a variety of advantages to using Lotus: Aftermarket products such as magazines, books templates, and training are more readily available for it than many competing products. However, Lotus can be complex. There are alternatives that are faster, less expensive, and that have just as many features. Consult your local computer/software dealer for these alternatives.

Some key areas to look at when comparing spreadsheets are speed of calculation, the richness of the formula set, reporting flexibility, and maximum spreadsheet size. You may also want to look at so-called integrated packages that include a spreadsheet and more.

You should also look at the standard review criteria: Does the program work properly? Is the documentation helpful? Is the program easy to learn and easy to use? Does it properly intercept errors or wipe out disks? Does the vendor/dealer support the product?

First, do some preliminary research. Read industry magazines for reviews. Ask your professional peers. Check professional research publications at a local technical library. *Software Digest* is good for quantitative analyses of different packages; the *Datapro Research Reports* have a broader range of less specific information; *Infoworld* has good specific reviews of software packages.

After you've drawn up a preliminary list of features and products, go to your local retailer and try each one. Browse through the documentation, insist on starting up the program and trying it. Run through the tutorial if the store will let you.

Once you find a spreadsheet package you like, buy it from the retailer that was the most courteous and helpful, even if you know you can get it cheaper through the mail. If something goes wrong, correcting it should be easier.

Selecting accounting software is a bit more complex. The products vary in the types of modules you can buy, data entry capabilities, special reporting flexibility, ease of use, integration of the various modules, and suitability for special industries.

You must analyze your business. Do you have any special information-handling requirements, such as unusual sales transactions, very heavy inventory tracking needs, government reporting requirements? Try to figure out how many transactions you generate during the year. Can you get by with a single-user system, or will you need a multiuser system?

Identify any special requirements you may have. Is yours a nonprofit organization, or do you have unusual payroll withholding or multiple pay scales for each employee? Do you have multiple departments, companies, or divisions, or other special requirements?

Talk to your bookkeeper or accountant; in fact, get him or her involved. Your bookkeeper/accountant will know better than anyone how the financial side of your business works. Also, he or she will be using whatever package you select.

As you develop a list of features based on your business needs, include things you might want to consider in the future. Will you want to generate custom sales reports? Will you need a way to load your accounting data into a spreadsheet, database management program, or word processor? Is expansion planned?

Next, draw up a preliminary list of products. Start by checking industry magazines. Talk to your professional peers—other business owners, and your accountant and banker. Professional research reports from Datapro™ can be very helpful.

Try each product on your list. Seek out packages that have the features you need. Apply the criteria of Table 4.7 as you're testing. Don't buy anything that doesn't score reasonably well in all four areas.

Finally, you may find the right accounting system. Don't assume that your work is finished, though. You still have to install the programs and apply them to your business. If you want to buy several modules, do so one at a time. Expect problems but, if you do your homework, you'll minimize your aggravation.

Word Processing Software. Everyone knows what makes a good word processor: It must be powerful enough to handle the most sophisticated tasks yet easy on the pocketbook; flexible enough to meet all contingencies but easy to learn and use.

However, what do all these cliches mean in practice? And how do you know when you've found enough "power" and "flexibility" to satisfy your needs?

There's no answer, just as there's no one word processor right for everybody. But there are things to look for before you buy. As with any software purchase, read the reviews, talk to friends, and above all, assess your needs first.

If you mainly like to manipulate fancy spreadsheets and only write an occasional letter or memo, you'll get by just fine with a simple editor that costs less than $100. It won't have many bells and whistles, but you'll also waste less time paging through the manual to recall obscure commands.

However, if you prepare elaborate reports complete with tables of contents, indexes, footnotes, and running headers, you'll need a top-of-the-line product with advanced formatting capabilities. Even this can set you back less than $300 if you shop carefully.

Next consider what your colleagues use. If everyone else in the office uses Brand X, chances are you should too. It may not be the best but you'll be able to swap files and find friendly support across the aisle.

If associates aren't on hand to show you the ropes, who is? Does your dealer know the program well enough to answer questions? Does the manufacturer offer a toll-free number? Even experienced users need support; make sure it is available before purchasing any word processor product.

Now, assuming you can make sense of the manual, take whichever package you're considering for a test drive. Does it appeal to novice users by guiding them through every step with handy menus, lists of options that require a keystroke to choose from? That works great until you're no longer a novice. Once you want real action, the program delivers only more menus.

Don't despair; some word processors allow you to bypass menus as you learn. Others include tutorials to ease the learning process but rely on direct commands to attack your work without interruption. Check for these signs of quality software design.

Look next for raw speed—the lack of which is the downfall of many a high-end program. You didn't buy your computer to wait around, after all. Can the program keep up with a fast typist? Can it jump from one screen of text to another in an instant? Does it delete or move words without delay? You'd be surprised how many cannot.

In actual use, speed depends greatly on program design. Some word processors offer every function ever conceived, but each requires four keystrokes. Even if your memory doesn't balk, your fingers won't forgive you. For the IBM PC, look especially for intelligent use of the function keys.

Make sure common actions, such as copying or deleting, are handled with a minimum of effort. For heavy editing, being able to move the cursor by sentence or paragraph and to instantly define them for block operations (copy, move, delete), are tremendously advantageous.

Finally, don't forget to check if your program forgives human error. Will it recover mistakenly erased text? Does it automatically make backup copies? Are help screens a keystroke away?

Beyond these basics, you may need advanced features for particular jobs. Most important, does the program support your printer's specialized capabilities?

That's a lot to check out. But when you've made up your mind, relax. Your choice may not be perfect, but with a little practice you'll leave your old typewriter behind in a cloud of dust.

Databases and File Managers. It's not easy to choose "the best" file manager or database software, even when the characteristics of an application are well known. It's harder when software and hardware, and even your needs, are constantly changing. You want to organize pieces of information, and you want to find them again without any trouble. Where do you start?

When you decide to invest money and time in software, three guides are important: First, purchase only as much capacity and complexity as you will be able to use in the clearly foreseeable future. Next, make sure you have the required hardware and support. Last, and equally important, be sure to leave yourself a "doorway" to use when you outgrow your present choice.

To compare your needs with the capabilities of available software, you need to define those needs in terminology that is useful for comparisons. A "file" is a single collection of information, organized in a uniform manner. Common examples of files are a telephone book and a list of customers with relevant information about each one. Each piece of information, such as the name or address, is a "field," and a collection of fields for each item in the file is a "record." Each line in the phone book is one record.

A "file manager" is a program with which you can build and use individual files of many different types. You could use the same file manager for an address list, a customer file, or a list of your home movies, including almost any reference data.

In contrast, a "database" is also a collection of fields, but it is more complex than a file. A "database manager" is the comparable software—it is often referred to simply as a database. Databases for personal computers range from a very large single file, to complex multiple structures with different organizational schemes. Many of the more complex databases are called "relational databases" because their structures allow you to define and use relationships between different groups of fields.

Databases, like personal computers themselves, give a user more flexibility and control than a specialized computer program or a file manager. They are used for customized systems, such as accounting systems, inventory and invoicing systems, and rental management and reporting systems, for which existing programs are not satisfactory.

Conventional wisdom says that you should choose the software and then buy hardware that fits. In reality, however, you may already own hardware or be affected by the choices of employers or friends with whom you wish to be compatible. It's smart to examine the software already in use first and to look for convenient interfaces with spreadsheets, word processors, and other existing software. It may be smarter to choose software that has more features you want than to select widely used software that won't provide that doorway to help you convert data for other uses.

The clarity of the tutorials and user manuals and the availability of help from the publisher, the dealer, friends, and co-workers are all grouped under support, and that is a very important item to consider. Experience shows that the two most reliable of these are the documentation that comes with the software and the support of friends and co-workers. Be sure the tutorials and references are adequate and that the language is understandable. If possible, find other users of the same software through friends or a user group.

An essential function for both file and database software is the one that revises a file structure without losing existing data. Software that provides automatic data conversion and report revisions once the file is rebuilt is very desirable.

Once a computer and software are tentatively chosen, you may find you need additional hardware for optimum use. Although not necessary for other applications, you may need additional random-access memory or a hard disk for data storage or for faster and easier operation.

In case this all sounds too difficult, there are a few things to remember: There is no one "right" choice; in fact, you probably can't find software that fits all your needs and has everything we specified here. However, if you consider these criteria in relation to your needs and then find the program that you think most suitable, you'll do better than average.

Graphics Software. In the introductions to the various sections throughout this book, one theme keeps reappearing: "First of all, define your needs." It is a sensible dictum for selecting any major purchase, but it is particularly important in the field of graphics because of the umbrella nature of the word "graphics" as applied to software.

Mention graphics software to a marketing or sales manager, and the image immediately conjured is one of bar graphs, pie charts, and line charts. The more technologically sophisticated marketer will also think in terms of organizational charts, flow charts, and maps. Mention graphics to an artist, and unique creations of electronic images come to mind.

Basically, there are three kinds of packages for the generation of microcomputer graphics: business graphics, integrated software, and drawing programs.

A business graphics package typically is used for data presentation. These are by far the most common and are used for bar, pie, and line charts. These programs range from the basic to the fairly complex. The more complex may include color potential, multiple text sizes and fonts, variegated fill-patterns all the way up to three-dimensional appearance, annotation or overlay capability, and drawing and slide show features.

In the review-for-purchase process, there are multiple considerations. Most of these considerations involve an anticipation of actual applications in the near future and down the road.

Naturally, memory capability of the microcomputer is uppermost importance, but it is also imperative to anticipate support products and how easy it is to use. What kind of printing capabilities are required for any given program? What do you have available? Will users be generating graphics on an everyday basis, or will it be only an occasionally used feature? Is it a program that can be booted and it will run, or is it necessary to keep changing disks during the program's performance? The latter can be bothersome for everyone but the graphics specialist.

Graphics programs are, by nature, fairly complicated to use—even the simplest among them. Thus if the usage anticipated is only occasional, perhaps ease of learning and use should be a priority factor. The idea, of course, is to eliminate the need to relearn the process each time graphics are needed.

It is safe to say that there is no perfect business graphics program on the market today encompassing all the capabilities possible. Of necessity, your buying decision will be a compromise. Are the anticipated graphics uses a major thrust of your business or are they supplemental to the main theme?

The next discussion is on integrated software. Just about all of the programs reviewed there have some form of business graphics capabilities integrated into the overall package. It stands to reason that any program packaged with three or four others—no matter how well designed—will be less versatile that a well-designed stand-alone program. This is particularly true of graphics programs, if only because of the heavy memory requirements compared to microcomputer capacity.

Perhaps this limited versatility, when packaged with two, three, or four other functional packages, is more than adequate for all of your needs. The fundamentals of charting and graphing should all be present to a satisfactory degree. Call it a compromise, call it a trade-off, call it sheer economics, but typically, the graphics capabilities of an integrated program—played against the much higher cost of separate programs for each individual function—will have all that's necessary to illustrate your business point.

A drawing software package is really an image creator. From basic elements such as lines, boxes, circles, and arcs, the user can create anything from an organizational chart to a full-scale illustration. The needs here speak for themselves. You will know whether these capabilities are a critical part of your business plan and purchase accordingly.

Make every effort to review potential purchases in great depth before you make any commitment. Try to run the potentials on the proper equipment and don't get sold by the sales pitch. The graphics are going to reflect you and/or your company. They're expensive; analyze products carefully and personally and don't buy a Mercedes when a Volkswagen will do.

Integrated Software. Technologies generate "technobabble." New terms suddenly appear and we use them as though they were precisely defined and commonly understood. Integrated software is just such a term. What, in fact, does it mean?

In the broadest sense, an integrated program is one that encompasses at least two (any two) distinct features (e.g., subprograms). Thus a word processor of any degree of complexity would not be considered integrated software, although a simple word processor and a simple spelling checker under one roof certainly could be. The extent of organized diversity, therefore, rather than the degree of complexity is the issue.

Perhaps the first significant software integration came with Wordstar™, which offered a spelling checker and a mail merger, which are accessible through the program's main menu, as add-ons to the basic word processor.

The notion of putting several operations under the control of a single menu emerged in another way: the operating system shell program that allowed the user to bundle all the programs on a disk under a single command structure. And, although the "menu-maker" program provides a relatively easy-to-use environment for getting at programs and text files, it doesn't allow one program to talk directly to another.

A step beyond the customized menu came with software that consists of sets of formerly independent programs managed under an executive menu, allowing for movement from program to program. However, direct communication among the programs—typically, a word processor, spreadsheet, and file manager—was no more possible with this technique than with the shell or menu-maker. The parent program's executive menu simply acted as a shell.

Some recently developed packages integrate spreadsheet, word processor, data manager, graph maker, and telephone manager into what some call "kitchen-sinkware." The integration extends even to matched definitions of special-function and cursor-control keys across all the modules. The programs come with hefty manuals and demand vast random access memory and disk space. The relatively long learning curve needed to master such elaborate software has spawned a small industry of explainers: books, tutorial programs, and seminars.

For those who are happy with a particular single-function program, perhaps one's old reliable word processor, the "electronic desk manager"—as exemplified by Sidekick™—will serve as a kind of software integrator. The desk manager typically comes with a notepad, a multifunction calculator, a card file, and a telephone dialer and resides in computer memory, out of sight until needed. If in the middle of writing a report, you need to do some arithmetic, you can pull down the calculator and go to work. Some of these programs will even allow transfer of data to your text file.

Another approach to custom integration is through the windows type of program (Windows™, Topview™, and Gem™). These are sophisticated descendents of the menu-maker shell programs, providing for access to several programs simultaneously.

Basic question: Who needs what? Capability, costs, and equipment requirements vary widely. The notion that bigger is better drives many of us to buy hardware and software that may far exceed our present needs or those of the foreseeable future. However, it would be shortsighted to prepare only for the moment.

The question persists. In trying to answer it, you should make a list of your "productivity software" requirements as you perceive them and try to match the list with the software available for testing at local dealers. Is your business operation more amenable to computerization through the word processor, the spreadsheet, or the database? Some integrated packages are weighted more toward text handling, some more toward numbers. Do you really need to graph your data? All of the big programs come with a graphic module—a module you are paying for whether you use it or not. Perhaps a few small enhancements to the good old reliable, familiar, single-function piece of software you are currently using would do the job well. Or perhaps you'll be best served by a singleton with built-in hooks to alien files.

Integrated software such as Symphony™, Framework™, and Smart™ tease the mind and can puzzle the will. Do you really need state of the art? Read on, try on, and don't let the salesperson dazzle you.

Business Planning Integrated Software. An intelligent business planning and development tool called "Business Plan Expert" is designed to help you think strategically about your business using a question and answer format focusing on key areas of a business plan. After answering the questions, the user can print out a business strategy profile that can become the backbone of a business plan. For more information and a PC compatible demo disk, contact Expert Technologies Corporation, 3618 Burlington, Houston, TX 77006 (713) 526-0909.

Venture—The Entrepreneur's Handbook is designed specifically to help emerging businesses plan, analyze and control their own growth. It guides the user through the steps necessary to create a comprehensive and usable business plan, not just a set of financial projections. *Venture* also includes a spreadsheet program, word processor, general ledger, file manager, and templates of critical documents. Available from Star Software Systems, 363 Van Ness Way, Torrance, CA 90501 (213)533-1190.

Your business plan may be the most important document you'll ever create. It's both a road map for you and an enticement for investors. But it's ticklish to write. Many seasoned entrepreneurs often don't know where to begin when they have to put their ideas into words and numbers.

BizPlanBuilder is aimed at entrepreneurs, managers, and consultants; it can help you launch or expand a new company or product line. The program (IBM, Macintosh compatible) starts with a template. The disk contains an 85 page document containing incomplete statements such as: "Based on and XXX percent market share for our XXX product by 19XX, we estimate our return on investment to be XXX percent." The idea is that it's easier to fill in and edit an existing plan than it is to start from scratch.

There's more to that process than meets the eye. By focusing your attention on certain statements and numbers, the program prompts you to better articulate an analysis of your market—and also of your company's objectives, strategy, and financial projections.

At various points within the plan, the computer also asks questions like: "What do you want for yourself (personally and financially) 5 years from now?" You're forced to think through all facets of your operation and their impact on your life, helping you avoid pitfalls that frequently trip up new ventures.

For the financial side of your plan, you don't have to set up any spreadsheets from scratch. Projections are already laid out on-screen; wherever they don't match yours, all you need to do is type your company's numbers in over the existing ones. The software automatically recalculates the totals for you.

To obtain *BizPlanBuilder* write: Success, P.O. Box 2, Church Hill, MD., 21690-0002.

Venture Capital Directory is an on-disk directory to venture capital firms and financial advisory and consulting firms. It gives information on each firm including what industries it invests in, preferred stages, and preferred investment range. Available from: Infoprobe, 620 Iris Ave. #229, Sunnyvale, CA 94086 (408)730-4636.

Selective Software, 903 Pacific Ave., Santa Cruz, CA 95060 (408)423-3556, has a group of three software packages that allow you to produce a business plan, loan application package, and a company and personnel policy document.

The business plan program (*Develop Your Business Plan*) enables you to develop a comprehensive business plan that will: (1) define your concept, (2) evaluate the competition, and (3) determine your risks and estimate your costs. It gives you the expertise needed to make realistic projections for balance sheets, cash flow, income planning, market size and penetration, sales planning, and ratios.

The Loan Package is a program that works with the above business plan program (they can be bought as a package), gives you ways to analyze your cash needs, step-by-step instructions for anticipating lenders requirements and other loan application insights.

The company and personnel policy document writer (*A Company Policy and Personnel Workbook*) is a text-based software package that gives you over 40 already written personnel policies which you can customize or use as is. This assists you in meeting the requirements of the Labor Board and avoiding any future labor disputes.

These are a few of the business applications and business planning software packages available. They seem to be the best for their designed purpose. There are many more on the market and more being introduced to the market practically on a daily basis. Become familiar with the selection criteria and terminology noted earlier and then, with the help of someone familiar with computers, write down your selection criteria and begin the actual selection process of "shopping around" for a system (hardware and software) that meets your specific needs.

EXHIBIT 1
Strategic Planning Session: Agenda

Dates:
Location:
Facilitator:
Scribe:

Day 1

Time	Topic	Responsibility
8:00 - 8:05	Opening comments	President
8:05 - 8:15	Review agenda Review procedures for session Review roles of facilitator and scribe	Facilitator
8:15 - 8:30	Review completed analysis of external environment	Preparer of Analysis
8:30 - 10:00	SWOT analysis, Part I Round table discussion aimed at identifying and documenting on the flip chart, all of the company's strengths, opportunities, weaknesses and threats	Facilitator and Group
10:00 - 10:15	Coffee break	
10:15 - 12:00	SWOT analysis, Part II Continuance of SWOT analysis	Facilitator and Group
12:00 - 12:45	Lunch	
12:45 - 2:30	Develop or redefine "mission statement" for organization (statement of purpose)	Facilitator and Group
2:30 - 2:45	Coffee and soft drink break	
2:45 - 3:30	Analysis and identification of key results areas (areas in which the company must achieve significant results in order to achieve the kind of revenues and profits desired)	Facilitator and Group
3:30 - 5:00	Establish strategic objectives Within each key results area establish a small number of strategic objectives (objectives that are descriptive of a condition you want to achieve)	Facilitator and Group
5:00 - 6:30	Dinner	

Day 2

8:00 - 8:05	Opening comments	President
8:05 - 8:15	Review of where group left off	Facilitator
8:15 - 10:00	Establishing tactical objectives to address SWOTs, Part I	Facilitator and Group
10:00 - 10:15	Coffee break	
10:15 - 12:00	Establishing tactical objectives to address SWOTs, Part II	Facilitator and Group
12:00 - 12:45	Lunch	
12:45 - 1:45	Integration of budgeting process into the strategic plan	Facilitator and Group
1:45 - 2:00	Coffee and soft drink break	
2:00 - 4:00	Prioritizing objectives, assignment of responsibilities, and establishment of target dates	Facilitator and Group
4:00 - 4:30	Discussion of business plan Coordinating and monitoring (including discussion of business plan format and appointment of business plan coordinator who will handle monitoring and keep everyone advised when shortfalls or reforecast situations arise)	Facilitator and Group
4:30 - 4:45	Agreement on timing of written report and method of communicating the plan to all employees of the organization	Facilitator and Group
4:45 - 5:00	Closing comments	President

EXHIBIT 2

Internal Business Plan Format

- Coversheet
- Table of contents
- Mission statement
- Summary of key strategies
- Objectives, responsibilities, and targets
  - For (enter key strategy area 1)
  - For (enter key strategy area 2)
  - For (enter key strategy area 3)
  - For (enter key strategy area 4)
  - For (enter key strategy area 5)
  - For (enter key strategy area 6)
  - For (enter key strategy area 7)
  - For (enter key strategy area 8)
  - For (enter key strategy area 9)
  - For (enter key strategy area 10)
  - For (enter key strategy area 11)
  - For (enter key strategy area 12)
- Individual objectives summaries/status reports
  - For (enter employees's name)
  - For (enter employees's name)
  - For (enter employees's name)
  - For (enter employees's name)
  - For (enter employees's name)
  - For (enter employees's name)
  - For (enter employees's name)

EXHIBIT 3

Objectives/Responsibilities and Targets

Key strategy area:

Strategy statement:

Tactical Objectives	Responsibility	Target Date	Status

EXHIBIT 4

Individual Objectives Summary/Status Report

Employee Name:			
Tactical Objectives	Key Strategy Area	Target Date	Status

5

WRITING THE BUSINESS PLAN

At the beginning of this book the emphasis of business plan writing was placed on knowing who your audience is and what they expect, want to know, see, and hear from a business plan. This is a necessary prelude to writing and presenting an effective plan. If your audience is your department or general manager who will be reviewing your next year's plan, your plan and presentation will be different from one prepared for the corporate executive staff or the financial community.

There is one common thread woven through all plans regardless of the audience, namely, brevity. However, it is brevity with all the necessary facts to enable a decision. Busy executives and investors do not generally like or want to be deluged with a morass of detail. They usually want the essence of a plan or program. Each plan section should be summarized into one page if possible, but no more than two or three at the most. And the lead section, the executive summary, should then contain a summary paragraph or two on each section. The detailed, backup data can be included as an addendum or kept in reserve until asked for by the person(s) reviewing it.

If your audience is a department manager or even a general manager of a small firm, the plan can include many specific details of the operation, including references to departments, personnel, equipment, and products. The working vocabulary of the operation or the industry should be used in the plan. This type of audience is likely to demand more details than a plan prepared for an executive staff or financial community because of its familiarity with the organization's detail. It is best at the outset to pinpoint what this audience wants and tailor the product (your plan) to fit its needs.

If your audience is the executive staff or the financial community, chances are they are not intimately familiar with the details of your operation. Because they are not, detailed references to personnel and equipment, and certain specialized language should be omitted unless they add some special significance to the discussion.

A good rule of thumb to follow regarding the page count of a business plan is that it should be approximately 30 pages of single-spaced, easily readable print. And, certainly, never more than 60 pages of double-spaced print. This is inclusive of the title page, table of contents, and body. Any appendixes may increase the page count beyond these limits.

A business plan for an external audience which is too lengthy will probably be unable to hold that audience's attention. Keep it brief.

A note of interest, when presenting a business plan to a government agency under the SBIR program, any plan containing more than 30 pages is automatically rejected.

SUGGESTED ORGANIZATION

Each of the elements for a successful business plan has been carefully developed in the preceding sections. In a successful plan, the individual elements must be organized in a logical sequence that will make sense to your audience. Enough information must be included to convey your intended message but not so much as to overwhelm and confuse. Remember, it is primarily facts that are of interest. Rhetoric, extolling the virtues of the product or company, is not what your potential investors want. They are interested in how much will be returned on their investment and when.

To secure their attention, keep your plan short and informative. Divide your plan into four or five sections. Your first section should provide an overview of the business opportunity, product plan, market overview, and competitive summary. This will provide an overview of the entire proposed company.

Your second section should provide more of the details pertinent to the company's operation, and is the heart of the plan. It should include your charter, company organization, personnel profiles, and all of the pro forma (forecasted) financial reports. These financial statements may include the income statement, cash flow analysis, balance sheet, depreciation schedule, income tax schedule, and ratio analyses.

Your third section should delve more into the operational details with a presentation of the department plans for finance and administration, marketing, engineering, and manufacturing. Your last section should be reserved for market studies, resumes of key personnel, and detailed product specifications.

The business plan organization should allow the plan to be tailored to the prospective audience. If investors are being approached for the first time, only the first section need be given to them and an emphasis should be made on the ROI and the organization and qualification of the management team. It provides enough information to let them know what is being attempted without "giving away the store." If they are still interested, give them section two, the pertinent details of the company, during the next meeting. Further interest warrants giving them the remainder of the plan.

It is only through experience that the planner will learn what works best for a given industry and audience.

QUESTIONS TO ASK YOURSELF BEFORE WRITING THE BUSINESS PLAN

Before starting to write your business plan, ask yourself the following questions and be sure you can answer them. If you can't answer the questions, restudy the points covered in the previous chapters and your business situation until you can answer them.

1. Exactly what is your project? Describe its operation, functions, structure, use, or purpose.
2. What is the current status of the project?
3. Does the project have protection through patent, copyright, regulation, and so on?
4. Who are the principle leaders and managers in the project? Describe their backgrounds, education, and responsibilities. Describe company organization and job functions.

5. Why will you and your company succeed in this project better than anyone else?
6. What facilities and equipment do you have? What distribution networks are established? What are your expansion plans?
7. What suppliers will you use? What is the relationship for price, delivery, credit, and quality?
8. What are the risks of the project? How have you prepared for them? What are your contingency plans to meet these risks?
9. Who will be the users of the project? Explain why you believe there is a demand for it. What need does it fill?
10. How is the marketing effort organized? What are the advertising plans?
11. Who are your competitors? What are their strengths, weaknesses, and market shares? How will they respond to your project?
12. What share of the market will you capture? What contracts, commitments, or interest have you established with potential customers?
13. What is the industry background for the project? What are the trends and peculiarities?
14. What amount of money are you seeking for the project? How will the funds be used? What benefit are you willing to give to an outside investor?
15. How much money and time has been devoted to the project to date?
16. What is the potential for the project? For the next 5 years, estimate monthly sales and revenue.
17. For the next 5 years, give as much detail as possible for estimated monthly expenses and detailed costs.
18. Explain the price structure for your project.
19. Provide the following items to support your answers to the above questions:
    a. Flowcharts, diagrams, drawings, photographs, illustrations, audiotapes, videotapes
    b. Patents, license agreements, contracts
    c. Schedule of equipment or property acquisition
    d. Manpower growth plan
    e. Recommendations of feasibility studies
    f. Personal, professional, technical references
    g. Letters of intent or contracts from potential customers

WRITING THE PLAN: THE FORMAT

While answering the questions in the last section and in previous chapters, you have developed an evaluation of your company's present status, your industry, and your environment; a set of objectives with specific tactics, assigned responsibilities, time frames, and reporting structures; and the financial analyses and projections to support those objectives.

Now you must take the information you have gathered and prepare the written business plan for your company. You can follow the suggested outline which follows, keeping each section as brief as possible, and stressing the points you wish to make with the plan's audience(s), whether they are investors and lenders, your internal staff, or other groups such as boards of directors or stockholders.

In each case, you should review your responses to the questions in the appropriate sections and write summaries of your planning conclusions.

Business Plan Outline I: General and/or Internal

Cover Sheet

This is generally one page that should include the name of the business, address, phone number(s), principals, date of plan, and any other appropriate information about your company or plan.

Executive Summary

The executive summary captures and presents succinctly the essence of the plan. It is, in effect, a capsulized version of the entire plan. The executive summary is neither a background statement, nor an introduction. In fact, the balance of the plan basically supports the statements made in the summary. If this section is poorly written or provides insufficient or misleading facts, the audience may not read further. This opportunity summary simply, clearly, and succinctly presents the facts of the business opportunity in three pages or less.

The executive summary should begin by identifying your product or service and the industry or market it will serve. These introductory remarks can be followed by a paragraph about the industry's size and growth rate. How large was the market last year and this year, and what are the expectations 3 years into the future? What is the percentage of growth this year over last? What is contributing to growth, and how long is it likely to be sustained? And why?

Note: Few people want to enter an industry or market that is not growing because its chances for success are reduced. If an industry is stagnating, it generally means that the companies already participating are probably fighting desperately with one another just to stay alive.

Include a few short paragraphs about the company or program under discussion, its location and products, what market segment(s) it will serve, when it can begin serving it, its expected profits, and when they will be realized.

The company's location should be identified, along with the reason(s) for its being there. A location is generally chosen for its natural resources, proximity to the company's market, low labor rates, or other good business reason(s).

The description of the product and market segment it is expected to serve should not be in glowing technological terms but in simple, down-to-earth language. What the product does and how it fits into the market picture should be discussed. A few clear statements about why the product is as good as, or better than, current products on the market should be included. If it is worse than existing competitive products, a statement should be included as to why it is expected to succeed.

Any special circumstances surrounding the product such as license to build an already successful device should be discussed here. Also, a statement about when the company will begin to serve the market should be included.

The most important statement to investors or the financial community is one about expected profits: how much and when. Profit is the basic reason for investing. The forecast should be short and factual and taken from the prepared income statement.

A concluding summary statement should state the business opportunity and the advantages that can be realized from its pursuit and the action desired of the plan's audience.

Table of Contents

A business plan's table of contents serves the same function as a table of contents for a book. The page(s) should be specific enough to enable the reader to locate any particular item of interest. As with a book's table of contents, some readers will judge the plan's thoroughness based on what is included on this page alone.

Product Plan

The product plan should be a brief, descriptive overview of the initial product offering (what it is and what it does) in very general terms. Operational details should be left to specifications or other documentation that should be included in an appendix that is either made available with the plan or upon request. Any special features that will make the product more marketable should be mentioned, also in general terms. If there is going to be a product enhancement or even a second-generation product, this should be noted.

When describing the products/services include a product photograph or illustration of the service delivery method. It is important not to overemphasize this area as most people reading the plan are more interested in the market response to the product/service and view the product/service as merely a vehicle to solicit that response.

Market Overview

The market discussion should be no more than one or two pages in length. It should state what market segment the product offering will serve and the size of that market. Market figures in dollars should be included for several years to provide an overall growth perspective. Expected product prices should be included for these years to illustrate price increases or erosion. Some justification of a product's price may also be included, such as a competitor's advertised price, to demonstrate credibility.

Competitive Summary

The competitive summary, while very brief, should completely state what other companies are offering for a similar product, their model numbers, and any other points that may highlight the competition's products' strengths and weaknesses. Investors want to see at a glance what it is that they are up against and what may prevent them from earning a profit on their investment. Facts should not be hidden.

History

This section is tailored to your needs as either a startup venture or an existing business. If your history is brief, this section should explain how your venture came to exist, its organization to date, and the backgrounds of the founders. If yours is an existing company, you should explain the major highlights of your history, keeping it brief and adding detail through appendixes as needed.

The general description of the company should take no more than a few pages. It should present the fundamental activities and nature of the company. Included should be a description of what the company is—manufacturer, retailer, or service business—

what its product or service is and how it is to be made available to the customer base, where the company is located, and the geographical boundaries of its market—local, national, or international. Also, the company's current stage of activity and its future objectives.

Definition of the Business

This section describes exactly what needs your business meets, whose needs these are, and how you meet those needs.

Definition of the Market

Outlined in this section is detailed information on the targeted customers, customer profile, size and location of the market, projected market share, and why the company will be able to obtain the targeted market share. This is the portion of the plan where you discuss your competition and the tactics you use to participate in the marketplace. Your advertising and promotion campaign should be briefly explained.

The marketing section is one of the two most important parts of a business plan (the other is the management structure section) because it communicates most directly the nature of the intended business and the manner in which that business will be able to succeed. Reviewers give a great deal of attention to this section when evaluating a business plan. The purpose of this section is to explain how the business intends to manipulate and react to market conditions in order to generate sales. The plan cannot simply explain a concept; it must sell the business as an attractive investment opportunity, a good credit risk, or a valued vendor of a product or service. It should include information regarding the market definition and opportunity, competition and other market influences, marketing strategy, market research, sales forecast, and key material references supporting all assertions made.

Products or Services Description

This section of the plan may be placed before the marketing section if your product or service is new or requires extensive explanation. In this section you explain how you will meet an identified need with a specific product or service. The status of your R&D efforts should be detailed with any information pertaining to copyrights, patents, trademarks, and so on. Technical information and catalog sheets or pictures may be appended as appropriate.

The operational section of the plan must explain the general approach to manufacturing or how the service is to be provided, where and how needed materials or support services are to be acquired, what processes will be used to produce and deliver the product or service to the customer, the labor requirements, time requirements to provide the product, and what suppliers and vendors are going to be used and how they will be used. It is wise to write a very detailed operational section for internal use but merely include the most straightforward processes in the business plan. If more detail is requested by the reviewer it can be provided.

Management Structure

The management structure section describes who will enact the plan, providing the basic background information on the principals, the organizational structure, staffing, employee policies, and the reporting structure. Much of the detail should be appended, such as resumes and organizational charts.

The legal form of the business and how the business will be capitalized is also identified here. This is one of the most critical parts of the proposal and as such must be concise and precise with detail that pertains to the proposition being presented to the specific reviewer. It should be organized to first show the business structure: its legal form and the manner of financial participation (who owns the business and how much they own). Then it must detail the capital requirements: present sources of funds and expected future sources of funds—complete disclosure of equity distribution and borrowings is necessary for the simple reason that action taken by the reviewer in reliance on these facts can determine the legal liability of the founders if something should go wrong in the future.

The management and organization section of the plan is the second of the two most important sections of the plan. Reviewers have been known to read this section first, after the summary, to make a determination of whether it is worthwhile to continue the review process. Their reasoning is that many businesses fail because the proper talent was not assembled to manage the concern. Individuals with strong technical backgrounds might ignore the importance of including on a management team people with the appropriate business background, and vice versa. Some of the management team philosophies and principals should be noted. An organization chart with brief descriptions of each positions' function and interrelation should be presented along with a statement of management policy and strategy. The names and brief backgrounds, including successes and failures, of the founding members, active investors, key employees, directors, and consultants should be included in this section.

The structure and capitalization sections of the plan allow the entrepreneur to wrap up the business proposition. It says to the reviewer: "You've reviewed the business plan. If you are interested here's what the business requires."

Objectives and Goals

This section includes varying amounts of detail depending on the purpose of your plan. It is in this section where you list your objectives, the specific tactics you will use to achieve those objectives, the timeframes involved, and why you think the set of objectives is doable and advantageous.

The major milestones section of the plan is to present a time frame for the business's accomplishments to date, its current plans and objectives, and its plans and objectives for the future. This can be presented in the form of Gantt charts, that present the major milestone accomplishments on a time base showing how each milestone relates to the next, or PERT charts, that illustrate the activity flow of the project, but an explanation of major events should be included.

Financial Data

The purpose of the financial section of the plan is to formulate a credible, comprehensive set of projections (pro forma statements) reflecting the business venture's anticipated financial performance. While the preceding parts of the plan communicates a basic understanding of the nature of the enterprise, projected financial performance addresses itself most directly to the bottom-line concerns of both the entrepreneur and the reviewer. With a start-up business there is no financial history. Therefore, you should emphasize the reliability of the supporting data. The quality of research is directly reflected in the accuracy and acceptability of the projections. The reviewer will likely do his or her own research to verify the data. There are only so many reference sources available and if your source information is verified the reviewer has no reason to doubt your projections.

The following information is generally included in the financial section:

- A set of assumptions on which the projections are based.
- Projected income statements, typically for 5 years but can be for 3 years. The first year is presented on a monthly basis, the second and third years on a quarterly basis, and the remainder on a yearly basis.
- Projected cash flow statements for the first 2 years in as great detail as possible.
- Current and projected balance sheets reflecting the financial position of the business at its inception or present condition and projected year-end balance sheets for each year presented.
- Break-even analysis that demonstrates when the business will start becoming profitable. And further break-even analyses or financial summaries that reflect the contribution of each product or service of a multiproduct/service business.

The financial section explains how you will fund your operations over the planning period. You may include forecasted (pro forma) balance sheets, for example:

> Balance sheets summarize the assets in your business and (through liabilities) show how these assets are to be financed. They are the primary source of information for: debt to equity ratios, working capital, inventory turnover, and so forth. These are all necessary data concerning the soundness of your endeavor. Prepare balance sheets and other forecasts—quarterly for the first year and annually for subsequent years.

A forecasted balance sheet might include the following headings:

Assets
- Cash
- Accounts receivable
- Inventory
- Other current assets

Total current assets
- Land
- Building and improvements
- Furniture and equipment

Total fixed assets
- Less accumulated depreciation

Net fixed assets
- Other assets

Total assets

Liabilities and shareholders' equity
- Short-term debt
- Accounts payable
- Dividends payable
- Income taxes payable

Accrued compensation
Other current liabilities
Total current liabilities
Long-term debt
Other noncurrent liabilities
Shareholders' equity
Common stock
Retained earnings
Total shareholders' equity
Total liabilities and shareholders' equity

Forecasted statements of earnings, for example, might include information for the planning period under the following headings (by quarter and year):

Sales
Cost of sales (The detailed cost of sales schedule will vary by type of business)
Gross profit
Operating expenses
Fixed expenses
Interest
Depreciation
Amortization
Operating profit (loss)
Other income (expenses)
Interest income
Earnings (loss) before income taxes
Income taxes
Net earnings (loss)

An example of forecasted statements of changes in financial position, on a cash basis is:

Sources (uses) of cash
Net earnings (loss)
Depreciation & amortization
Cash provided by operations
Dividends
Cash provided by (used for) changes in
Accounts receivable
Inventory
Other current assets
Accounts payable
Income taxes
Accrued compensation
Dividends payable
Other current liabilities
Other assets
Net cash provided by (used for) operating activities
Investment transactions
Furniture and equipment
Land

Building and improvements
Net cash from investment transactions
Financing transactions
Short-term debt
Long-term debt
Other noncurrent liabilities
Sale of common stock
Net cash from financing transactions
Net increase (decrease) in cash
Cash: beginning of year
Cash: end of year

Forecasted cash flow analyses, cost-volume-profit analysis, and the company's projected break-even point. This section should be detailed and as well documented and supported as possible.

Disclose the accounting policies and the major assumptions made in your plan. Any financing requests made with the plan as a backup should be justified in this section.

Appendixes

Include in appendixes any specific supporting information or detail which you feel your plan requires but which does not fit into the context of the sections previously discussed.

Business Plan Outline II: Venture Capital

The following is another suggested business plan outline which lends itself to the venture capital community. Only the major sections are presented and their definition and points of inclusion are the same as those given earlier but with emphasis on the management team and the return on investment justified by a marketing study (research). The details of which would be included in the appendix.

I. Table of Contents
II. Executive Summary
III. General Company Description
IV. Product and Services
V. Marketing Plan
VI. Operational Plan
VII. Management and Organization
VIII. Capitalization and Structure
IX. Financial Plan

Appendixes

A. Resumes of Principles
B. Summary of Competitors
C. Projection of Sales by Markets and Product Line
D. Product Line Profit Analysis: Markets X and Y

Business Plan Outline III: Lender/Bank

The following is a suggested business plan outline which lends itself to the banking and lending community. Again, only the major sections are presented and their definition and points of inclusion are the same as those given earlier but with emphasis on the loan repayment schedule justified by a marketing study (research) that supports the projected cash flow that allows the repayment schedule to be met. The details of the marketing study would be included in the appendix.

I. Executive Summary
II. Resume(s)
III. Product Description
IV. Company Management and Organization
V. Company Operations
VI. Marketing Program
VII. Financial Statements & Forecasts
    Income Statement Summary
    Expense & Revenue Detail
VIII. Exhibits

6

AFTER THE PLAN IS WRITTEN

After the business plan has been written the entrepreneur must circulate it to the proper people (the intended audience) and get them sufficiently interested in it to at least browse through it. And hopefully they will read it. This can be even more difficult than researching and writing the plan.

The intended audience is normally very busy and only something very extraordinary will jog them from their current interest sufficiently to take time to review a new proposal. Here is where the creative and patient genius of the entrepreneur is truely put to the test. However, with determination, perseverance, and dedication—and especially imagination—the entrepreneur will generate that interest. The targeted audience will respond and review the plan. And, if interested, will ask questions.

If real interest is generated and the audience begins discussions the first thing that will be questioned will be the basis of the projected figures. Your market research will be questioned. The audience will challenge those figures and probably present their market figures with a request for you to run these figures through your planning calculations to determine a more "realistic" projected performance of the proposed business. You are now in the midst of negotiation. With lenders this is the process of determining the security of the payback. With investors and venture capitalists this is where they determine their ROI and what portion of the company they must obtain in order to attain their desired ROI.

During this negotiation phase you may be required to revise your figures and other management, organizational, and operational strategies three or four times and possibly more. It all depends on how well you can support your projections against the challenges of the audience. Remember, the audience has the advantage in that their organizations have not only studied the same market data you have but have also investigated many similar proposals—some successful and some not so successful.

The following pages present two business plans and their required modifications. The first is a loan application plan for a low-tech (auto repair shop) business venture where the potential lender questioned the colateral and its value and required a detailed breakdown of each item and rejected some items entirely. This, of course, reduced the colateral value and thus the potential loan amount. But it all had to be refigured by the applicant before the lender would consider any further action on the application.

The second plan is for a high-tech business (medical imaging products) with a target audience of investors and venture capitalists and later potential buyers of the company. Each modification was made necessary by the initial questioning of the basis of the projections, to the restatement of the ventures progress toward producing the envisioned product, to the search for a potential buyer.

BUSINESS PLAN
XYZ AUTO
REPAIR

Walter Jones, General Manager.
434 Any Ave.
Anytown, XA 95635
796/555-6666

EXECUTIVE SUMMARY

The business venture described in this plan is an automobile fleet maintenance service to be known as "XYZ Auto Repair" and will be located in the city and state of Anytown, State. Growth plans include engine rebuilding and automobile restoration services.

Mission Statements:

> To provide those businesses within a 25 mile radius of the city of Anytown a fleet maintenance service which is scheduled, reliable, and cost effective.
>
> To provide the general public a cost-effective engine rebuilding service.
>
> To locate and acquire popular ventage model automobiles for the purpose of restoring and reselling. Specializing in model years prior to 1970.

The target market is those businesses with fleets of 5 to 15 vehicles (i.e., Motorola Service Co., 8 vehicles; Tiffany Plant Rentals, 10 vehicles).

A review of the local (Anytown) auto mechanic businesses reveals that no member is targeting a specific customer area. Instead, they rely on the general public to respond to local advertising or merely "drop in" as the need occurs. Thus the proposed market is without any real competition in the planned area of service.

The two principals of the business, Walter Jones and Fred Smith are well experienced in their respective areas. Walter has over 20 years in the design, development, implementation, and management of service support programs for electronic and electromechanical systems. Fred has over 5 years experience in the automotive repair industry in general mechanics: tune-ups, lube, oil change, tire rotation, transmission service, road testing, differential service, and engine rebuilding.

The purpose of the loan funds is to provide working capital until the business is through the "breakeven" point—approximately 6 to 9 months. It will also provide funds for the purchase of some major items of capital equipment over the first 5 months of operation.

The amount being requested is $150,000 which will be paid back over 15 years at prime plus 2 percent. The funds are to be secured by the assets of the business which include over $92,000 worth of hand tools and heavy equipment such as air compressor, engine hoist, and engine rack.

CONTENTS

1. Name of Firm
   The business will be known as "XYZ Auto Repair."
2. Ownership
   The business is to be formed as a partnership consisting of two partners: Walter Jones as to an undivided fifty-one percent (51%) interest and Fred Smith as to an undivided forty-nine percent (49%) interest.
3. Information on the Business
   a. Type of business and product or service
      The proposed business venture is an automobile fleet maintenance service targeting those businesses with fleets of 5 to 15 vehicles. With growth plans to include engine rebuilding and automobile restoration services.

      Mission Statements:

      To provide those businesses within a 25 mile radius of the city of Anytown a fleet maintenance service which is scheduled, reliable, and cost effective.

      To provide the general public a cost-effective engine rebuilding service.

      To locate and acquire popular vintage model automobiles for the purpose of restoring and reselling. Specializing in model years prior to 1970.
   b. History
      This business is a start-up business venture and as such has no history of previous operation to relate. However, both principals forming the business have histories in the maintenance business. The general manager (Walter Jones) has been in computer maintenance management for the past 20 years (refer to resume attached) and the operations manager (Fred Smith) has been in the automobile repair industry for over 5 years. Both of these people have demonstrated progressive success in their respective areas of expertise and feel that by combining their talents a new automotive repair niche market can be profitably addressed.
   c. Office hours

      Business hours: 10:00 A.M. to 9:00 P.M.
      Thursday through Tuesday

      These hours are considered best for the convenience of the target customer; the customer does not want to be bothered with fleet unit "shuffling" during the busy morning hours when trying to dispatch deliveries, and so forth, and, in some cases, cannot deliver vehicles for servicing during normal working hours of 8:00 A.M. to 5:00 P.M. and/or during the normal work days of Monday through Friday. Thus 4 hour availability during the week from 5:00 P.M. to 9:00 P.M. and weekend (Saturday and Sunday) availability provides the most convenient time for fleet maintenance needs.
   d. Economic/accounting
      The business will produce revenue by providing a cost-effective vehicle service facility for businesses with fleet maintenance needs. These services will be provided under a semiannual or annual contract basis at a stated monthly charge for the fleet. Repair items not included in the contract will be provided at extra charge which will provide extra revenue over and above the contract revenue.

      Prices will be determined by the general manager with consultation from the operations manager and will initially be determined by estimate using industry standards, and later, once a history has been obtained, by experience. The general formula for pricing will be: all costs (parts, labor, overhead) plus 50 percent. This may be modified depending on "what the market will bear."

Full accounting records will be kept by the administrative manager Jane Smith (wife of Fred) for all supplies purchased, parts purchased and sold, as well as labor and overhead costs. This complete recording system will be implemented as a computerized system specific to the auto repair industry.

e. Inventory, supplies, suppliers, and equipment
Inventory will consist primarily of consumable office supplies (forms, pens, etc.). Very little inventory of high cost parts will be kept on hand since there are many parts stores in the general area which can supply most needed parts within a one working day period, or less. Therefore, it is the intent to practice the "JIT" inventory strategy with only a few specific exceptions which affect signed contract obligations.

f. Legal
The business is to be formed as a partnership consisting of two partners: Walter Jones as to an undivided fifty-one percent (51%) interest and Fred Smith as to an undivided forty-nine percent (49%) interest.

Responsibilities of the business will be divided into two general areas. Those being: administration and operation. Walter Jones will be responsible for the administration and general management of the business and Fred Smith will be responsible for managing the day-to-day shop operations.

g. Future plans
The company mission will be accomplished in three phases starting with the operation that provides the greatest opportunity for immediate cash flow and profit. And, once phase one is proven stable and profitable, adding the necessary resources to incorporate the phase two objective. Then, using the same criteria of stability and profitability, to expand to the third phase operation. Each progressive phase requiring greater human, capital, and time resources.

4. Market Analysis
The target market is those businesses with fleets of 5 to 15 vehicles (i.e., Motorola Service Co., 8 vehicles; Tiffany Plant Rentals, 10 vehicles).

A review of the local (Anytown) auto mechanic businesses reveals that no member is targeting a specific customer area. Instead, they rely on the general public to respond to local advertising or merely "drop in" as the need occurs.

The objective of this targeting is to attract and retain a group of 40 to 45 accounts averaging 8 vehicles each. The vehicles will require servicing (tune-up, lube, oil change) twice per year (minimum) and use approximately 2 hours to service. (43 × 8 = 344 vehicles; 344 × 2 = 688 servicings; 688 × 2 hours = 1376 hours per year; 1376 hours/1980 total working hours per year = .70 or 70% annual capacity.) (1980 working hours per year × .7 = 1386, 1386/4 vehicles per day per mechanic = 347 vehicles per year per mechanic at 70% efficiency.) (Servicing price: $127.00. Servicing cost: $92.00. Gross net per service: $35.00. $35.00 × 347 = $12,145.00 at 70% efficiency.)

The target market will be attracted to the service being offered because they will no longer need to track the service record of each vehicle. That will be provided for them via a computer printout. Also, a reminder call will be made when the estimated time for service is near. Thus they can plan for a vehicle or series of vehicles to be out of service, reducing the impact on their work scheduling. The yearly vehicle maintenance cost will also be a known, easily budgeted figure, since the service will be provided under a contract agreement. Not, as potential competition would offer, a no-contract variable rate.

Any problems found that require work beyond that agreed to under contract would be first recommended and a cost bid submitted. The customer would then have the option to go ahead with the work or check the general market for competitive bids.

Anytown Chamber of Commerce information indicates that industry is moving into the Anytown area encouraged by the fact that the city government has set aside 7000 acres for industrial purposes. Currently 4000 acres are zoned industrial, and there are 50 industrial parks and districts at different levels of development.

As of 1987 there are in excess of 400 plants in the city of Anytown. Leading group classes of products are: electronic, fabricated metal products, automobiles, metal container fabricating, roofing, and printing.

Job growth rate during the past year has been 4 percent and is expected to continue. The initial growth rate of the business is expected to be 15 percent per month. This is justified by the fact that the service offered has virtually no competition in the area and there is already a large customer base potential established in the area. This potential must first be addressed, then the expected growth rate of 19 percent factored into the projections. (Telephone Company Yellow Pages demographic study indicates a 19 percent area growth rate.)

5. Products and Services
   a. XYZ Auto Repair will provide fleet maintenance service to surrounding businesses in the Anytown area. This will include:

Tune-up	Wheel replacement
Lubrication	Engine analysis
Oil change	Engine repair
Brake rebuild	Exhaust maintenance
Tire replacement/balancing	Transmission repair/service
Electrical repair	Chassis repair
Suspension maintenance	

   (Note: Wheel alignments and smog checks are to be subcontracted.)

   b. Comparison to competitors' products
   The service being proposed is a standard automotive service but will be offered to a specific target market in an attractive package (contract form) which no other organization offering this type service is now doing.

   Competition remains the standard auto repair service which is "location" bound to attract the transient customer which is normally the single-vehicle owner with standard maintenance needs. Thus there is no competition for the service being offered by XYZ Auto Repair.

6. Marketing Strategy
   a. Promotion strategy
   The service will be promoted by targeted telemarketing methods. This means that via a demographic study specific businesses will be identified as fleet owners. These businesses will be contacted and the person responsible for fleet management will be identified. That person will be contacted with a description of the service and

its benefits to that person. An interview will be arranged where a full discussion and explanation of the service will be presented and specific information on the fleet will be obtained. A bid contract will then be generated and presented for the person (customer) to read and sign.

Other promotional aids will be mailings directed to the specific person responsible for fleet management (if known, otherwise the general manager) explaining the benefits of the service and with a return mail inquiry card enclosed.

Initial promotion will be kept to the Anytown area to accomplish market test and contain costs. Budgeted promotion costs will average, at maturity, the industry standards. These are:

Auto Dealers and Gas Station Advertising to Sales Ratios:

1.6% Ad $ as % of Sales
6.1% Ad $ as %of Margin

(*Source*: "Advertising-to-Sales Ratios, 1985," *Advertising Age*, September 15, 1986, p. 60.)

b. Pricing policy
Pricing will be established to encourage multiple-vehicle maintenance contracts. The advantage to the customer is a constant set monthly cost for ease in budgeting. The advantage to the business is a constant, dependable cash flow.

c. Sales strategy
Sales will be accomplished by personal interview with people responsible for fleet maintenance. These interviews will be generated by telemarketing and/or direct-mail response. During these interviews the full explanation of the services provided and the cost of these services will be discussed, a contract written to the customers specific needs, and the contract priced, conditions of payment noted, and presented for signature.

7. Management Plan
   a. Form of business organization
   A partnership consisting of two (2) partners:

      Walter Jones
      Fred Smith

   b. Board of directors composition

Board of Directors

Chairperson:	Walter Jones, owner/general manager
	Fred Smith, owner/operations manager
	Betty Jones
	Jane Smith

Advisory Board

Chairperson:	Walter Jones, owner/general manager
	Fred Smith, owner/operations manager
Attorney:	Dave Neverwantsto, advise as needed
CPA:	Eugene Numbersgame, advise as needed, audit accounts, and prepare tax filings
Insurance:	Paul Notenough, insurance broker, advise as needed

c. Officers: organization chart and responsibilities

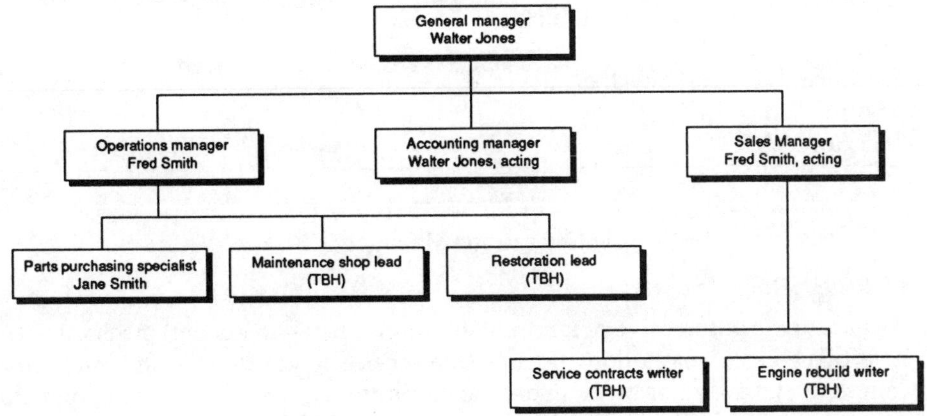

d. Resumes of key personnel

WALTER JONES, Ph.D.
General Manager

BACKGROUND SUMMARY

Over 20 years in the design, development, and implementation of sales support programs for electronic and electromechanical systems.

Director of Technical Support, Technical Sales Support Manager, and Project Manager for microcomputer and peripheral computer products.

SPECIFIC AREAS OF EXPERTISE

Technical support administration
Maintainability engineering
Reliability engineering
Program management
Field technical operations management
Material control systems
Customer relations
Technical training
Technical documentation

EXPERIENCE APPLIED TO THE FOLLOWING SYSTEMS

Microcomputers and word processors
Computer peripherals: Matrix and drum printers, disk and tape-storage devices
Telecommunications
Networks

EDUCATION

B.S. Business Management	(LaSalle University)
B.S.E.E.	(Loyolla University)
B.S. Business Administration	(Columbia Pacific University)
Ph.D. Business Administration	(Columbia Pacific University)

COMPANY AFFILIATIONS

E.D.P. Division of Honeywell, Inc.
Hewlett-Packard Co.
Microform Data Systems, Inc.
Osborne Computer Corp.
Ferix Corp.

FRED SMITH
Operations Manager

BACKGROUND SUMMARY

Over 5 years in the automotive repair industry apprenticing in general mechanics: tune-ups, lube, oil change, tire rotation, transmission service, road testing, differential service.

Completed Journeyman work in engine rebuilding, transmission repair, and clutch replacement of most foreign and domestic automobiles and 4-wheel drive trucks.

SPECIFIC AREAS OF EXPERTISE

Engine rebuilding
Transmission rebuilding
Clutch replacement

EDUCATION

Reynolds High School, (1983)
Sequoia Institute
Chabot Jr. College

COMPANY AFFILIATIONS

Mowry Automotive, Anytown, XA.
Winner Chevrolet, Trans, XA.
Anytown Ford, Anytown, XA.
Shamrock Ford, Dubland, XA.
Dan's Car Repair, Anytown, XA.
Osborne Computer Corporation, Hayward, XA.
SoutherlandConstructionCo., Anytown, XA.

---

e. Staffing plan/number of employees
Initially staffing will consist of Walter Jones and Fred Smith who will be responsible for assuring the accounting books are in order and that the job flow is maintained through the shop respectively. These two people will share the responsibility of soliciting business and answering the telephone and handling necessary correspondence.

This will be the mode of operation until on-going cash flow justifies the hiring of additional personnel. The first to be hired will be a maintenance shop apprentice. The intent will be for Fred Smith to supervise and train the individual in the proper shop processes so as to allow the trainee's promotion to maintenance shop lead. When this occurs, Fred will begin setting up the engine rebuilding facility. When that department's cash flow justifies another person, that person will be hired as an apprentice and trained by Fred in the proper procedures of rebuilding engines. Fred will then move on to the third and last operation of establishing the restoration shop. The same rules for hiring will apply here: cash flow justification, and apprentice to journeyman growth.

The primary source of apprentice type personnel will be the Sequoia Institute. However, other sources will not necessarily be refused or rejected.

Additional personnel that may be necessary, again justified by cash flow, will be service contract writer, engine rebuild writer, and restored auto sales. These positions are primarily sales positions whose salaries will be a combination of base salary and commission.

The basic philosophy of personnel management will be to hire from outside the company but promote from within the company. Thus assuring a career growth path which is not offered by many in the industry. This will promote loyalty and longevity of the individual employee.

8. Financial Plan
   a. Explanation of key financial points

Manpower Budgets:

There are two budgeted departments: administration and operations. It is indicated that the initial manpower will consist of one primary person in each department with a part-time person assisting with the clerical and data-entry duties in administration. This will continue for approximately 6 months or until the business growth justifies additional help in each department.

Budget Worksheets:

Again, there are two budgeted deparments. Each showing the projected cash flow needs of that specific department. The major expenses for capital equipment are called out. Those being:

$10000	Computer system for accounting purposes in administration
$5000	Chassis lift
4500	Tire mounting equipment and Brake lathe
5000	Engine analyzing equipment

These purchases are spread through the first 6 months of operation.

Cash Flow Projections:

This is a combined projection for XYZ Auto Repair operations and includes the budgeted items mentioned above.

Cash receipts reflect what is expected from miscellaneous repair work which is outside the targeted market of maintenance contract work. This is expected to increase at the same rate as the maintenance contract work which is 15 percent per month.

Cash disbursements include all disbursements of both the administrative and operations departments.

Depreciation is based on 5-year straight-line method against the capital equipment purchases mentioned above.

Accounts receivable reflects the income from the sale of fleet maintenance contracts and the expected increase at a 15 percent per month rate.

Accounts payable are expenses for fleet maintenance contract parts purchases.

Payment of other Expenses reflects the cost of parts purchases for work other than fleet maintenance accounts.

Purchase of equipment shows the expected expenditures for capital equipment.

Increase in funds invested reflects the average of the long-term loan principal payback of approximately $500 per month.

b. Financial projections
   1. Manpower budget: Administration
   2. Budget worksheet: Administration
   3. Manpower budget: Operations
   4. Budget worksheet: Operations
   5. Cash flow projections: First running year
   6. Pro forma balance sheets: First running year
   7. Pro forma income statements: First running year
   8. Pro forma balance sheets: Three continuing years
   9. Pro forma income statements: Three continuing years
   10. Pricing strategy

MANPOWER BUDGET: ADMINISTRATION

	MONTH 1	2	3	4	5	6	7	8	9	10	11	12	YR END TOTAL
EMPLOYEES	1	1	1	1	1	2	2	2	2	2	2	2	2
TEMP.EMP.	1	1	1	1	1	0	0	0	0	0	0	0	0
ADDITIONS						1	1	1	1	1	1	1	1
HIRE/PROMOTION DATE / POSITION													
Mo. 1 Admin Mgr	2500/mo												
Mo. 1 Data Entry/Recept	5.50/hr				6.50/hr								
TOTAL SALARIES & WAGES	2940	2940	2940	2940	3020	3020	3020	3020	3020	3020	3020	3020	35920
MERIT INCREASE (10% ANN)													
OVERTIME													
TEMP.													
TOTAL SALARY & WAGES	2940	2940	2940	2940	3020	3020	3020	3020	3020	3020	3020	3020	35920 35920

BUDGET WORKSHEET: ADMINISTRATION

ACCT	DESCRIPTION		MONTH 1	2	3	4	5	6	7	8	9	10	11	12	TOTAL
0100	SALARIES AND WAGES		2940	2940	2940	2940	3020	3020	3020	3020	3020	3020	3020	3020	35920
0110	OVERTIME PREMIUM														0
0150	ENGINEERING PROJECT														0
0200	PAYROLL BENEFITS	23% of hrly	676	676	676	676	695	695	695	695	695	695	695	695	8262
0210	EMPLOYEE DEVELOPMENT	5% of hrly	147	147	147	147	151	151	151	151	151	151	151	151	1796
0450	ADVERT PRINTING SERVICES	1.6% of Sales													0
0460	CONTRACT LABOR - TEMP	$5.50/hr													0
0500	OFFICE SUPPLIES	$20.00/mo	20	20	20	20	20	20	20	20	20	20	20	20	240
0510	EXPENSED EQUIPMENT	$500/qtr	500			500			500			500			2000
0530	EQUIPMENT RENTAL														0
0540	EQUIPMENT MAINTENANCE	$50.00/mo	50	50	50	50	50	50	50	50	50	50	50	50	600
0560	OPERATING SUPPLIES														0
0700	TRAVEL & ENTERTAIN														0
0790	MISC. EXPENSE	5% of Sales													0
	CAPITAL EQUIPMENT		10000												10000
0830	DEPRECIATION & AMORT			-167	-167	-167	-167	-167	-167	-167	-167	-167	-167	-167	-1833
0890	OTHER	$50.00/mo	50	50	50	50	50	50	50	50	50	50	50	50	600
	DEPARTMENT TOTAL		14383	3717	3717	4217	3819	3819	4319	3819	3819	4319	3819	3819	57584
														ck sum	57584

MANPOWER BUDGET: OPERATIONS

		MONTH												YR END
		1	2	3	4	5	6	7	8	9	10	11	12	TOTAL
EMPLOYEES		1	1	1	1	1	1	2	2	2	3	3	3	3
TEMP. EMP.						1	1		1	1				0
ADDITIONS								1			1			2
HIRE/PROMOTION DATE	POSITION													
1	Oper Mgr	20.00/hr												
5	Flt Maint App					5.50/hr								
7	Flt Maint Lead							6.50/hr						
8	Flt Maint App								5.50/hr					
8	Flt Maint Lead										6.50/hr			
10	Eng Rebld App										7.50/hr			
	TOTAL SALARIES & WAGES	3200	3200	3200	4080	4080	4240	5120	5120	5440	5440	5440	5440	54000
	MERIT INCREASE (10% ANN)													
	OVERTIME													
	TEMP.													
	TOTAL SALARY & WAGES	3200	3200	3200	4080	4080	4240	5120	5120	5440	5440	5440	5440	54000 54000

BUDGET WORKSHEET: OPERATIONS

ACCT	DESCRIPTION		MONTH 1	2	3	4	5	6	7	8	9	10	11	12	TOTAL
0100	SALARIES AND WAGES		3200	3200	3200	4080	4080	4240	5120	5120	5440	5440	5440	5440	54000
0110	OVERTIME PREMIUM														0
0150	ENGINEERING PROJECT														0
0200	PAYROLL BENEFITS	23% of hrly	736	736	736	938	938	975	1178	1178	1251	1251	1251	1251	12420
0210	EMPLOYEE DEVELOPMENT	5% of hrly	160	160	160	204	204	212	256	256	272	272	272	272	2700
0450	PRINTING SERVICES														0
0460	CONTRACT LABOR - TEMP	$5.50/hr													0
0470	OTHER PURCHASED SERV	$100.00/mo	100	100	100	100	100	100	100	100	100	100	100	100	1200
0500	OFFICE SUPPLIES	$20.00/mo	20	20	20	20	20	20	20	20	20	20	20	20	240
0510	EXPENSED EQUIPMENT	$500/qtr	500			500			500			500			2000
0520	SMALL TOOLS	$20.00/mo	20	20	20	20	20	20	20	20	20	20	20	20	240
0530	EQUIPMENT RENTAL														0
0540	EQUIPMENT MAINTENANCE	$50.00/mo	50	50	50	50	50	50	50	50	50	50	50	50	600
0560	OPERATING SUPPLIES														0
0700	TRAVEL & ENTERTAIN														0
0710	DUES & SUBSCRIPTIONS	$200.00/yr	20			20	20	20	20	20	20	20	20	20	200
0790	MISC. EXPENSE	5% of Sales													0
0800	JANITORIAL & MAINT.	5.50/hr,6hr/wk	143	143	143	143	143	143	143	143	143	143	143	143	1716
0810	INSURANCE	$3500.00/yr	292	292	292	292	292	292	292	292	292	292	292	292	3504
0820	FREIGHT & POSTAGE	Eng rebld $50/mo							1	50	50	50	50	50	251
	CAPITAL EQUIPMENT		5000	4500				5000							14500
0830	DEPRECIATION & AMORT			-83	-158	-158	-158	-158	-242	-242	-242	-242	-242	-242	-2167
0840	TELEPHONE & TELEX	$60.00/mo	60	60	60	60	60	60	60	60	60	60	60	60	720
0850	RENT	1325ft/$600/mo	600	600	600	600	600	600	600	600	600	600	600	600	7200
0860	UTILITIES	$100.00/mo	100	100	100	100	100	100	100	100	100	100	100	100	1200
0870	TAXES	28% of Sales													0
0890	OTHER	$100.00/mo	100	100	100	100	100	100	100	100	100	100	100	100	1200
	DEPARTMENT TOTAL		11101	9998	5423	7069	6569	11774	8318	7867	8277	8777	8277	8277	101724

CASH FLOW PROJECTIONS
FIRST RUNNING YEAR
($000's omitted)

	MONTH 1	2	3	4	5	6	7	8	9	10	11	12	Total
Beg Cash Balance	.00	106.35	235.22	371.97	505.17	637.88	758.73	886.33	1013.48	1138.82	1261.82	1384.51	8300.28
Cash Receipts													
Cash from Operations (net income)	1.00	1.15	1.32	1.52	1.75	2.01	2.31	2.66	3.06	3.52	4.05	4.65	29.00
Add Depreciation	.00	.25	.33	.33	.33	.33	.49	.49	.49	.49	.49	.49	4.51
Interest Income (6%)	.00	1.50	1.49	1.47	1.46	1.44	1.42	1.41	1.39	1.38	1.36	1.34	15.65
Increase in Curr Liab	.00	.00	.00	.00	.00	.00	.00	.00	.00	.00	.00	.00	.00
Decrease in Inventory	.00	.00	.00	.00	.00	.00	.00	.00	.00	.00	.00	.00	.00
Decrease in A/R	.00	3.15	3.62	4.16	4.78	5.50	6.33	7.28	8.37	9.62	11.07	12.73	76.60
Total Receipts	1.00	6.05	6.75	7.48	8.32	9.28	10.55	11.83	13.31	15.01	16.96	19.21	125.76
Cash Disbursements													
Cash for Operations (net loss)	25.48	13.78	9.14	11.29	10.39	15.59	12.64	11.69	12.10	13.10	12.10	12.10	159.37
Less Depreciation	.00	-.25	-.33	-.33	-.33	-.33	-.41	-.41	-.41	-.41	-.41	-.41	-4.00
Increase in Inventory	.00	.00	.00	.00	.00	.00	.00	.00	.00	.00	.00	.00	.00
Increase in A/R	3.15	3.62	4.16	4.78	5.50	6.33	7.28	8.37	9.62	11.07	12.73	14.64	91.24
Decrease in Other Liab	.00	1.50	1.50	1.50	1.50	1.60	1.60	1.60	1.60	1.60	1.60	1.60	17.20
Accts Payable	.92	.93	.93	.93	.94	.94	.94	.95	.95	.95	.96	.96	11.29
Payment of Other Exp.	.10	.10	.10	.10	.10	.10	.10	.10	.10	.10	.10	.10	1.22
Total Disbursements	29.65	19.67	15.51	18.28	18.10	24.24	22.15	22.29	23.96	26.41	27.07	28.99	276.32
NET CASH FOR OPERATIONS	-28.65	92.72	226.47	361.17	495.38	622.93	747.13	875.88	1002.82	1127.42	1251.71	1374.74	8149.72 ck sum 8149.72
Sale of Capital Stock													.00
Purchase of Equipment	-15.00	-4.50	.00	.00	.00	-5.00	.00	.00	.00	.00	.00	.00	-24.50
Long-term Borrowings (-repayments)	150.00	148.50	147.00	145.50	144.00	142.40	140.80	139.20	137.60	136.00	134.40	132.80	1698.20
Decrease (-Increase) in Funds Invested	.00	-1.50	-1.50	-1.50	-1.50	-1.60	-1.60	-1.60	-1.60	-1.60	-1.60	-1.60	-17.20
ENDING CASH BALANCE	106.35	235.22	371.97	505.17	637.88	758.73	886.33	1013.48	1138.82	1261.82	1384.51	1505.94	9806.22 ck sum 9806.22

NOTE: Minor footing differences are the results of rounding. See explanation of key financial points, page 171.

PROJECTION OF FINANCIAL STATEMENTS
FIRST OPERATING YEAR
Actual Projections ->

Submitted For: XYZ AUTO REPAIR
Spread in hundreds ( )
Spread in thousands (X)

	MONTH 1	2	3	4	5	6	7	8	9	10	11	12	TOTAL
PROFIT AND LOSS													
Direct Sales	4.15	2.98	2.00	2.27	2.15	2.58	3.10	3.72	4.46	5.35	6.42	7.70	46.87
Contract Sales	.00	2.00	3.98	4.93	6.46	7.75	9.30	11.16	13.40	16.07	19.29	23.15	117.49
NET SALES	4.15	4.98	5.98	7.20	8.61	10.33	12.40	14.88	17.85	21.42	25.71	30.85	164.37
Less: Materials Used	.92	.92	.93	.93	.93	.94	.94	.94	.94	.95	.95	.95	11.24
Direct Labor	3.20	3.20	3.20	4.08	4.08	4.24	5.12	5.12	5.44	5.44	5.44	5.44	54.00
Other Oper. Expense	.10	.10	.10	.10	.10	.10	.10	.10	.10	.10	.10	.10	1.20
COST OF GOODS SOLD	4.22	4.22	4.23	5.11	5.11	5.28	6.16	6.16	6.48	6.49	6.49	6.49	66.44
GROSS PROFIT	-.07	.76	1.75	2.09	3.50	5.05	6.24	8.72	11.37	14.93	19.22	24.36	97.93
Less: Sales Expense (8% sales)	.33	.40	.48	.58	.69	.83	.99	1.19	1.43	1.71	2.06	2.47	13.15
Warranty(.1% sales)	.00	.00	.01	.01	.01	.01	.01	.01	.02	.02	.03	.03	.16
Gen. and Admin. Exp.	2.94	2.94	2.94	2.94	3.02	3.02	3.02	3.02	3.02	3.02	3.02	3.02	35.92
Burden (50% labor)	1.60	1.60	1.60	2.04	2.04	2.12	2.56	2.56	2.72	2.72	2.72	2.72	27.00
OPERATING PROFIT	-4.95	-4.18	-3.27	-3.47	-2.26	-.92	-.35	1.93	4.19	7.46	11.40	16.12	21.69
Less: Other Exp. or Inc. (Net)	.00	.00	.00	.00	.00	.00	.00	.00	.00	.00	.00	.00	.00
Income Tax Provision (28%)	-1.38	-1.17	-.92	-.97	-.63	-.26	-.10	.54	1.17	2.09	3.19	4.51	6.07
NET PROFIT	-3.56	-3.01	-2.36	-2.50	-1.63	-.67	-.25	1.39	3.02	5.37	8.21	11.61	15.62
												check sum	15.62
P & L RATIO ANALYSIS													
Sales	1.00	1.00	1.00	1.00	1.00	1.00	1.00	1.00	1.00	1.00	1.00	1.00	1.00
Cost of Goods Sold	1.02	.85	.71	.71	.59	.51	.50	.41	.36	.30	.25	.21	.40
Gross Margin	-.02	.15	.29	.29	.41	.49	.50	.59	.64	.70	.75	.79	.60
Net Profit on Sales	-.86	-.60	-.39	-.35	-.19	-.06	-.02	.09	.17	.25	.32	.38	.10
Marketing (Sales Exp. + Wty)	.08	.08	.08	.08	.08	.08	.08	.08	.08	.08	.08	.08	.08
Admin. (Gen. and Admin. + Burden)	1.09	.91	.76	.69	.59	.50	.45	.38	.32	.27	.22	.19	.38
CASH PROJECTION													
CASH BALANCE (Opening)	1.00	128.39	113.64	104.97	96.87	89.15	77.16	69.75	63.02	53.15	50.87	52.16	
Plus RECEIPTS: Receivable Coll.	.00	.00	2.00	3.98	4.93	6.46	7.75	9.30	11.16	13.40	16.07	19.29	
Interest Inc. (cash bal x .06/12)	.00	.64	.57	.52	.48	.45	.39	.35	.32	.27	.25	.26	
Return of Net Profit	.00	.00	.00	.00	.00	.00	.00	.00	1.39	3.02	5.37	8.21	
Bank Ln Proceeds	150.00												
Total	151.00	129.03	116.21	109.47	102.29	96.06	85.30	79.40	75.89	69.82	72.57	79.92	
Less: DISBURSEMENTS: Trade Payables	.92	.92	.93	.93	.93	.94	.94	.94	.94	.95	.95	.95	
Direct Labor	3.20	3.20	3.20	4.08	4.08	4.24	5.12	5.12	5.44	5.44	5.44	5.44	
Other Manuf Exp.													
Sales,Gen & Adm Exp	4.88	4.94	5.02	5.56	5.76	5.98	6.58	6.79	7.19	7.48	7.82	8.24	
Fixed Asset Adds	15.00	4.50	.00	.00	.00	5.00	.00	.00	5.00	.00	.00	.00	
Income Taxes	-1.38	-1.17	-.92	-.97	-.63	-.26	-.10	.54	1.17	2.09	3.19	4.51	
Dividends or Withdrawals	.00	.00	.00	.00	.00	.00	.00	.00	.00	.00	.00	.00	
Bank Ln Repaym't	.00	3.00	3.00	3.00	3.00	3.00	3.00	3.00	3.00	3.00	3.00	3.00	
Total	22.61	15.39	11.24	12.60	13.14	18.90	15.55	16.39	22.74	18.95	20.40	22.14	
CASH BALANCE (Closing)	128.39	113.64	104.97	96.87	89.15	77.16	69.75	63.02	53.15	50.87	52.16	57.78	

BALANCE SHEET												
ASSETS: Cash	1.00	128.39	113.64	109.97	96.87	89.15	77.16	93.75	63.02	53.15	50.87	52.16
Marketable Securities	.00	.00	.00	.00	.00	.00	.00	.00	.00	.00	.00	.00
Receivables (Net)	.00	.00	2.00	3.98	4.93	6.46	7.75	9.30	11.16	13.40	16.07	19.29
Inventory (Net)	19.00	19.00	19.00	19.00	19.00	19.00	19.00	19.00	19.00	19.00	19.00	19.00
Spec. Auto Inventory	34.00	34.00	34.00	29.00	29.00	29.00	29.00	5.00	.00	.00	.00	.00
Total Current Assets	54.00	181.39	168.64	161.95	149.80	143.61	132.91	127.05	93.18	85.54	85.94	90.45
Fixed Assets (Net)	37.50	52.50	57.00	57.00	57.00	57.00	62.00	62.00	67.00	72.00	72.00	72.00
Deferred Charges												
TOTAL ASSETS	145.50	415.28	394.28	380.90	356.61	344.22	327.82	316.11	253.36	243.08	243.89	252.91
LIABILITIES: Notes Payable - Banks	150.00	148.50	147.00	145.50	144.00	142.50	141.00	139.50	138.00	136.50	135.00	133.50
Trade Payables	.92	.92	.93	.93	.93	.94	.94	.94	.94	.95	.95	.95
Income Tax	-1.38	-1.17	-.92	-.97	-.63	-.26	-.10	.54	1.17	2.09	3.19	4.51
Accruals (ins. $3500/yr.)	.29	.29	.29	.29	.29	.29	.29	.29	.29	.29	.29	.29
CURRENT LIABILITIES	149.83	148.54	147.31	145.75	144.59	143.47	142.14	141.27	140.40	139.83	139.43	139.26
CAPITAL STOCK - Net Worth for	-4.33	266.74	246.97	235.15	212.02	200.75	185.69	174.83	112.95	103.25	104.45	113.65
SURPLUS - Ptnrship or Indiv.												
TOTAL LIABILITIES AND NET WORTH	145.50	415.28	394.28	380.90	356.61	344.22	327.82	316.11	253.36	243.08	243.89	252.91
BALANCE SHEET RATIO ANALYSIS												
Current Ratio	.36	1.22	1.14	1.11	1.04	1.00	.94	.90	.66	.61	.62	.65
Debt-to-Equity	-34.63	.56	.60	.62	.68	.71	.77	.81	1.24	1.35	1.33	1.23
Return on Assets	-.03	-.01	-.01	-.01	-.01	.00	.00	.01	.02	.03	.05	.06
Return on Equity	.82	-.01	-.01	-.01	-.01	.00	.00	.01	.03	.05	.08	.10
Investment Turnover	.03	.01	.02	.02	.02	.03	.04	.05	.07	.09	.11	.12
Return on Investment (ROI)	-.02	-.01	-.01	-.01	.00	.00	-.00	.00	.01	.02	.03	.05
Working Capital (acid test)	.01	.86	.79	.78	.70	.67	.60	.73	.53	.48	.48	.51

PRO FORMA INCOME STATEMENTS
FIRST RUNNING YEAR
($000's omitted)

	MONTH												
	1	2	3	4	5	6	7	8	9	10	11	12	Total
Unit Sales													0
Sales ($)	4.15	4.77	5.73	6.87	8.25	9.90	11.88	14.25	17.10	20.52	24.63	29.55	157.59
Cost of Sales:													
Warranty (.1% sales)	.00	.00	.01	.01	.01	.01	.01	.01	.02	.02	.02	.03	.16
Labor	3.20	3.20	3.20	4.08	4.08	4.24	5.12	5.12	5.44	5.44	5.44	5.44	54.00
Material	.92	.92	.93	.93	.93	.94	.94	.94	.94	.95	.95	.95	11.24
Burden (50% labor)	1.60	1.60	1.60	2.04	2.04	2.12	2.56	2.56	2.72	2.72	2.72	2.72	27.00
Total Cost of Sales	5.72	5.73	5.73	7.06	7.06	7.31	8.63	8.64	9.12	9.13	9.14	9.14	92.40
												ck sum	92.40
Gross Margin	-1.57	-.96	.00	-.18	1.19	2.59	3.25	5.61	7.98	11.39	15.49	20.41	65.19
Gross Margin (%)	-.38	-.20	-.00	-.03	.14	.26	.27	.39	.47	.56	.63	.69	.41
Operating Expenses:													
Marketing (10% sales)	.42	.33	.27	.21	.17	.14	.11	.09	.07	.06	.04	.04	1.93
General Admin.	2.94	2.94	2.94	2.94	3.02	3.02	3.02	3.02	3.02	3.02	3.02	3.02	35.92
Depreciation	.00	.25	.33	.33	.33	.33	.49	.49	.49	.49	.49	.49	4.51
Total	3.36	3.52	3.54	3.48	3.52	3.49	3.62	3.60	3.58	3.57	3.55	3.55	42.36
												ck sum	42.36
Operating Profit	-4.93	-4.48	-3.54	-3.67	-2.33	-.90	-.37	2.02	4.40	7.83	11.93	16.86	22.82
Operating Profit (%)	-1.19	-.94	-.62	-.53	-.28	-.09	-.03	.14	.26	.38	.48	.57	.14
Other Income/Expense:													
Interest Exp.(11.75%)	.00	1.50	1.50	1.50	1.50	1.50	1.40	1.40	1.40	1.40	1.40	1.30	15.80
Interest Inc. (6%)	.00	.50	.49	.49	.48	.47	.46	.45	.45	.44	.43	.42	5.08
NET INCOME (-LOSS) BEFORE TAXES	-4.93	-5.48	-4.55	-4.68	-3.36	-1.93	-1.31	1.07	3.45	6.87	10.97	15.98	12.10
												ck sum	12.10
Federal Income Tax (28%)	-1.38	-1.53	-1.27	-1.31	-.94	-.54	-.37	.30	.96	1.92	3.07	4.48	
NET INCOME (-LOSS) AFTER TAX	-3.55	-3.94	-3.27	-3.37	-2.42	-1.39	-.94	.77	2.48	4.94	7.90	11.51	12.10

EXPRESSED AS PERCENTAGE OF SALES:													
Sales	1.00	1.00	1.00	1.00	1.00	1.00	1.00	1.00	1.00	1.00	1.00	1.00	1.00
Cost of sales	1.38	1.20	1.00	1.03	.86	.74	.73	.61	.53	.44	.37	.31	.59
Gross margin	-.38	-.20	-.00	-.03	.14	.26	.27	.39	.47	.56	.63	.69	.41
Marketing	.10	.07	.05	.03	.02	.01	.01	.01	.00	.00	.00	.00	.01
General and admin.	.71	.62	.51	.43	.37	.31	.25	.21	.18	.15	.12	.10	.23
Depreciation	.00	.05	.06	.05	.04	.03	.04	.03	.03	.02	.02	.02	.03
Total operating exp	.81	.74	.62	.51	.43	.35	.30	.25	.21	.17	.14	.12	.27
Income from oper.	-1.19	-.94	-.62	-.53	-.28	-.09	-.03	.14	.26	.38	.48	.57	.14
Interest inc (-exp) net	.00	-.21	-.18	-.15	-.12	-.10	-.08	-.07	-.06	-.05	-.04	-.03	-.07
NET INCOME (-LOSS) BEFORE TAXES	-1.19	-1.15	-.79	-.68	-.41	-.19	-.11	.08	.20	.33	.45	.54	.08
NET INCOME (-LOSS) AFTER TAXES	-.86	-.83	-.57	-.49	-.29	-.14	-.08	.05	.15	.24	.32	.39	.08

NOTE: Minor footing differences are the results of rounding. See expanation of key financial points, page 171.

PRO FORMA BALANCE SHEETS
3 CONTINUING YEARS - BY QTR
$000's omitted)

	YEAR 2 1	2	3	4	YEAR 3 1	2	3	4	YEAR 4 1	2	3	4		CUMUL. TOTALS
ASSETS														
Current Assets:														
Cash	908.28	944.61	982.40	1021.69	1021.69	1042.13	1062.97	1084.23	1084.23	1105.91	1128.03	1150.59		12536.75
Investments	.00	.00	.00	.00	.00	.00	.00	.00	.00	.00	.00	.00		.00
Inventory	.00	.00	.00	.00	.00	.00	.00	.00	.00	.00	.00	.00		.00
Total	908.28	944.61	982.40	1021.69	1021.69	1042.13	1062.97	1084.23	1084.23	1105.91	1128.03	1150.59		12536.75
													ck sum	12536.75
Equipment	.00	.00	.00	.00	.00	.00	.00	.00	.00	.00	.00	.00		.00
TOTAL ASSETS	908.28	944.61	982.40	1021.69	1021.69	1042.13	1062.97	1084.23	1084.23	1105.91	1128.03	1150.59		12536.75
													ck sum	12536.75
LIABILITIES AND STOCKHOLDERS' EQUITY														
Current Liabilities:														
Accounts Payable	.96	1.00	1.04	1.08	1.08	1.10	1.12	1.15	1.15	1.17	1.19	1.22		13.25
Accrued Liabilities	12.10	11.62	11.15	10.71	10.71	10.50	10.29	10.08	10.08	9.88	9.68	9.49		126.27
Total	13.06	12.61	12.19	11.79	11.79	11.60	11.41	11.23	11.23	11.05	10.87	10.70		139.52
													ck sum	139.52
Long-term Debt	130.60	127.10	121.80	114.50	108.80	104.90	98.90	90.70	84.30	79.90	73.20	63.90		
Stockholders' equity:	.48	.49	.50	.52	.53	.55	.56	.58	.59	.61	.63	.64		
Preferred Stock														.00
Common Stock														.00
Deficit	764.14	804.41	847.91	894.89	900.57	925.08	952.10	981.72	988.11	1014.35	1043.33	1075.35		11191.95
Total	764.62	804.90	848.41	895.41	901.10	925.63	952.66	982.30	988.70	1014.96	1043.96	1075.99		11198.63
													ck sum	11191.95
TOTAL LIABILITIES	908.28	944.61	982.40	1021.69	1021.69	1042.13	1062.97	1084.23	1084.23	1105.91	1128.03	1150.59		12536.75
													ck sum	11338.15
STATISTICS:														
Current Ratio	69.55	74.88	80.59	86.69	86.66	89.86	93.17	96.58	96.58	100.11	103.75	107.50		89.86
Debt-to-Equity Ratio	.19	.17	.16	.14	.13	.13	.12	.10	.10	.09	.08	.07		.01
Working Capital	1025.82	1059.10	1092.01	1124.41	1118.70	1135.43	1150.46	1163.70	1157.30	1174.76	1190.36	1203.79		12397.23
Net Worth	1529.24	1609.79	1696.81	1790.81	1802.20	1851.26	1905.32	1964.60	1977.40	2029.93	2087.91	2151.97		23595.86
													ck sum	22397.26
Check - Assets-Liab.	.00	.00	.00	.00	.00	.00	.00	.00	.00	.00	.00	.00		.00

PRO FORMA INCOME STATEMENT
3 CONTINUING YEARS - BY QTR
($000's omitted)

	YEAR 2					YEAR 3					YEAR 4				
	1	2	3	4	TOTAL	1	2	3	4	TOTAL	1	2	3	4	Total
Sales ($)	163.89	170.45	177.26	184.35	695.95	191.73	199.40	207.37	215.67	814.17	224.29	233.27	242.60	252.30	952.46
TOTAL SALES ($)	163.89	170.45	177.26	184.35	695.95	191.73	199.40	207.37	215.67	814.17	224.29	233.27	242.60	252.30	952.46
Cost of Sales:															
Warranty(.1% sales)	.16	.17	.18	.18	.70	.19	.20	.21	.22	.81	.22	.23	.24	.25	.95
Labor (Oper.)	3.20	3.33	3.46	3.60	13.59	3.74	3.89	4.05	4.21	15.90	4.38	4.55	4.74	4.93	18.60
Material	11.58	11.92	12.28	12.65	48.43	13.03	13.42	13.82	14.24	54.51	14.67	15.11	15.56	16.03	61.36
Burden (labor x 1.5)	4.80	4.99	5.19	5.40	20.38	5.62	5.84	6.07	6.32	23.85	6.57	6.83	7.11	7.39	27.90
Total Cost of Sales	19.74	20.41	21.11	21.83	83.10	22.58	23.35	24.15	24.98	95.07	25.84	26.73	27.64	28.59	108.80
					83.10					95.07				ck sum	108.80
Gross Margin	144.15	150.03	156.15	162.52	612.85	169.15	176.04	183.22	190.69	719.10	198.46	206.54	214.95	223.71	843.66
Gross Margin (%)	87.95	88.02	88.09	88.16	88.06	88.22	88.29	88.35	88.42	88.32	88.48	88.54	88.61	88.67	88.58
Operating Expenses:															
Marketing	16.39	17.04	17.73	18.44	69.60	19.17	19.94	20.74	21.57	81.42	22.43	23.33	24.26	25.23	95.25
General Admin.	35.92	35.92	35.92	39.51	147.27	39.51	39.51	39.51	43.46	162.00	43.46	43.46	43.46	47.81	178.20
Deprec. (SL. 5yr.)	1.02	1.02	1.02	1.02	4.10	1.02	1.02	1.02	1.02	4.10	1.02	1.02	1.02	1.02	4.10
Total	53.33	53.99	54.67	58.97	220.97	59.71	60.48	61.27	66.05	247.51	66.92	67.81	68.75	74.06	277.54
					220.97					247.51				ck sum	277.54
Operating Profit	90.82	96.04	101.48	103.55	391.89	109.44	115.57	121.95	124.63	471.58	131.54	138.73	146.21	149.64	566.12
Operating Profit (%)	55.41	56.35	57.25	56.17	56.31	57.08	57.96	58.80	57.79	57.92	58.65	59.47	60.27	59.31	59.44
Other Income/Expense:															
Interest Expense	3.83	3.68	3.52	3.36	14.39	3.19	3.02	2.84	2.66	11.71	2.47	2.28	2.08	1.87	8.70
Interest Income	.11	2.72	2.88	3.04	8.76	3.11	3.28	3.47	3.66	13.51	3.74	3.95	4.16	4.39	16.23
NET INCOME (-LOSS)	87.09	95.09	100.84	103.23	386.25	109.35	115.83	122.57	125.63	473.39	132.81	140.39	148.29	152.16	573.65
					386.25					473.39				ck sum	573.65

PRICING STRATEGY
MARCH 25, 1988

ITEM	TIME REQ.	TIME COST	PARTS COST	TOTAL COST	LABOR CHARGE	PARTS CHARGE	PRICE
Single Vehicle							
Tune-up	1.50	30.00	30.00	60.00	60.00	45.00	105.00
Chassis Lube	.50	10.00	2.00	12.00	20.00	3.00	23.00
Oil Change	.50	10.00	10.00	20.00	20.00	15.00	35.00
Brake Rebuild	4.00	80.00	65.00	145.00	160.00	97.50	257.50
Tire Replace	1.50	30.00	5.00	35.00	60.00	7.50	67.50
Wheel Replace	1.50	30.00		30.00	60.00	.00	60.00 Plus Pts
Engine Anal.	1.00	20.00		20.00	40.00	.00	40.00 Plus Pts
Engine Repair	16.00	320.00	300.00	620.00	640.00	450.00	1090.00
Exhaust Maint.	3.00	60.00		60.00	120.00	.00	120.00 Plus Pts
Trans Service	1.00	20.00		20.00	40.00	.00	40.00 Plus Pts
Trans Repair	8.00	160.00		160.00	320.00	.00	320.00 Plus Pts
Chassis Repair		.00		.00	.00	.00	.00 Plus Pts
Suspension		.00		.00	.00	.00	.00 Plus Pts
MULTIPLE VEHICLE DISCOUNT SCHED. 3 to 6							
Tune-up	1.20	24.00	30.00	54.00	48.00	45.00	93.00
Chassis Lube	.40	8.00	2.00	10.00	16.00	3.00	19.00
Oil Change	.40	8.00	10.00	18.00	16.00	15.00	31.00
Brake Rebuild	3.20	64.00	65.00	129.00	128.00	97.50	225.50
Tire Replace	1.20	24.00	5.00	29.00	48.00	7.50	55.50
Wheel Replace	1.20	24.00		24.00	48.00	.00	48.00 Plus Pts
Engine Anal.	.80	16.00		16.00	32.00	.00	32.00 Plus Pts
Engine Repair	12.80	256.00	300.00	556.00	512.00	450.00	962.00
Exhaust Maint.	2.40	48.00		48.00	96.00	.00	96.00 Plus Pts
Trans Service	.80	16.00		16.00	32.00	.00	32.00 Plus Pts
Trans Repair	6.40	128.00		128.00	256.00	.00	256.00 Plus Pts
Chassis Repair	.00	.00		.00	.00	.00	.00 Plus Pts
Suspension	.00	.00		.00	.00	.00	.00 Plus Pts
MULTIPLE VEHICLE DISCOUNT SCHED. 6 to 10							
Tune-up	.96	19.20	30.00	49.20	38.40	45.00	83.40
Chassis Lube	.32	6.40	2.00	8.40	12.80	3.00	15.80
Oil Change	.32	6.40	10.00	16.40	12.80	15.00	27.80
Brake Rebuild	2.56	51.20	65.00	116.20	102.40	97.50	199.90
Tire Replace	.96	19.20	5.00	24.20	38.40	7.50	45.90
Wheel Replace	.96	19.20		19.20	38.40	.00	38.40 Plus Pts
Engine Anal.	.64	12.80		12.80	25.60	.00	25.60 Plus Pts
Engine Repair	10.24	204.80	300.00	504.80	409.60	450.00	859.60
Exhaust Maint.	1.92	38.40		38.40	76.80	.00	76.80 Plus Pts
Trans Service	.64	12.80		12.80	25.60	.00	25.60 Plus Pts
Trans Repair	5.12	102.40		102.40	204.80	.00	204.80 Plus Pts
Chassis Repair	.00	.00		.00	.00	.00	.00 Plus Pts
Suspension	.00	.00		.00	.00	.00	.00 Plus Pts

* Wheel alignment to be subcontracted
Smog checks to be subcontracted

* * *

After discussions with the potential lender the following revised plan was submitted. This revision detailed the collateral (tools and equipment) inventory by its item value. The reduced value collateral, of course, caused the amount of the lender capital to be reduced. This lender would only lend to twice the collateral value. Thus the amount supported by the collateral was requested, discussed in view of the total proposition, and granted.

BUSINESS PLAN
XYZ AUTO REPAIR

(rev. 6/1/90)
Walter Jones, General Manager.
434 Any Ave.
Anytown, XA 95635
796/555-6666

EXECUTIVE SUMMARY

The business venture described in this plan is an automobile fleet maintenance service to be known as "XYZ Auto Repair" and will be located in the city and state of Anytown, XA. Growth plans include engine rebuilding and automobile restoration services.

Mission Statements:

> To provide those businesses within a 25 mile radius of the city of Anytown a fleet maintenance service which is scheduled, reliable, and cost effective.
>
> To provide the general public a cost-effective engine rebuilding service.
>
> To locate and acquire popular vintage model automobiles for the purpose of restoring and reselling. Specializing in model years prior to 1970.

The target market is those businesses with fleets of 5 to 15 vehicles (i.e., Motorola Service Co., 8 vehicles; Tiffany Plant Rentals, 10 vehicles).

A review of the local (Anytown, Othertown) auto mechanic businesses reveals that no member is targeting a specific customer area. Instead, they rely on the general public to respond to local advertising or merely "drop in" as the need occurs. Thus the proposed market is without any real competition in the planned area of service.

The two principals of the business, Walter Jones and Fred Smith are well experienced in their respective areas. Walter has over 20 years in the design, development, implementation, and management of service support programs for electronic and electromechanical systems. Fred has over 5 years experience in the automotive repair industry in general mechanics: tune-ups, lube, oil change, tire rotation, transmission service, road testing, differential service, and engine rebuilding.

The purpose of the loan funds is to purchase capital equipment and provide working capital until the business is through the "breakeven" point—approximately 6 to 9 months.

The amount being requested is $50,000 which will be paid back over 5 years at prime plus 2 percent. The funds are to be secured by the assets of the business which include over $20,000 worth of hand tools and heavy equipment such as air compressor, engine hoist, and engine rack.

CONTENTS

1. Name of Firm
   The business will be known as "XYZ Auto Repair."

2. Ownership
   The business is to be formed as a partnership consisting of two partners: Walter Jones as to an undivided fifty-one percent (51%) interest and Fred Smith as to an undivided forty-nine percent (49%) interest.

3. Information on the Business
   a. Type of business and product or service
      The proposed business venture is an automobile fleet maintenance service targeting those businesses with fleets of 5 to 15 vehicles. With growth plans to include engine rebuilding and automobile restoration services.

      Mission Statements:

      > To provide those businesses within a 25 mile radius of the city of Anytown a fleet maintenance service which is scheduled, reliable, and cost effective.
      >
      > To provide the general public a cost-effective engine rebuilding service.
      >
      > To locate and acquire popular vintage model automobiles for the purpose of restoring and reselling. Specializing in model years prior to 1970.

   b. History
      This business is a start-up business venture and as such has no history of previous operation to relate. However, both principals forming the business have histories in the maintenance business. The general manager (Walter Jones) has been in computer maintenance management for the past 20 years (refer to resume attached) and the operations manager (Fred Smith) has been in the automobile repair industry for over 5 years. Both of these people have demonstrated progressive success in their respective areas of expertise and feel that by combining their talents a new automotive repair niche market can be profitably addressed.

   c. Office hours

      Business hours: 10:00 A.M. to 9:00 P.M.
      Thursday through Tuesday

      These hours are considered best for the convenience of the target customer; the customer does not want to be bothered with fleet unit "shuffling" during the busy morning hours when trying to dispatch deliveries, and so forth, and, in some cases, cannot deliver vehicles for servicing during normal working hours of 8:00 A.M. to 5:00 P.M. and/or during the normal work days of Monday through Friday. Thus 4 hour availability during the week from 5:00 P.M. to 9:00 P.M. and weekend (Saturday and Sunday) availability provides the most convenient time for fleet maintenance needs.

   d. Economic/accounting
      The business will provide revenue by providing a cost-effective vehicle service facility for businesses with fleet maintenance needs. These services will be provided under a semiannual or annual contract basis at a stated monthly charge for the fleet. Repair items not included in the contract will be provided at extra charge which will provide extra revenue over and above the contract revenue.

      Prices will be determined by the general manager with consultation from the operations manager and will initially be determined by estimate using industry standards, and later, once a history has been obtained, by experience. The general formula for pricing will be: all costs (parts, labor, overhead) plus 50 percent. This may be modified depending on "what the market will bear."

Full accounting records will be kept by the administrative manager (Jane Smith (wife of Fred)) for all supplies purchased, parts purchased and sold, as well as labor and overhead costs. This complete recording system will be implemented as a computerized system specific to the auto repair industry.

e. Inventory, supplies, vendors, and equipment
Inventory will consist primarily of consumable office supplies (forms, pens, etc.). Very little inventory of high cost parts will be kept on hand since there are many parts stores in the general area which can supply most needed parts within a 1 working day period, or less. Therefore, it is the intent to practice the "JIT" inventory strategy with only a few specific exceptions which affect signed contract obligations.

f. Legal
The business is to be formed as a partnership consisting of two partners: Walter Jones as to an undivided fifty-one percent (51%) interest and Fred Smith as to an undivided forty-nine percent (49%) interest.

Responsibilities of the business will be divided into two general areas. Those being: administration and operation. Walter Jones will be responsible for the administration and general management of the business and Fred Smith will be responsible for managing the day-to-day shop operations.

g. Future plans
The company mission will be accomplished in three phases starting with the operation that provides the greatest opportunity for immediate cash flow and profit. And, once phase one is proven stable and profitable, adding the necessary resources to incorporate the phase two objective. Then, using the same criteria of stability and profitability, to expand to the third phase operation. Each progressive phase requiring greater human, capital, and time resources.

4. Market Analysis
The target market is those businesses with fleets of 5 to 15 vehicles (i.e., Motorola Service Co., 8 vehicles; Tiffany Plant Rentals, 10 vehicles).

A review of the local (Anytown, Other Town) auto mechanic businesses reveals that no member is targeting a specific customer area. Instead, they rely on the general public to respond to local advertising or merely "drop in" as the need occurs.

The objective of this targeting is to attract and retain a group of 40 to 45 accounts averaging 8 vehicles each. The vehicles will require servicing (tune-up, lube, oil change) twice per year (minimum) and use approximately 2 hours to service. (43 × 8 = 344 vehicles; 344 × 2 = 688 servicings; 688 × 2 hours = 1376 hours per year; 1376 hours/1980 total working hours per year = .70 or 70% annual capacity)

(1980 working hours/year × .7 = 1386, 1386/4 vehicles per day per mechanic = 347 vehicles per year per mechanic at 70% efficiency. Servicing price: $127.00. Servicing cost: $92.00. Gross net per service: $35.00. $35.00 × 347 = $12,145.00 at 70% efficiency.)

The target market will be attracted to the service being offered because they will no longer need to track the service record of each vehicle. That will be provided for them via a computer printout. Also, a reminder call will be made when the estimated time for service is near. Thus they can plan for a vehicle or series of vehicles to be out of service, reducing the impact on their work scheduling. The yearly vehicle maintenance cost will also be a known, easily budgeted figure, since the service will be provided under a contract agreement. Not, as potential competition would offer, a no-contract variable rate.

Any problems found that require work beyond that agreed to under contract would be first recommended and a cost bid submitted. The customer would then have the option to go ahead with the work or check the general market for competitive bids.

Anytown Chamber of Commerce information indicates that industry is moving into the Anytown area encouraged by the fact that the city government has set aside 7000 acres for industrial purposes. Currently 4000 acres are zoned industrial, and there are 50 industrial parks and districts at different level of development.

As of 1987 there are in excess of 400 plants in the city of Anytown. Leading group classes of products are: electronic, fabricated metal products, automobiles, metal container fabricating, roofing, and printing.

Job growth rate during the past year has been 4 percent and is expected to continue. The initial growth rate of the business is expected to be 15 percent per month. This is justified by the fact that the service offered has virtually no competition in the area and there is already a large customer base potential established in the area. This potential must first be addressed, then the expected growth rate of 19 percent factored into the projections. (Telephone Yellow Pages demographic study indicates a 19 percent area growth rate.)

5. Products and Services
   a. XYZ Auto Repair will provide fleet maintenance service to surrounding businesses in the Anytown area. This will include:

      Tune-up
      Lubrication
      Oil change
      Brake rebuild
      Tire replacement/balancing
      Electrical repair
      Suspension maintenance
      Wheel replacement
      Engine analysis
      Engine repair
      Exhaust maintenance
      Transmission repair/service
      Chassis repair

   (Note: Wheel alignments and smog checks are to be subcontracted.)
   b. Comparison to competitors' products
   The service being proposed is a standard automotive service but will be offered to a specific target market in an attractive package (contract form) which no other organization offering this type service is now doing.

   Competition remains the standard auto repair service which is "location" bound to attract the transient customer which is normally the single-vehicle owner with standard maintenance needs. Thus there is no competition for the service being offered by XYZ Auto Repair.

6. Marketing Strategy
   a. Promotion strategy
   The service will be promoted by targeted telemarketing methods. This means that via a demographic study specific businesses will be identified as fleet owners. These businesses will be contacted and the person responsible for fleet management will

be identified. That person will be contacted with a description of the service and its benefits to that person. An interview will be arranged where a full discussion and explanation of the service will be presented and specific information on the fleet will be obtained. A bid contract will then be generated and presented for the person (customer) to read and sign.

Other promotional aids will be mailings directed to the specific person responsible for fleet management (if known, otherwise the general manager) explaining the benefits of the service and with a return mail inquiry card enclosed.

Initial promotion will be kept to the Anytown-Othertown areas to accomplish market test and contain costs. Budgeted promotion costs will average, at maturity, the industry standards. These are:

Auto Dealers and Gas Station Advertising to Sales Ratios:

1.6% Ad $ as % of Sales
6.1% Ad $ as %of Margin

(Source: "Advertising-to-Sales Ratios, 1985", *Advertising Age*, September 15, 1986, p. 60.)

b. Pricing policy
Pricing will be established to encourage multiple vehicle maintenance contracts. The advantage to the customer is a constant set monthly cost for ease in budgeting. The advantage to the business is a constant, dependable cash flow.

c. Sales strategy
Sales will be accomplished by personal interview with people responsible for fleet maintenance. These interviews will be generated by telemarketing and/or direct-mail response. During these interviews the full explanation of the services provided and the cost of these services will be discussed, a contract written to the customers specific needs, and the contract priced, conditions of payment noted, and presented for signature.

7. Management Plan
   a. Form of business organization
   A partnership consisting of two (2) partners:
   Walter Jones
   Fred Smith
   b. Board of directors composition

Board of Directors

Chairperson:	Walter Jones, owner/general manager
	Fred Smith, owner/operations manager
	Betty Jones
	Jane Smith

Advisory Board

Chairperson:	Walter Jones, owner/general manager
	Fred Smith, owner/operations manager
Attorney:	Dave Neverwantsto, advise as needed
CPA:	Eugene Numbersgame, advise as needed, audit accounts, and prepare tax filings
Insurance:	Paul Notenough, insurance broker, advise as needed

c. Officers: organization chart and responsibilities

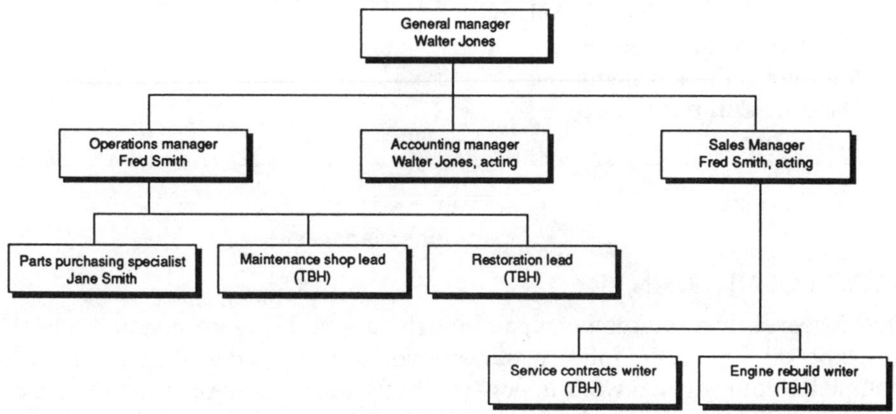

d. Resumes of key personnel

WALTER JONES, Ph.D.
General Manager

BACKGROUND SUMMARY

Over 20 years in the design, development, and implementation of sales support programs for electronic and electromechanical systems.

Director of Technical Support, Technical Sales Support Manager, and Project Manager for microcomputer and peripheral computer products.

SPECIFIC AREAS OF EXPERTISE

Technical support administration
Maintainability engineering
Reliability engineering
Program management
Field technical operations management
Material control systems
Customer relations
Technical training
Technical documentation

EXPERIENCE APPLIED TO THE FOLLOWING SYSTEMS

Microcomputers and word processors
Computer peripherals: Matrix and drum printers, disk and tape-storage devices
Telecommunications
Networks

EDUCATION

B.S. Business Management	(LaSalle University)
B.S.E.E.	(Loyolla University)
B.S. Business Administration	(Columbia Pacific University)
Ph.D. Business Administration	(Columbia Pacific University)

COMPANY AFFILIATIONS

E.D.P. Division of Honeywell, Inc.
Hewlett-Packard Co.
Microform Data Systems, Inc.
Osborne Computer Corp.
Ferix Corp.

FRED SMITH
Operations Manager

BACKGROUND SUMMARY

Over 5 years in the automotive repair industry apprenticing in general mechanics: tune-ups, lube, oil change, tire rotation, transmission service, road testing, differential service. Completed Journeyman work in engine rebuilding, transmission repair, and clutch replacement of most foreign and domestic automobiles and 4-wheel drive trucks.

SPECIFIC AREAS OF EXPERTISE

Engine rebuilding
Transmission rebuilding
Clutch replacement

EDUCATION

Reynolds High School, (1983)
Sequoia Institute
Chabot Jr. College

COMPANY AFFILIATIONS

Mowry Automotive, Anytown, XA.
Winner Chevrolet, Trans, XA.
Anytown Ford, Anytown, XA.
Shamrock Ford, Dubland, XA.
Dan's Car Repair, Anytown, XA.
Osborne Computer Corporation, Hayworth, XA.
SoutherlandConstructionCo., Anytown, XA.

---

e. Staffing plan/number of employees

Initially staffing will consist of Walter Jones and Fred Smith who will be responsible for assuring the accounting books are in order and that the job flow is maintained through the shop respectively. These two people will share the responsibility of soliciting business and answering the telephone and handling necessary correspondence.

This will be the mode of operation until on-going cash flow justifies the hiring of additional personnel. The first to be hired will be a maintenance shop apprentice. The intent will be for Fred Smith to supervise and train the individual in the proper shop processes so as to allow the trainee's promotion to maintenance shop lead. When this occurs, Fred will begin setting up the engine rebuilding facility. When that department's cash flow justifies another person, that person will be hired as an apprentice and trained by Fred in the proper procedures of rebuilding engines. Fred will then move on to the third and last operation of establishing the restoration shop. The same rules for hiring will apply here: cash flow justification, and apprentice to journeyman growth.

The primary source of apprentice type personnel will be the Sequoia Institute. However, other sources will not necessarily be refused or rejected.

Additional personnel that may be necessary, again justified by cash flow, will be service contract writer, engine rebuild writer, and restored auto sales. These positions are primarily sales positions whose salaries will be a combination of base salary and commission.

The basic philosophy of personnel management will be to hire from outside the company but promote from within the company. Thus assuring a career growth path which is not offered by many in the industry. This will promote loyalty and longevity of the individual employee.

8. Financial Plan (Revised)
   a. Explanation of key financial points

   Manpower Budgets:

   There are two budgeted departments: administration and operations. It is indicated that the initial manpower will consist of one primary person in each department with a part-time person assisting with the clerical and data-entry duties in administration. This will continue for approximately 6 months or until the business growth justifies additional help in each department.

   Budget Worksheets:

   Again, there are two budgeted deparments. Each showing the projected cash flow needs of that specific department. The major expenses for capital equipment are called out. Those being:

$5000	Computer system for accounting purposes in administration (revised from $10000 due to reduced hardware pricing in the computer industry)
$5000	Chassis lift
$4500	Tire mounting equipment and brake lathe
$5000	Engine analyzing equipment

   These purchases are spread through the first 6 months of operation.

   Cash Flow Projections:

   This is a combined projection for XYZ Auto Repair operations and includes the budgeted items mentioned above.

   Cash receipts reflect what is expected from miscellaneous (direct) repair work which is outside the targeted market of maintenance contract work. This is expected to be the major billable work during the first 2 to 3 months of operation but decline, due to maintenance contract concentration, during the first 6 months. It will then increase at the same rate as the maintenance contract work which is 20 percent per month. However, this increase will be due to work likely to be required by contract clients that is outside the contracted services.

   Cash disbursements includes all disbursements of both the administrative and operations departments.

   Depreciation is based on 5-year straight-line method against the capital equipment purchases mentioned above.

Accounts receivable reflects the income from the sale of fleet maintenance contracts and their expected value increase at a 15 percent per month rate. Accounts Payable are expenses for fleet maintenance contract parts purchases.

Payment of other expenses reflects loan interest expense.

Purchase of equipment shows the expected expenditures for capital equipment.

An increase in net worth is reflected in the last quarter of the first year due to the beginning of the return of net profit to the business. Prior to that time the net worth is a reflection of the use of borrowed funds to meet the working capital needs of the business.

Note: All net profit will be returned to the business until a current ratio of 2 is obtained. This will occur sometime in the third or fourth quarter of operation. At that time limited ownership withdrawals will be permitted (Rule: Maintain a current ratio of 2 after any withdrawal.)

At the end of the financials, for additional information, is a detailed equipment inventory list having a total current value of $20,899.21.

PROJECTION OF FINANCIAL STATEMENTS
FIRST OPERATING YEAR
Actual Projections -->

Submitted For: XYZ AUTO REPAIR
Spread in hundreds ( )
Spread in thousands (X)

						MONTH							
A	1	2	3	4	5	6	7	8	9	10	11	12	TOTAL
PROFIT AND LOSS													
Direct Sales	4.00	3.00	2.00	2.30	2.00	3.00	4.00	5.00	6.00	8.00	10.00	12.00	61.30
Contract Sales	.00	2.00	4.00	5.00	6.00	7.00	9.00	10.00	12.00	14.00	17.00	20.00	106.00
NET SALES	4.00	5.00	6.00	7.30	8.00	10.00	13.00	15.00	18.00	22.00	27.00	32.00	167.30
Less: Materials Used	.92	.92	.93	.93	.93	.94	.94	.94	.94	.95	.95	.95	11.24
Direct Labor	3.00	3.00	3.00	4.00	4.00	4.00	5.00	5.00	5.00	5.00	5.00	5.00	51.00
Other Oper. Expense	.10	.10	.10	.10	.10	.10	.10	.10	.10	.10	.10	.10	1.20
COST OF GOODS SOLD	4.02	4.02	4.03	5.03	5.03	5.04	6.04	6.04	6.04	6.05	6.05	6.05	63.44
GROSS PROFIT	-.02	.98	1.97	2.27	2.97	4.96	6.96	8.96	11.96	15.95	20.95	25.95	103.86
Less: Sales Expense (8% sales)	.32	.40	.48	.58	.64	.80	1.04	1.20	1.44	1.76	2.16	2.56	13.38
Warranty(.1% sales)	.00	.01	.01	.01	.01	.01	.01	.02	.02	.02	.03	.03	.17
Gen. and Admin. Exp.	2.00	2.00	2.00	2.00	3.00	3.00	3.00	3.00	3.00	3.00	3.00	3.00	32.00
Burden (50% labor)	1.50	1.50	1.50	2.00	2.00	2.00	2.50	2.50	2.50	2.50	2.50	2.50	25.50
OPERATING PROFIT	-3.84	-2.93	-2.02	-2.32	-2.68	-.85	.41	2.25	5.00	8.67	13.26	17.86	32.81
Less: Other Exp. or Inc. (Net)	.00	.00	.00	.00	.00	.00	.00	.00	.00	.00	.00	.00	.00
Income Tax Provision (28%)	-1.08	-.82	-.56	-.65	-.75	-.24	.11	.63	1.40	2.43	3.71	5.00	9.19
NET PROFIT	-2.77	-2.11	-1.45	-1.67	-1.93	-.61	.29	1.62	3.60	6.24	9.55	12.86	23.62
												check sum	23.62
P & L RATIO ANALYSIS													
Sales	1.00	1.00	1.00	1.00	1.00	1.00	1.00	1.00	1.00	1.00	1.00	1.00	1.00
Cost of Goods Sold	1.01	.80	.67	.69	.63	.50	.46	.40	.34	.28	.22	.19	.38
Gross Margin	-.01	.20	.33	.31	.37	.50	.54	.60	.66	.73	.78	.81	.62
Net Profit on Sales	-.69	-.42	-.24	-.23	-.24	-.06	.02	.11	.20	.28	.35	.40	.14
Marketing (Sales Exp. + Wty)	.08	.08	.08	.08	.08	.08	.08	.08	.08	.08	.08	.08	.08
Admin. (Gen. and Admin. + Burden)	.88	.70	.58	.55	.63	.50	.42	.37	.31	.25	.20	.17	.34
CASH PROJECTION													
CASH BALANCE (Opening)	2.50	35.83	28.01	24.79	21.05	17.62	14.20	10.66	9.43	5.80	10.77	20.71	
Plus RECEIPTS: Receivable Coll.	.00	4.00	5.00	6.00	7.30	8.00	10.00	13.00	15.00	18.00	22.00	17.00	
Interest Inc. (cash bal x .06/12)	.00	.18	.14	.12	.11	.09	.07	.05	.05	.03	.05	.10	
Return of Net Profit	.00	.00	.00	.00	.00	.00	.00	.00	1.62	3.60	6.24	9.55	
Bank Ln Proceeds	50.00												
Total	52.50	40.01	33.15	30.92	28.45	25.71	24.27	23.72	26.10	27.43	39.06	47.37	
Less: DISBURSEMENTS: Trade Payables	.92	.92	.93	.93	.93	.94	.94	.94	.94	.95	.95	.95	
Direct Labor	3.00	3.00	3.00	4.00	4.00	4.00	5.00	5.00	5.00	5.00	5.00	5.00	
Other Manuf Exp.													
Sales,Gen & Adm Exp	3.82	3.91	3.99	4.59	5.65	5.81	6.55	6.72	6.96	7.28	7.69	8.09	
Fixed Asset Adds	10.00	4.00	.00	.00	.00	.00	.00	.00	5.00	.00	.00	.00	
Income Taxes	-1.08	-.82	-.56	-.65	-.75	-.24	.11	.63	1.40	2.43	3.71	5.00	
Dividends or Withdrawals	.00	.00	.00	.00	.00	.00	.00	.00	.00	.00	.00	.00	
Bank Ln Repaym't	.00	1.00	1.00	1.00	1.00	1.00	1.00	1.00	1.00	1.00	1.00	1.00	
Total	16.67	12.01	8.35	9.87	10.83	11.51	13.61	14.28	20.30	16.66	18.35	20.04	
CASH BALANCE (Closing)	35.83	28.01	24.79	21.05	17.62	14.20	10.66	9.43	5.80	10.77	20.71	27.32	

XYZ AUTO REPAIR: EQUIPMENT INVENTORY
NOVEMBER 1, 1989

ITEM	MANUF.	QTY	VALUE EACH	TOTAL VALUE	ITEM	MANUF.	QTY	VALUE EACH	TOTAL VALUE
Pliers, spark plug wire	Duro	1	12.48	12.48	Die grinder, small	Mac	1	63.50	63.50
Pliers, spark plug (ra)	Blue Point	1	12.48	12.48	Die grinder, 1/4"	Mac	1	116.00	116.00
Vice grips, 8"	Allied	1	10.30	10.30	Drill, air	Mac	1	101.95	101.95
Channel locks, 6"	C/M	1	14.85	14.85	Ball bearing tool	Sioux	1	287.50	287.50
Cutters, wire 5"	Duro	2	15.35	30.70	Light, timing	Allied	4	36.95	147.80
Cutters, wire 6"	Duro	1	15.90	15.90	Coil spring tool, sgl act	Mac	1	67.65	67.65
Cutters, wire 7"	Duro	7	17.80	124.60	Guage, feeler, metric	Duro	10	1.00	10.00
Pliers 6"	C/M	1	6.80	6.80	Gappers, spark plug	C/M	1	5.80	5.80
Pliers 6.5"	C/M	1	7.10	7.10	Screwdriver, fh, 1/8"	Allied	5	6.50	32.50
Pliers 7"	Optica	2	18.20	36.40	Screwdriver, fh, 3/16"	Allied	11	6.65	73.15
Pliers 8"	Pexto	1	13.45	13.45	Screwdriver, fh, 3/8"	Allied	5	14.80	74.00
Sheers 8"	C/M	1	8.00	8.00	Screwdriver, fh, 1/4"	Duro	4	8.10	32.40
Sheers 10"	C/M	1	8.00	8.00	Screwdriver, ph, #1	Allied	9	7.35	66.15
Pliers, snap ring (adj)	Mac	1	10.95	10.95	Screwdriver, ph, #2	Allied	3	7.95	23.85
Pliers, snp rng (adj agl)	Mac	1	13.95	13.95	Screwdriver, ph, #3	C/M	4	12.95	51.80
Pliers, crimping	Mac	1	11.80	11.80	Screwdriver, ph, #4	Allied	4	14.25	57.00
Spreaders	Duro	1	13.95	13.95	Pencil, electric	BVI	1	6.00	6.00
Hammer, #1 plastic lip	C/M	1	25.95	25.95	Meter, VOM	Micronta	1	109.95	109.95
Hammer, ball peen 24z	C/M	1	20.95	20.95	Tester, electrical cont.	Mac	3	7.95	23.85
Hammer, ball peen 4z	Vaughrn	1	11.45	11.45	Wrench, oil filter	Mac	5	7.35	36.75
Hammer, ball peen 32z	Mac	1	15.95	15.95	Micrometer	Ammco	1	55.95	55.95
Hammer, framing 20z	Vaughrn	1	13.95	13.95	Micrometer	C/M	1	55.95	55.95
Hammer, sledge 32z	Mac	1	15.95	15.95	Univ. carb. adj. tool	Mac	1	10.25	10.25
Hammer, body sm	Mac	1	22.25	22.25	Punch, roll pin 1/16"-1/2"	Duro	8	12.85	102.80
Hammer, body med	Mac	1	23.85	23.85	Wrench, torgue mic/adj	Mac	1	118.00	118.00
Pliers, standard 5"	C/M	1	6.80	6.80	Cleaner, file	Colton	1	7.00	7.00
Pliers, ndl nose 5.5"	C/M	1	15.20	15.20	Wrench, torque 1/2"	Allied	1	209.00	209.00
Pliers, ndl nose 7"	C/M	1	15.50	15.50	Drive, manifold 1/2"	Matco	1	55.00	55.00
Pliers, ndl nose 7.5"	C/M	1	15.75	15.75	Drive, ext. bar 3/8"x24"	Duro	1	28.00	28.00
Punch, starter 6/32"	Power Kraft	1	4.25	4.25	Ratchet, air 3/8"	Allied	2	81.25	162.50
Leverage bar 18"	Mac	1	75.95	75.95	Impact gun, 3/8"	Mac	1	153.75	153.75
Handle, speed 3/8"	Duro	1	30.95	30.95	Impact gun, 1/2"	Mac	1	117.95	117.95
Guage, manifold set	Robinair	1	162.95	162.95	Impact gun, 1/2"	Mac	1	117.95	117.95
Guage, compres tstr	Mac	1	418.40	418.40	Grinder, valve, air	Mac	1	110.00	110.00
Guage, pump pres	Mac	1	85.10	85.10	Hydra-lifter removal tool	Mac	1	38.55	38.55
Bit, drill set 1/16"-3/8"	Blk & Dkr	1	16.20	16.20	Compressor, ring	Mac	1	7.25	7.25
Bit, drill set 1/16"-1/2"	Union	1	64.80	64.80	Tester, cooling sys. pres.	Mac	1	25.80	25.80
Bit, hs drl set 1/16"-3/8"	Matco	1	57.60	57.60	Cleaner, pist. rng. grv.	Mac	1	23.50	23.50
		Total value		1471.46			Total value		2786.80

XYZ AUTO REPAIR: EQUIPMENT INVENTORY
NOVEMBER 1, 1989

ITEM	MANUF.	QTY	VALUE EACH	TOTAL VALUE	ITEM	MANUF.	QTY	VALUE EACH	TOTAL VALUE
Gun, rivet	Mac	1	38.00	38.00	Cabinet, metal 72"x36"	Mac	2	75.00	150.00
Hammer, piston dead blow	Mac	1	26.00	26.00	Cabinet, metal 78"x35"	Mac	1	75.00	75.00
Compressor, strut spring	Mac	1	112.00	112.00	Cabinet, metal 21"x26.5"	Mac	1	100.00	100.00
Compressor, pist.rng..slv	Mac	1	86.00	86.00	Cabinet, metal 24"x25"	Sioux	1	100.00	100.00
Iron, tire	Nissan	1	10.95	10.95	Work bench, metal 70"x31"	Allied	1	225.00	225.00
Hoist, engine	Dayton	1	345.00	345.00	Shelves, metal (4)	Mac	1	75.00	75.00
Lift, center load, 500lb.	Vermette	1	900.00	900.00	Shelves, metal (6)	Duro	1	100.00	100.00
Lift, hydro, 3000lb.	Presto	1	1687.00	1687.00	Cover, fender	C/M	5	24.95	124.75
Guage, vac./press.	Mac	1	43.00	43.00	Vice, bench	Allied	4	85.00	340.00
Gun, air blow	Mac	2	26.15	52.30	Cab., rolawy 10drw MB5200	Mac	1	795.00	795.00
Gun, air blow	C/M	2	23.95	47.90	Cab., hng-on 5drw MB5050	Mac	1	425.00	425.00
Metric thread repair kit	Helicoil	1	20.00	20.00	Cab., sideshelf MB300S	Mac	1	65.00	65.00
Compressor, air	Sanborn	1	650.00	650.00	Cab., hng-on 6drw MB302	Mac	1	215.00	215.00
Hose, air comp. 50ft.	Gates	4	33.95	135.80	Screwdriver, ph set 8pc	Mac	1	52.00	52.00
Hose, air comp. 25ft.	Gates	6	28.95	173.70	Extractor, screw set 5pc	Grt Neck	1	20.00	20.00
Cam bearing inst. tool	Mac	1	312.00	312.00	Extractor, screw set 5pc	Matco	1	21.50	21.50
Wrench, torgue 1/2"	Mac	1	223.00	223.00	Extractor, screw set metric	Mac	1	23.00	23.00
Wrench, cresent 12"-300mm	Sears	1	32.95	32.95	Nutdriver,set 5m-12mm, 8pc	Mac	1	22.00	22.00
Wrench, cresent 12"-300mm	Diamalloy	1	28.95	28.95	Nutdriver,set 3/16-1/2", 8pc	Mac	1	18.00	18.00
Wrench, cresent 10"	Diamond	1	22.95	22.95	Ratchet, reverse drive set	Allied	1	25.00	25.00
Wrench, cresent 10"-250mm	Crestoloy	1	20.95	20.95	Tap & Die set	Mac	1	295.55	295.55
Wrench, cresent 6"	Grt Neck	1	17.10	17.10	Cotter key set	Zomax	1	49.95	49.95
Wrench, cresent 6"	Diamond	1	15.95	15.95	Caliper, dial 6"	General	1	29.10	29.10
Wrench, cresent 8"	McK -Hatch	1	17.65	17.65	Wrench, hex key set, 050-3/8"	Royal	1	17.00	17.00
Wrench, pipe set	C/M	5	99.00	495.00	Wrench, hex key set 2mm-14mm	Royal	1	22.00	22.00
Wrench, cresent 4"	C/M	1	12.35	12.35	Flaring tool kit, FT158	Mac	1	31.45	31.45
Wrench, distributor 9/16"	Mac	1	18.00	18.00	Deflectors, rockerarm oil	Mac	1	8.00	8.00
Ratchet, air 1/4"	Mac	1	99.95	99.95	Puller, wheel kit (27pc)	Matco	1	39.95	39.95
Ratchet, air 3/8"	Mac	2	98.95	197.90	Setscrew, hollow key(8pc)	C/M	1	26.00	26.00
Ratchet, drive set 3/8"	C/M	6	81.25	487.50	File, 8Aset(HRB,MBF,RBF,SBF)	Mac	1	34.60	34.60
Ratchet, drive 3/8"	Mac	1	98.95	98.95	Plier, snap ring set	Mac	2	31.00	62.00
Ratchet, drive set 1/4"	C/M	2	75.95	151.90	Plier, 5"	Duro	1	8.30	8.30
Ratchet, drive set 1/2"	C/M	3	101.95	305.85	Screwdriver, 4" standard	Duro	1	6.50	6.50
Ratchet, drive 1/2"	Mac	1	98.95	98.95	Wrench, set (15/64"-1/2")	Duro	1	53.95	53.95
Tank, solvent	Allied	1	300.00	300.00	Socket, set 3/16"-8/16"std	Mac	1	24.70	24.70
Gun, staple	Arrow	1	10.75	10.75	Socket, set 7/16"-1-1/4"dp	Mac	1	41.10	41.10
Gun, soldering	Ungar	1	15.95	15.95	Socket, set 6mm-19mm dp	Matco	1	87.60	87.60
Bench, metal 72"x30"x32"	Matco	1	250.00	250.00	Socket, set 7/16"-1"std	CR-V	1	24.90	24.90
			Total Value	7562.20				Total Value	3833.90

XYZ AUTO REPAIR: EQUIPMENT INVENTORY
NOVEMBER 1, 1989

ITEM	MANUF.	QTY	VALUE EACH	TOTAL VALUE	ITEM	MANUF.	QTY	VALUE EACH	TOTAL VALUE
Socket, 17pc set w/Univ. Imp.	C/M	1	475.15	475.15	Ext., 3/8" 1"	Walden	1	10.75	10.75
Socket, 16pc set w/Univ. Imp.	Mac	1	447.20	447.20	Ext., 3/8" 3-1/2"	Walden	1	12.85	12.85
Socket, Torx drive set (6pc)	Matco	1	30.00	30.00	Ext., 3/8" 3"	Duro	1	11.40	11.40
Socket, Torx 3/8" male	Mac	1	4.90	4.90	Ext., 3/8" 10"	Duro	1	17.30	17.30
Socket, Torx 3/8"female	Mac	1	4.90	4.90	Ext., 1/4" 6"	C/M	1	14.30	14.30
Socket, Torx 3/8"std	Proto	1	4.90	4.90	Ext., 1/4" Univ. 1-1/2"	Easco	1	17.95	17.95
Socket, set Allen 3/8"	Mac	1	4.90	4.90	Ext., 1/4" 1"	Mac	1	10.75	10.75
Adapter, hex 1/4"-3/8"	Mac	1	2.20	2.20	Ext., 1/4" 6"	Allied	1	14.30	14.30
Socket, set Allen 3/8" metric	Mac	1	136.90	136.90	Ext., 1/4" 1"-6" (6pc)	C/M	6	12.85	77.10
Wrench, set O/E 8mm-19mm	Mac	1	89.95	89.95	Ext., 3/8" 1"	C/M	1	12.85	12.85
Extension, set 1/2"/5"-15"	Mac	1	92.95	92.95	Ext., 1/4" 3"	Easco	1	11.40	11.40
Extension, set 3/8"/3"-7.5"	Snap-on	1	95.95	95.95	Socket, 1/4" dp 3/8" (6pc)	Trucraft	1	6.85	6.85
Socket, set 1/4"/4mm-10mm	C/M	1	105.30	105.30	Socket, 1/4" metric 7mm	Blackhawk	1	4.95	4.95
Die grinder, bit set (12pc)	Mac	1	40.00	40.00	Socket, 1/4" metric 4mm	C/M	1	4.95	4.95
Wrench, set combo 8mm-19mm	Duro	1	75.00	75.00	Socket, 1/4"sh1/4-3/8"(3pc)	Duro	3	4.15	12.45
Wrench, set combo 8mm-24mm	Algo	1	120.00	120.00	Socket, 1/4"sh3/8-1/2"(6pc)	Duro	6	4.15	24.90
Crows feet, set 3/8"-13/16"	Mac	1	116.55	116.55	Socket, 1/4"sh1/4-11/32"(13)	Mac	13	4.15	53.95
Wrench, set combo 3/8"-3/4"	Mac	1	104.65	104.65	Socket, holder rack	Mac	3	7.10	21.30
Wrench, set combo 3/8"-3/4"	Duro	1	98.95	98.95	Rachet, air 1/4"	G/P	1	53.25	53.25
Wrench, set com 13/16-1-1/4"	Duro	1	103.95	103.95	Rachet, air 3/8" CP828	Mac	1	155.95	155.95
Wrench, offset ratchet (5pc)	Mac	1	69.95	69.95	Drill, st hdl h/s 1-1/4"	SDG	1	75.00	75.00
Wrench, offset bxend (4pc)	Mac	1	160.00	160.00	Brakeshoe, ret.spring remv	Mac	1	4.10	4.10
Wrench,o ffset bxend (4pc)	Mac	1	169.95	169.95	Grinder, wheel/wire	Dayton	1	75.95	75.95
Wrench, ignition O/E set	C/M	1	46.95	46.95	Wrench, organizer DWO-2	Mac	3	8.50	25.50
Wrench, hex keyset15/64-1/4"	Grt Neck	1	7.20	7.20	Wrench, torque	Sturtevant	1	161.00	161.00
Stamp, steel set letters	DJ	1	39.95	39.95	Mirror, inspection 14" MC-2	Mac	2	5.95	11.90
Stamp, steel set numbers	DJ	1	19.95	19.95	Screwdriver, mag. 5-1/4"	Mac	1	11.95	11.95
Stethoscope, dbl head	Baxter	1	126.50	126.50	Screwdriver, mag. 9-1/2"	Mac	1	12.95	12.95
Extension, 1/2"/3"	C/M	1	12.50	12.50	Knife, X-Acto	X-Acto	4	3.40	13.60
Ext., Univ.swivel imp 1/2"/2"	Mac	1	12.55	12.55	Chisel, set of 4	Mac	4	9.75	39.00
Ext., Univ.svl imp 1/2"/2.5"	Mac	1	23.75	23.75	Scrapper, 6" pointed	Snap-on	1	6.30	6.30
Ext., Univ.svl imp 1/4"/1.5"	Mac	1	17.95	17.95	Screwdriver, ph 4-3/4" #1	Snap-on	1	9.50	9.50
Ext., Univ. 1/2"/2.5"	Japan	1	15.55	15.55	Wrench, flat 4"-3/8"x5/8"	Mac	1	17.60	17.60
Ext., 1/2" 5"	S-K	1	12.75	12.75	Wrench, flt 3-1/2"-5/8"x3/4"	Mac	2	21.45	42.90
Ext., 3/8" 1-1/4"	Duro	1	10.75	10.75	Wrench, O/E 5"-9/16"x1/2"	M/H	1	10.30	10.30
Ext., 3/8" 1-1/4"	Duro	1	10.75	10.75	Wrench, O/E 4.5"-7/16"x3/8"	Mac	1	9.25	9.25
Ext., Univ. 3/8" /2"	C/M	1	8.75	8.75	Wrench, O/E 5-1/4"-7/16x3/8	Mac	1	9.25	9.25
Ext., 3/8" 3"	Mac	1	11.40	11.40	Wrench, O/E 6"-9/16x1/2"	Mac	1	10.55	10.55
			Total Value	2931.45				Total Value	1096.10

XYZ AUTO REPAIR: EQUIPMENT INVENTORY
NOVEMBER 1, 1989

ITEM	MANUF.	QTY	VALUE EACH	TOTAL VALUE	ITEM	MANUF.	QTY	VALUE EACH	TOTAL VALUE
Wrench, O/E 6.5-11/16x1/2"	Mac	1	16.90	16.90	Stone, grinding 13/4"	Disston	1	19.90	19.90
Wrench, O/E 5.5-7/16x3/8"	Proto	1	9.25	9.25	Grinder, surface 5"	Dayton	1	3.00	3.00
Wrench, O/E 4.5-1/4x5/16	C/M	1	8.20	8.20	Grinder, surface 4"	Dayton	1	3.00	3.00
Wrench, O/E 5.25-3/8x7/16"	C/M	1	9.25	9.25	Grinder, surface 2"	Dayton	3	3.00	9.00
Wrench, O/E 8-5/8x3/4"	C/M	1	19.85	19.85	Grinder, surface 13/4"	Dayton	1	3.00	3.00
Wrench, O/E 5"-9mmx7mm	C/M	1	13.45	13.45	Wheel, abrasive 3"	Cratex	1	24.00	24.00
Wrench, O/E 4.5"-6mmx8mm	C/M	1	13.45	13.45	Chisel, flat 5" air	Mac	2	9.50	19.00
Wrench, O/E 6.25"-12mmx14mm	C/M	1	14.95	14.95	Cutter, sgl blade 5" air	Mac	1	10.40	10.40
Wrench, O/E 8"-16mmx18mm	C/M	1	17.95	17.95	Punch, tapered 5" air	Mac	1	9.95	9.95
Wrench, O/E 5"-12mmx13mm	Dreed	1	14.95	14.95	Punch, tapered 33/4"air	Mac	1	7.95	7.95
Wrench, O/E 10mm rt angl	Trucraft	1	16.20	16.20	Drill, 1/2"	B & D	1	104.00	104.00
Wrench, combo 5.5" 11mm	S&K	1	16.70	16.70	Kit, #KB152	Mac	1	8.10	8.10
Wrench, combo 6" 10mm	Trucraft	1	16.10	16.10	Stand, engine	Dayton	6	70.00	420.00
Wrench, combo 6" 13mm	Proto	1	18.55	18.55					.00
Wrench, combo 5-3/4" 1/2"	Mac	1	15.60	15.60					.00
Wrench, combo 4.5" 11/32"	Bill/Vital	1	14.60	14.60					.00
Wrench, combo 6-1/4" 13mm	C/M	1	18.55	18.55					.00
Wrench, flywheel 8-3/4"	Mac	1	13.65	13.65					.00
Wrench, tubing 5.5-3/8x7/16"	Duro	1	15.70	15.70					.00
Wrench, tubing 5.5-3/8x7/16"	Duro	1	15.70	15.70					.00
Wrench, tubing 6.5-1/2x9/16"	Duro	1	16.40	16.40					.00
Wrench, tubing 8-3/4x5/8"	Duro	1	26.25	26.25					.00
Wrench, tubing 6.5-10mx12mm	Easco	1	16.60	16.60					.00
Wheel, camshaft degreeing	Crower	1	20.00	20.00					.00
Cleaner, battery term	Duro	1	6.80	6.80					.00
Extractor, finger 24.5"	Mac	1	3.00	3.00					.00
Extractor, magnetic 18"	Mac	1	4.00	4.00					.00
Extractor, magnetic 25"	Mac	1	4.25	4.25					.00
Extractor, magnetic 24.5"	Mac	1	4.00	4.00					.00
Measure, tape 6ft	Quality	1	8.00	8.00					.00
Measure, tape 25ft	Pro-Pak	2	13.00	26.00					.00
Measure, tape 50ft	Pro-Pak	2	18.00	36.00					.00
Chisel, air tool	Mac	1	7.95	7.95					.00
Wheel, wire 3.5"	Dayton	1	2.00	2.00					.00
Wheel, wire 1.25	Dayton	2	2.00	4.00					.00
Wheel, wire 2"	Dayton	1	2.25	2.25					.00
Stone, grinding 2"	Disston	3	24.00	72.00					.00
Stone, grinding 13/8"	Disston	1	16.95	16.95					.00
			Total Value	576.00				Total Value	641.30

* * *

In the following presentation of marketing plans and business plan revisions the development and evolutionary process of business plan presentation to the investment community is demonstrated.

The first marketing plan was developed to give the founding team members the same fundamental information and guidelines for an extended market strategy meeting which would result in the first marketing iteration plan (all information available to date but not necessarily the final plan). This plan was made available to interested qualified investors and venture capitalists.

This first iteration marketing plan was used to support the assumptions of the business plan and, of course, had detailed marketing research documents supporting it as well as the consensus of the founding team.

The format of the first plan presentations has been modified for the convenience of printing this book. The format most commonly used in all presentations is demonstrated in the final business plan starting on page 258. Note the placement of each primary heading (section title) on a separate page. This creates a much more formal type presentation and makes the material easier for the reader to refer to and absorb.

MARKETING PLAN FUNCTIONAL CARDIAC DISPLAYS, INC.

CORPORATE MISSION

Functional Cardiac Displays, Inc. (FCD) is dedicated to exploring, developing, and exploiting noninvasive medical imaging technologies. The entry product targeting cardiovascular imaging using standard Electrocardiograph (ECG) sensing technology and state-of-the-art three-dimensional computer display.

TARGET MARKET(S)

In order to maintain a conservative marketing analysis for the proposed product, CASE 2000, we have selected the current ECG market as a reference point. However, it should be understood that CASE 2000 provides information beyond the current ECG capabilities.

The primary competition existing for this product is the ECG based products, which, by introduction of this product, may be rendered obsolete in the future. This product may also negatively impact the radio isotope imaging market as well as the magnetic resonance imaging (MRI) and ultrasonic imaging markets. These markets will be affected to the extent that they address the practice of cardiovascular imaging.

When the product is introduced and in production, it is expected that the company will experience a high growth period. This will be controlled by the sale of licensed production rights to meet geographic areas of demand throughout the United States and international markets.

Sales and distribution will be in the continental United States during the Beta testing period and most of the first year after product release. This allows us to closely track the product performance under field conditions. In addition, the anticipated domestic market is such that FCD, Inc. may be hard pressed to keep up with that demand.

The sales force will be trained to act as the staff to train the Beta sites and ongoing site staffs in the proper use of the product. The salespeople will be paid a base salary initially. Following product acceptance, compensation will change to the more traditional base salary plus commission/bonus.

Three to five Beta sites will be selected. These sites will be cardiovascular training hospitals and clinics. One site has been approved for the clinical study at LBJ Memorial Hospital and one site is under consideration in Utah. (These sites will be requested to purchase the Beta units, which is a unique action for new products in the medical industry.)

TARGET MARKET(s)

The targeted market is the cardiology specialty of the medical industry. This market is represented by:

- Cardiologist practitioners
- Cardiology clinics
- Hospitals
  - Emergency rooms
  - Intensive care units
- Paramedics
  - Ambulance services
  - Fire department rescue units

The first market area to be approached will be hospitals and clinics which are recognized as primary cardiovascular training facilities within the United States.

Market Phase I

- Hospitals
  - Type
  - Number
- Clinics
  - Type
  - Number

Market Phase II

- Physicians
  - Type
  - Number
  - Type
  - Number
  - Type
  - Number

MARKET AREAS (geographic)

FCD, Inc. will concentrate initially on satisfying the domestic market. This will take an estimated 3 to 5 years. As this satisfaction occurs the international markets for methods of penetration as well as profitability will be investigated.

SERVICES AND PRODUCTS

Initially, FCD, Inc. will be a "systems integrator." The company will produce software that will be loaded into a hardware configuration purchased from a vendor (i.e., SiliconGraphics and/or Sun Microsystems). The company will also contract with a manufacturer (Stateside) to produce the devices necessary for sensing a patient's heart signals.

These above stated elements will be brought together under the complete direction and control of FCD, Inc., and will remain in that control until it is found advisable to move that integration process outside FCD, Inc.

Product Profile and Sketches

(Refer to office material—President)

System Integration

Long-term supply of imaging product(s)
(President to supply this information.)

Advertising

Display and demo of the product at selected medical conventions and trade shows

Print advertising in cardiovascular and hospital journals as well as health and fitness magazines

Direct mail to the cardiovascular community

Promotion of discounted software updates

Financing assistance

On-line product technical support (telephone technical advice/troubleshooting)

TV and radio news (science announcements)

Press releases

FCD, Inc. MARKET ADVANTAGES

The major market advantage that FCD, Inc. has is that the company was founded by a highly respected group of medical practitioners from the cardiovascular specialty. These people lend a great deal of credibility and long-term prestige to this company and its entry product(s).

Another advantage is the fact that this imaging product is a noninvasive cardiovascular device. This greatly reduces medical risk. Thus it becomes much more attractive to the customer than those imaging products that are invasive.

A further advantage is that it is state-of-the-art equipment for alerting patients of potential heart disease dangers as well as for diagnosing the damage caused by a heart attack (i.e., latent ischemia).

FCD MARKET DISADVANTAGES

The company has no perceived market disadvantage. The product is new and, as such, it is difficult to accurately predict public and medical acceptance. All reactions thus far have been positive.

MARKETING RESEARCH PLANNING

Market research once began will be an ongoing activity to discover new areas if application for the current product and new uses of the unique imaging technology (associate cost(s) with Phase II).

Industry Analysis

The market being used for clinical study is the current ECG market which is represented by the medical application market.

FCD, Inc. expects to conservatively gain 15 percent of the ECG based market and to ship at least 80 units during the first year after product introduction and continue a minimum of 32 percent sales revenue growth rate through the first 5 years.

General Overview

The medical application market is approximately 10 years old

In 1986, the medical application:

Generated approximately 3.4 percent of the total 1986 factory revenue for all technical system applications

Produced an estimated 8.9 percent of the total unit shipments

Revenue in this market grew at a 16.7 percent compound rate, from $269 million in 1982 to $499 million in 1986

Sales Trends

The medical application market will grow 11.0 percent in revenue and 29.3 percent in units, compounded over 5 years

Average system prices are decreasing as the industry moves toward the use of micro and personal computers.

Future Industry Trends

The forces motivating the user to purchase computer tools for medical applications are:

Increasing malpractice insurance costs are causing doctors to perform as many nonsurgical diagnostic techniques as possible

Sophisticated medical diagnostic equipment is becoming increasingly more complex, requiring computerization

There is a need to integrate many instruments to improve productivity and increase utilization of expensive instruments

There are shortages of medical technicians and doctors with critical skills

Labor costs are increasing

Drastic attention has been projected for the 1990s to focus toward fitness and cardiovascular related progress

OUTSIDE INFLUENCES FACING THE INDUSTRY

Medical products are subject to the following restrictions and influences:

Liability insurance

Government regulators such as FDA (Federal Drug Administration) and FTC (Federal Trade Commission)

Medical associations sales and criterion

International trade policy (for exports)

Political status of medical environment

Insurance industry regulations

Healthcare cost containment

Third party pay regulators (e.g., Medicaid and Medicare)

These outside influences have generated the following recent activities:

Liability insurance for physicians has almost doubled making them more responsive to new, no-risk, noninvasive technologies which provide early warning of an impending disaster

Medical products have relatively short lives

Hospitals, physicians, and suppliers are competing among themselves for available funds since insurance companies and the government have capped spending for health programs

Monitoring of cardiac function in all surgical patients is becoming an industry standard

The trend is toward using micro, board, and personal computers in medical applications

PRICING

Projection price
Comparative analysis

Product Usage

Patient hookup

Procedure cost

Comparative procedure cost

The average price per unit in the medical applications market is $7500 ($499 million/66.5 thousand units). However, this represents the pricing of a fully matured product base.

Advertising and Promotion Costs

Total investment in product (15 to 20 percent) is normally spent on media by industrial firms. ("Sharing the Value Added: A Bonus Plan for a Growth Company," A.

Graham Sterling, Operating Model of a Hypothetical Growth Company, *Strategic Planning and Management Handbook,* New York: Van Nostrand Reinhold Company, p. 522)

Mini and micro computer industry spent an average of 15.7 percent of margin on advertising during 1985. Hospital services industry spent 12 percent of margin on advertising during 1985. (*Advertising Age,* September 15, 1986 p. 60)

Advertising will be done by:

Display and demo of the product at selected medical conventions and trade shows

Print advertising in cardiovascular and hospital journals as well as health and fitness magazines

Direct mail to the cardiovascular community

Promotion of discounted software updates

Financing assistance

On-line product technical support (telephone technical advice/troubleshooting)

TV and radio news (science announcements)

Press releases

DISTRIBUTION

Type
Channels
Cost(s)

PRODUCT IMPROVEMENTS

Enhancements
Software version(s)

TIMETABLE AND SCHEDULE

(Refer to office chart—President)

CASE 2000 MARKETING POTENTIAL CONCLUSION

Heart disease is the primary killer in the United States—this makes this product a necessity in the medical community.

The uniqueness and need for this product indicated that there is a lot of potential for it now. FCD, Inc. has the technical expertise to make this product and the medical industry specific contact and marketing experience to successfully sell it.

The imaging technology being used is new and noninvasive and shows potential for expanded use in brain scan applications as well as other industries in need of scanning methodologies.

The medical application market is estimated to grow at a compound annual growth rate of 11.0 percent for the years 1987 to 1991. The gross national product is forecasted to grow at a rate of 305 percent during the same time period. The cardiology segment is especially strong, and the penetration in the medical application field is relatively low. No new entries are foreseen in the medical application marketplace.

TARGET MARKET(s)

The targeted market is the cardiology specialty of the medical industry. This market is represented by:

- Cardiologist practitioners
- Cardiology clinics
- Hospitals
  - Emergency rooms
  - Intensive care units
- Paramedics
  - Ambulance services
  - Fire department rescue units

The first market area to be approached will be hospitals and clinics which are recognized as primary cardiovascular training facilities within the United States.

MARKETING PLANNING

Obstacles to marketing planning:

- Lack of information
- Forecasting problems
- Coordination problems within the organization
- Lack of top management commitment
- Time pressures

DEVELOPING CORPORATE STRATEGY

Conceptual foundations for strategic planning:

- Business definition
- Setting the company's mission
- Strategic fit
- Market attractiveness
- Economies of scale
- Matrix planning approaches

BCG business portfolio analysis
General Electric portfolio analysis
The PIMS database

MARKETING PLANNING PROCESS

The evolution of marketing planning
- Stage 1: No planning
- Stage 2: Budget planning
- Stage 3: Annual planning
- Stage 4: Long-term planning
- Stage 5: Strategic planning

The marketing planning concept
- Understand the corporate mission and objective(s)
- Analyze the present situation and environment
- Determine the marketing goals and objectives
- Develop the marketing strategies to achieve the desired results
- Design an action plan to implement the strategies with appropriate tactics
- Determine procedures for evaluating and controlling the implementation of the plan

ENVIRONMENTAL ANALYSIS

Assessing economic trends
- Sources of information about economic variables
- Forecasting economic variables

Legal and political analysis
- Risk analysis

Physical, social, and cultural analysis

Technological analysis
- Forecasting technological change
- Delphi technique
- Scenario planning
- Trend extrapolation

Competitive analysis
- Understanding the competition
- Identifying and assessing competitors' relative positions

MARKET ANALYSIS

Market size
- Market potential
- Market forecast
- Sales potential
- Sales forecast
- Market share

Sources of information for market size analysis
- Market measuring techniques

Analysis of market size
- Growth
- Trends
- Analysis of components

Buying process
- Distribution channels
- Customer purchase process

DEVELOPING MARKETING STRATEGIES

Target market selection and market segmentation
- Demographics
- Psychographics
- Product benefits
- Usage rate

Distribution strategy

Pricing strategy for existing and new products

Promotion strategy
- Advertising
- Personal selling
- Publicity
- Sales promotions

WRITING THE MARKETING PLAN DOCUMENT

Introduction and summary

Situation analysis

Key issues

Marketing and business objectives

Marketing strategies/programs

Marketing research and information systems

Exhibits

IMPLEMENTING THE MARKETING PLAN

Organizing for the planning process
- Functional
- Geographic
- Product management organization
- Product/market management system

Turning strategies into action
- Marketing programs
- Sequencing activities
- Determining responsibility

Sell the plan
Monitor for results
Recognize and diagnose problems
Implement plans
Evaluate results of implementation
Modify strategies and implementation as required to meet objectives

MARKETING PLAN FORMAT

Major Strategies

Two or three paragraphs stating the major strategies for the product. Should specify such actions as improving, maintaining, or relinquishing market share; vertical integration; depth of product line; market regulation.

Marketing Objectives

Five or six sentences stating the measurable marketing objectives that enforce the major strategies. These objectives should be concerned with what can be accomplished through sales, communications, and marketing research.

P&L Effect of the Recommendation

	Actual	Estimated	Proposed
Volume			
Value			
Cases			
Percent Increase			
Share			
Cost of goods			
Sales and distribution			
Adverting/promotion			
Other costs			
Pretax profits			

Communications Plan

1. Objectives
   Two or three sentences on what you want to accomplish to help meet your overall marketing objectives. Include specific goals, such as to increase brand recall from 25 to 32 percent in 1 year.
2. Strategies (How are you going to accomplish your objectives?)
   a. Creative Strategy
      Two or three sentences regarding your target audience, main message, positioning, and the type of execution.

b. Media Strategy
   Two or three sentences detailing how you are going to spend your advertising dollars: on what media, at what rate, in what part of the country? Include reach and frequency figures.
c. Sales Promotion Strategy
   Two or three sentences stating the type of promotional activities, the audience it is aimed at, and what it should accomplish.
d. Public Relations Strategy
   Two or three sentences on what you want to accomplish through public relations.

3. Specific Plans (How each strategy will be implemented.)
   a. Creative plan (layouts and copy, storyboards, radio/TV scripts, etc.)
   b. Media plan
   c. Sales promotion plan
   d. Public relations plan

Marketing Research Plan

1. Strategy
   Specify how research will provide information to assist in preparing and executing the marketing plan. Include communications research.
2. Plans
   Describe the specific plans necessary to execute the above strategies.

Sales Management Plan

This is the responsibility of the sales manager. Where the sales are coming from—by market, territory, size, price, and so forth. Includes planning, communications, and training of sales force.

MARKETING PLAN PROVING AND MONITORING

THE MARKETING FACT BOOK (outline)

I. The Market
   A. Total size in units and dollar value—last 5 years
   B. Product versus the competition—last 5 years
      1. Sales in units and dollar value—total and by package size, national and by market
      2. Sales in units and dollar value by market outlet—total and by package size, national and by market
      3. Share of market—total and by package size, national and by market
   C. Consumption
      1. By age, sex, income, education, psychographics, SIC number
      2. By season
      3. By geographic area

II. Advertising
   A. Media spending, product versus the competition—last 5 years
   B. Creative strategies, product versus the competition—last 5 years
      1. Samples of all advertising for product and the competition
      2. Analysis of competitive advertising

III. Sales Promotion
   (Same analysis as above section, but on sales promotion activity)

IV. Public Relations
   (Analysis on public relations activity.)

V. Financial Data
   A. Product price and profit structure
   B. P&L—last 5 years

Results of meeting with President 2/16/89

Need Market Plan to cover:

Pricing
   Projection price
   Comparative analysis
   Procedure cost(s)
   Comparative procedure cost(s)

Distribution
   Type
   Channels
   Cost(s)

Market
   Phase I: Hospitals
      Number
      Type
   Clinics
      Number
      Type

   Phase II: Physicians
      Number (see President)
      Type

System Integration
   Long-term supply of imaging product (see President for this)

Product Usage
   Patient hookup

Marketing Research Plan
   (cost associated as Phase II)

Product Improvements
- Enhancements
- Software version

Timetable and Schedule
- (refer to office)

Product Profile and Sketches
- (refer to office)

* * *

After the founders meeting in which the questions of the previous marketing plan were discussed and resolved as well as could be with the information available at that time, the following marketing plan was written for limited distribution to specific investor groups, who were primarily venture capitalists.

FUNCTIONAL CARDIAC DISPLAYS, INC.
MARKETING PLAN

(Rev. 1)

Prepared by:

The Marketing Dept.
Functional Cardiac Displays, Inc.
B. Thorough, PhD.
B. Good,PhD.

CONTENTS

CORPORATE MISSION

Functional Cardiac Displays, Inc. (FCD) is in the medical imaging business and is dedicated to exploring, developing, and exploiting noninvasive medical imaging technologies. The entry product will be targeting cardiovascular imaging using multilead ECG sensing technology and state-of-the-art three-dimensional computer display.

CORPORATE OBJECTIVES

Profit. To make a sufficient profit to supply the finances required to meet the other corporate objectives.

Customers. To supply our customers with products and services of the greatest possible value in our chosen business.

Growth. To grow at a rate which keeps FCD, Inc. the premier company in its market choice, and to provide its employees with opportunity for personal growth.

People. To assure that our people can benefit from the company's success; that their achievements are recognized; and that they are managed so that they can have personal satisfaction from their accomplishments. To hire and continue to hire the best people possible.

Management. To manage our company so that an equitable balance is struck between the needs for short-term financial performance and long-term product and customer growth. To allow individual freedom in attaining well-defined objectives.

CASE 2000 MARKETING POTENTIAL

The imaging technology being used is new and noninvasive and shows potential for expanded use in brain scan applications as well as other industries in need of scanning methodologies.

Heart disease is the primary killer in the United States—makes this product a necessity in the medical community.

In America, someone dies of cardiovascular disease every 32 seconds.

In 1986, heart and blood vessel diseases killed nearly one million Americans, almost as many as cancer, accidents, pneumonia, influenza, and all other causes or death combined.

Almost one in two Americans die of cardiovascular disease.

Ref: The American Heart Association, 1989 Heart Facts

The medical application market is estimated to grow at a compound annual growth rate of 11.0 percent for the years 1987 to 1991. The gross national product (GNP) is forecasted to grow at a rate of 305 percent during the same time period. The cardiology segment is especially strong, and the penetration in the medical application field is relatively low. No new entries are foreseen in the medical application marketplace.

MARKETING OBJECTIVES

It is the marketing groups objective to gain approximately 1 to 3 percent of the ECG market ($4 million to $20 million) within the first year of product introduction and increase that share at a rate greater than 32 percent per year until 30 to 40 percent of that market has been captured. At that time, the primary concentration will be on increasing product profit margin and cash flow rather than on market share.

MARKETING STRATEGIES

In order to maintain a conservative marketing analysis for CASE 2000, we have selected the current ECG market as a reference point. However, it should be understood that CASE 2000 provides information beyond the current ECG capabilities.

The primary competition existing for this product are the ECG based products, which, by introduction of this product, may be rendered obsolete in the future. This product may also negatively impact the radio isotope imaging market as well as the magnetic resonance imaging (MRI) and ultrasonic imaging markets. These markets will be affected to the extent that they address the practice of cardiovascular imaging.

When the product is introduced and in production, it is expected that the company will experience a high growth period. This will be controlled by the sale of licensed production rights to meet geographic areas of demand throughout the United States and international markets.

Sales and distribution will be in the continental United States during the Beta testing period and most of the first year after product release. This allows us to closely track the product performance under field conditions. In addition, the anticipated domestic market is such that FCD, Inc. may be hard pressed to keep up with that demand.

The marketing/sales force will be trained to act as the staff to train the Beta sites and ongoing site staffs in the proper use of the product.

Three to five Beta sites will be selected. These sites will be cardiovascular training hospitals and clinics. Two sites have been approved for the clinical study, LBJ Memorial Hospital and Althia Hospital, in Your City, and one site is under consideration in Utah.

Target Market(s)

The target market is the cardiology specialty of the medical industry. This market is represented by:

- Cardiologist practitioners
- Cardiology clinics
- General practitioners
- Hospitals
  - Emergency rooms
  - Intensive care units
- Internal medicine practices
- Paramedics
  - Ambulance services
  - Fire Department rescue units

The first market area to be approached will be hospitals and clinics which are recognized as primary cardiovascular training facilities within the United States.

Market Phase I

Hospitals *			6281
Federal hospitals		322	
Nonfederal hospitals		5959	
Hospitals, special	5517		
Cardiac care facilities (B)	178		
Cardiac care facilities (C)	74		
Hospitals, special/SD	190		

Clinics **
General
Cardiology

*Source: Weissber, Robert AMA/NET, Jan. 17, 1989.
Flaph, Bruce, Stanford Medical Library, Feb. 1989.
**(to be researched - *American Hospital Association Abridged Guide*)

Market Phase II

Physicians in U.S. market *		81788
Cardiovascular disease specialists	9439	
Critical care medicine specialists	131	
Family practitioners	31888	
Geriatrics specialists	448	
Internal medicine specialists	39882	

* *Source*: Clark-O'Neill, Fisher-Stevens, Fairview, New Jersey

MARKET AREAS (GEOGRAPHIC)

FCD, Inc. will concentrate initially on satisfying the domestic market. This will take an estimated 3 to 5 years. As this satisfaction occurs the international markets for methods of penetration as well as profitability will be investigated.

Domestic market penetration strategy is to concentrate marketing efforts in a region-by-region manner addressing the western most states first, then the eastern states, and finally the midwestern and southern areas.

MARKET PENETRATION STRATEGY

Advertising will be done by:

Presentation of the product at selected medical conventions and trade shows:

American Heart Association (AHA)	Nov.
American College of Cardiology (ACC)	Mar.
American Society of Hypertension (ASH)	May-June

American College Physicians (ACP) Apr.
American Academy of Family Practitioners (AAFP) Oct.
Critical Care Medical Show (CCM) May-June

Print advertising in cardiovascular and hospital journals:

Journal of American College of Cardiology
American Heart Journal
Circulation
Hypertension
Clinical Cardiology
Health and fitness magazines

Direct mail to the cardiovascular community

Promotion of discounted software updates

On-line product technical support (telephone technical advice/operational troubleshooting)

Public relations (TV and radio news public service announcements, medical science breakthrough announcements, press releases)

Further research into this penetration strategy is being done to identify the specific hospitals, clinics, and trade shows to contact and attend.

SERVICES AND PRODUCTS

Initially, FCD, Inc. will be a "systems integrator." (Refer to Product Profile and sketches.) The company will produce software that will be loaded into a hardware configuration purchased from a vendor (i.e., SiliconGraphics and/or Sun Microsystems). The company will also contract with a manufacturer (Stateside) to produce the devices necessary for sensing a patient's heart signals.

These above stated elements will be brought together under the complete direction and control of FCD, Inc., and will remain in that control until it is found advisable to move that integration process outside FCD, Inc. This strategy is practicable due to the software being developed on the Open Architecture system (UNIX) which causes the hardware used to be virtually transparent.

The initial product will have the following features:

Product will identify:

- Specific areas and volumes of infarction, acute injury, and ischemia. Areas include transmural and subendocardial determinations.
- Localization of areas and volumes of infarction, acute injury, and ischemia despite intraventricular conduction delays or bundle branch blocks.
- Locations of accessory bypass pathways in WPW syndromes.
- Localization of sites of ventricular ectopic complexes or sites of ventricular re-entry for use in mapping of ventricular tachycardia for ablation purposes.

Product will have:

- 3 to 5 minute sensor/screen refresh rate
- 32 sensor input band

- 32 sensor signal display and printout
- 3-dimensional image generation at normal size
  - Image display orientation (to be determined)
  - Interior and exterior views
  - 1 mm slicing
  - Zoom to approx. 5X
  - Full-image rotation
  - Panning
- Color print of screen image
- Patient data recorded on removable hard disc
  (60 heartbeat sample requiring less than 1 MBytes)
  (Disk cartridge capable of 380 MBytes storage)
- Free user training will be provided for each Beta unit.
- Installation and training will be provided at a cost of $5,000 per each production unit and option.

PRODUCT IMPROVEMENTS

Ongoing Product Development (1.5 to 2 years) Enhancements
- Ischemia mapping
- Surgical anesthesia monitoring
- Intensive care unit monitoring

Software Version(s)
- Treadmill application
- Angioplasty application
- Digital display of ischemic and infarction volume
- Stop time review

PRODUCT PROFILE AND SKETCHES

(To be supplied by engineering)

SYSTEM INTEGRATION

A comprehensive system integration diagram is currently on display at FCD, Inc. offices. Nonproprietary diagrams are included here.

FCD, INC. MARKET ADVANTAGES

The major market advantage that FCD, Inc. has is that the company was founded by a highly respected group of medical practitioners from the cardiovascular specialty. These people lend a great deal of credibility and long-term prestige to this company and its entry product(s).

Another advantage is the fact that this imaging product is a noninvasive cardiovascular device. This greatly reduces medical risk. Thus it becomes much more attractive to the customer than those imaging products that are invasive.

A further advantage is that it is state-of-the-art equipment for alerting patients of potential heart disease dangers as well as for diagnosing the damage caused by a heart attack (i.e., latent ischemia).

FCD, INC. MARKET DISADVANTAGES

The company has two primary market disadvantages: (1) a market that is currently satisfied with the status quo, and (2) the company size dictates limited resources. These disadvantages will be addressed in the following manner.

The market will be educated to the superiority of this product in relation to the ECG products now in use. This will be done by demonstration at major medical conventions and trade shows as well as strategically placing clinical test units in major cardiovascular training hospitals. Also, technical papers regarding the clinical use of the product will be written by the practicing board members and published in the appropriate medical journals and presented at the appropriate conventions.

The company size and limited distribution resources will be overcome by establishing a strategic alliance(s) with established major medical system suppliers such as Marquette, Hewlett-Packard, and so on.

PRICING

It is expected that the pricing of the product will follow the general software industry pricing trend. Initial price is currently set at $40,000 which is based on current hardware costs of $15,000 to $24,000 providing a gross margin of 40 to 63 percent which is comparable to the general software industry. Free user training will be provided for each Beta unit. Installation and training will be provided at a cost of $5000 per each production unit and option.

ADVERTISING AND PROMOTION COSTS

On an average 15 to 20 percent of gross sales product revenue is spent on media by industrial firms. FCD, Inc. is targeting less than that since it is expected that a strategic alliance(s) will be established, and we will not be required to bear the total of this burden.

TIMETABLE AND SCHEDULES

(Available at FCD, Inc. offices)

FINANCIAL PROJECTIONS

The ECG unit sales growth for the next 10 years is projected to grow at the rate of 10 percent per year. FCD, Inc. is targeting a growing yearly penetration of that market starting with 1% in year 1990 and continuing at 5, 10, and 15 percent during fiscal years

1991, 1992, and 1993, respectively. That being the case, FCD, Inc. expects its gross revenues for each of those years to be $3.67 million, $20.15 million, $43.45 million, and $71.10 million, respectively.

Anticipated gross net profit is targeted to be in the range of 30 percent of gross sales or greater; $.29 million, $7.25 million, $17.38 million, and $28.44 million for years 1990, 1991, 1992, and 1993, respectively.

Marketing expense is targeted at an average of 11 percent of projected gross sales and includes income statement items: marketing and delivery, salaries, fringes and taxes, and travel. The projected budget for this expense over years 1990 through 1993 is $1.1 million, $2.42 million, $4.35 million, and $7.11 million, respectively. This is to cover the expense of convention and show attendance and display, journal and magazine advertising, direct mail advertising, and public relations activities of TV, radio, and press release announcements of our technological breakthroughs.

FINANCIAL PROJECTIONS DETAILS

MARKET PENETRATION PROJECTIONS
FCD, INC.

	1990	1991	1992	1993	AVERAGE OPERATING RATIOS (%)
Potential Market	367.35	402.90	434.50	474.00	
Market Penetration	1%	5%	10%	15%	
Gross Sales	3.67	20.15	43.45	71.10	1.00
Cost of Sales	1.65	9.07	19.55	32.00	.45
Gross Profit	2.09	11.48	24.77	40.53	.57
Marketing Expense	1.10	2.42	4.35	7.11	.11
Operations Expense	.70	1.81	3.04	4.98	.08
Gross Net Profit	.29	7.25	17.38	28.44	.39
Estimated Taxes	.12	2.90	6.95	11.38	
Net Profit	.18	4.35	10.43	17.06	.23

MARKETING BUDGET PROJECTIONS
FCD, INC.
(millions)

	1990	1991	1992	1993
Potential Market	1.10	2.42	4.35	7.11
Marketing Expense				
Market Penetration				
Shows:				
ACC (Mar.)				
ACP (Apr.)				
ASH (May/June)		(detail budget to be determined upon market research completion)		
AAFP (Oct.)				
AHA (Nov.)				
CCM (May/June)				
Marketing Expense				
Journals:				
Amer. Col. Card.				
Amer. Heart				
Circulation				
Hypertension				
Clin. Card.				
Health/Fitness				
Direct Mail				
Public Relations:				
TV				
Radio				
Press release				

MARKETING RESEARCH

Market research once begun will be an ongoing activity to discover new areas of application for the current product and new uses of the unique imaging technology. This ongoing research is part of the costs associated with Phase II financing and will consist of at least the following activities.

Profile Testing. Evaluation of market product usage to establish improvements.

Distribution. Evaluate alternative channels:
- Strategic alliances
- Medical wholesalers
  - McKesson (Los Angeles)
  - Bergin Brunswig (San Francisco)
  - Foxmeyer (Dallas)

Pricing Study. Determine acceptable price for market being addressed.
- Areas to consider:
  - Procedure cost
    - Full ECG analysis currently costs patient $700 to $900
  - Comparative procedure cost (being researched - (B. Thorough))
    - Stress test
    - Echo
    - Thalium
    - Rhodiogram

Usage Study. Extension of profile testing but related to the question of who is going to use the product rather than how it is used.

Phase III Research. Phase III research will address the question of who are the major competitors and competing products. A competitive fact book analysis will be made and will cover ECG and imaging products as a minimum.

INDUSTRY ANALYSIS

The market being used for clinical study is the current ECG market which is represented by the medical application market. FCD, Inc. expects to conservatively gain 15 percent of the ECG based market and to ship at least 80 units during the first year after product introduction and continue a minimum of 32 percent sales revenue growth rate through the first 5 years.

Sales Trends

The medical application market will grow 11.0 percent in revenue and 29.3 percent in units, compounded over 5 years.

Average system prices are decreasing as the industry moves toward the use of micro and personal computers.

Future Industry Trends

The forces motivating the user to purchase computer tools for medical applications are:

Increasing malpractice insurance costs are causing doctors to perform as many non-surgical diagnostic techniques as possible

Sophisticated medical diagnostic equipment is becoming increasingly more complex, requiring computerization

There is a need to integrate many instruments to improve productivity and increase utilization of expensive instruments

There are shortages of medical technicians and doctors with critical skills

Labor costs are increasing

Drastic attention has been projected for the 1990s to focus toward fitness and cardiovascular related progress

OUTSIDE INFLUENCES FACING THE INDUSTRY

Medical products are subject to the following restrictions and influences:

Liability insurance

Government regulators such as FDA (Federal Drug Administration) and FTC (Federal Trade Commission)

Medical associations sales and criterion

International trade policy (for exports)

Political status of medical environment

Insurance industry regulations

Healthcare cost containment

Third party pay regulators (e.g., Medicaid and Medicare)

These outside influences have generated the following recent activities:

Liability insurance for physicians has almost doubled making them more responsive to new, no-risk, noninvasive technologies which provide early warning of an impending disaster

Medical products have relatively short lives

Hospitals, physicians, and suppliers are competing among themselves for available funds since insurance companies and the government have capped spending for health programs

Monitoring of cardiac function in all surgical patients is becoming an industry standard

The trend is toward using micro, board, and personal computers in medical applications

SALES MANAGEMENT

General end user sales methodology will be finally determined during the Phase II marketing research. Options to be studied are: strategic alliances, medical equipment distributors, direct sales force, and so forth.

Once the methodology is determined the method of management can be addressed.

* * *

Having developed and written the marketing plan, the next step is to write the business plan. This business plan is called the "summary" business plan because it combines all the previous material gathered and studied. The company founders want to convey accuracy as well as possibly pique the readers curiosity.

This first iteration of the business plan was distributed to a limited, specific group of potential investors. Just as the Marketing Plan was.

FUNCTIONAL CARDIAC DISPLAYS, INC.
SUMMARY BUSINESS PLAN

JANUARY 1989

A. Team Builder, Pres./CEO
3039 Cardiac Health Drive Anytown, Anywhere 90000
999/555-1234

CONTENTS

EXECUTIVE SUMMARY

As a result of three decades of accumulated research, Functional Cardiac Displays, Inc. (FCD, Inc.) of Anytown, Anywhere is proud to announce a successful breakthrough in the field of medical science and the resultant business opportunity.

The estimated market potential for medical products in 1989 is $1.5 billion. In 1986, the estimated worldwide revenues generated by medical applications products, the market area first being addressed by FCD, Inc., were $499 million. This represents a 12.6 percent increase over 1985. Forecasts through 1991 anticipate uninterrupted growth for the industry owing to a demand for cardiac diagnostic services. This situation has evolved because of the increased longevity of the world population, especially in the industrialized nations. Worldwide revenues for 1991 are forecast at $860 million, which represents an average annual growth rate of 12 percent.

This business plan describes Functional Cardiac Displays, Inc. a company which has currently completed feasibility studies (Phase I) for a product that addresses a particular segment of the medical applications marketplace: The EKG marketplace. Which affects 60 percent of that marketplace.

The Management Team

The FCD, Inc. management has a proven record of several successful start-up assignments and has guided numerous multimillion dollar programs in a timely manner. The management staff has served as executive officers of technical societies in local chapters and on a national basis.

FCD, Inc.'s work force consists of excellent professionals who are versed in a specific array of required disciplines. Each member of the team is a significant contributor in a particular element of this project and was selected for that expertise and for his or her fit with the other members. Exhibit A of the plan (not included in this published example) provides resumes of the FCD, Inc. team that detail the experience available for this project.

The principles of FCD, Inc. have a long established relation with a number of reliable technical resources that will assist through the development process of this product. Scientific reviews have been conducted with several members of reputable cardiovascular clinics, and a close relation with several hospitals has been established. These valuable resources and individuals will serve as consultants throughout the development stage of the project.

Market Environment

FCD, Inc. has performed a market survey based on Dun and Bradstreet financial data. Using established patterns of medical applications equipment, they were compared to an estimated distribution of CASE 2000. This estimated distribution was based on a conservative analysis of the market for the new product.

The general environment for the medical supply industry is still in the growth stage. The technological complexity of this new procedure requires a team with many valued and rare abilities to be able to develop such a new concept in cardiac diagnostic techniques. The difficulty of assembling such a team and the virtual impossibility of duplicating the proprietary information which is the basis of the product makes it unlikely that a competitor would soon arrive on the scene. As a result, we at FCD, Inc. believe we offer a unique opportunity to be first with a valuable advanced cardiac diagnostic tool for medical technology. A noninvasive procedure designed to provide an accurate evaluation of a patient, and at the same time allows for low cost and maximum safety.

The market for new advanced medical technology shows no direct dependency on sustained general economic status or substantial growth. The market for medical service is quite complex and one finds that some areas grow regardless of national economic conditions.

The cornerstone of this plan is the breakthrough mentioned earlier. This breakthrough provides a major leap forward for cardiovascular diagnostic technology using the proven EKG data sensing techniques as input to a computer system that compares that data with a mathematically synthesized heart model and presents a three-dimensional color display of the electrical function of the patient's heart highlighting the and presenting traditional EKG electrical signals.

Management Objectives

Gaining the medical communities confidence in the system will take time, effort, and training, since it is a new application of old technology. However, based on the response received from esteemed members of that community to the demonstrated prototype, which is the result of the feasibility study, the need and desire for such a product is there.

FCD, Inc.'s long-term objectives are to develop products related to imaging technology. CASE 2000 being the first product introduced in the market is just the threshold of a huge market existing the the medical area. FCD, Inc. is currently reviewing EEG (electroencephalograph) related product possibilities which uses the same technology principles. There are a number of advantages that arise as a result of the use of this imaging technology:

1. The product has proven itself to be reliable from an engineering standpoint, since the hardware has been in use in the medical community for a number of years. The components used in this product have been approved by the American Heart Association and it takes little effort to obtain FDA (Federal Drug Administration) approval.
2. The basis product family is known in the marketplace and has a good reputation.
3. The product will become available at a time when the market segment is expected to expand rapidly because of the growing percentage of older people in the general world population growth pattern.
4. A greater demand for advanced technology.
5. The investment in hardware engineering required by FCD, Inc. is low in comparison to similar start-up manufacturing concerns.
6. Because the product is primarily software based, FCD, Inc. will act primarily as a systems integrator with software that is easily adaptable to many hardware sources. This provides the additional opportunity of licensing the software to the international market for additional revenue without added effort.

Near-Term Objectives

FCD, Inc. is now in the position that in order to make the product marketable additional development is necessary which will last 1 year to 18 months. This is the effort that needs $1.5 million funding now to move through Phase II of the plan.

At the end of Phase II, FCD, Inc. will hold a design specification for each of the hardware and software components to the system. This, by itself, provides a tangible asset. With this, FCD, Inc. could employ other vendors to manufacture/distribute the product. This would develop a selection of opportunities allowing FCD, Inc. alternatives of market approach thus securing the best advantage for the investors. This asset would also provide FCD, Inc. alternatives in financing on-going objectives.

Long-Term Objectives

Manufacturing activities (Phase III) are planned to start at the end of Phase II and will require an additional cash infusion of $5.5 million if FCD, Inc. sets up a manufacturing facility. However, management is looking into other alternatives such as a strategic alliance to support existing manufacturing needs.

First shipments will be made during the second quarter after the start of manufacturing. In the period between start-up and shipments, the sales effort will be supported by a small quantity of CASE 2000 systems to be used for customer evaluation and demonstration.

Financial Forecasts

Estimated sales during the first year of production are $3.7 million (starting 1990), rising to $20 million and $40 million in the second and third years, respectively.

Gross margin in the first quarter of the second year is calculated to be 68 percent and before-tax income at the end of the second year is forecast to be 21 percent. Positive cash flow is expected in the early part of the third year.

Conclusion

The business opportunity presented here is an opportunity to capitalize on an information base it has taken over 25 years and uncounted hours to accumulate. The product uses this information base in such a way as to greatly benefit the cardiovascular medical services in saving lives.

The market for this product is proven by marketing survey and the enthusiasm of significant members of that potential market.The total required capital to bring the product to manufacturing prototype (Phase II) and on to production (Phase III) is estimated at $7 million with positive cash flow expected in the early part of the third year.

The investor is expected to realize a return on investment in the order of 5 to 10 times that investment in approximately 3 years.

In summary, this plan identifies an opportunity to enter a marketplace that has enormous potential for revenue and profit growth, using an already established product technology and an experienced and seasoned management.

INTRODUCTION

The modern science of the interpretation of the electric signals from the heart began almost 100 years ago (1907) with Einthoven's application of the string galvanometer to the recording of the ECG. The next major step forward was the development of Wilson unipolar chest leads some 50 years ago. The standardization of ECG recordings to consist of 6 precordial leads and 6 limb leads followed soon after. The electrocardiographer reading these 12 scalar ECG traces consisting of the familiar P-QRS-T waveforms reconstructs a three-dimensional (3D) image in his mind of the electrical activity in the upper and lower chambers of the heart. The result of this mental image building is the ECG interpretation, that is, "Complete Heart Block," "Left Ventricular Hypertrophy," or "Acute and Extensive Anterior Myocardial Infarction." The recording, processing, and interpretation of the ECG has been assisted by digital computers to an ever-increasing extent in recent years. The primary signal is, however, still the 12 lead set of ECG waveforms.

With the advent of high speed colorgraphic digital image technology it is now possible (in addition to the standard 12 lead ECG processing) to reconstruct a 3D color image of the electrical activity of the heart directly from multiple body surface lead measurement. The local area of "Block," "Hypertrophy," "Injury," or "Infarction," for example, can be directly imaged and shown in 3D color on a high resolution color monitor. The image can be rotated and magnified to optimize the definition of the local injury or disordered electrical activity. The enhancement of the mental image building by this direct imaging process can be expected to lead to clearer, simpler, and more quantitative and accurate diagnosis.

The development of such a high resolution 3D color cardiac local electric field imaging system is underway at Functional Cardiac Displays, Inc. in Anytown, Anywhere.

Dr. Donald Z. Smithson, MD

Prof. of Med.: Univ. of Estonia
Dir: Biomathematics and ECG Research Group
Editor-in-Chief: *Journal of Cardiac Technology*
Dir. and Chief Scientist: Cardiac Local Field Imaging, FCD, Inc.

HISTORY

Approximately 25 years ago Dr. Donald Z. Smithson, MD conceived that electrical signals of the heart could be used as input data to a computer. This data could then develop an accurate image of a patient's heart. At this time, the technology did not exist that would make this economically feasible. However, the trend of technology development indicated that it would be available in the near future. He teamed up with Mr. J. Computer, a computer expert, and together they began the arduous task of collecting the data necessary to develop the database, to construct the mathematical model of the heart. Initially, this data was gathered on a Digital Equipment (DEC) computer system.

During this period Mr. Computer took a healthy human heart, dissected it, and took approximately 280,000 data point measurements to accurately define the database math model. This information is proprietary and with patent pending to FCD, Inc.

The resulting database and math model can now be demonstrated, in a time intensive manner, using the DEC system. FCD is now addressing the conversion of that data to a UNIX system for use with the more cost-effective, high speed, engineering workstations being produced today by companies such as SiliconGraphics and Sun Microsystems.

To date, FCD, Inc. has converted a sufficient amount of the data to prove and demonstrate the feasibility of the DEC-UNIX conversion process. This effort by a team of three full-time personnel has taken 6 months. This represents the successful completion of Phase I of the project. The next phase (Phase II) consists of completing the data conversion process, developing and verifying the prototype system, starting clinical studies, and beginning development of the marketing program.

Through the contributions of private investors, including many of the founders and first employees, sufficient resources of money, manpower, facilities, and equipment have been made available. This has accomplished a $5 million work effort for under $500,000. FCD, Inc. is now at the point where contributed manpower will not accomplish the task. Additional technical and marketing expertise must now be adopted in order to move the project forward to the commercial market.

PRODUCT DEFINITION

FCD, Inc. is in the "noninvasive medical imaging" business. The company has started with the electrical imaging of the heart based on the founders devoted time to cardiovascular study. This study base has given FCD, Inc. a head start in this highly specialized area of medical imaging.

Since 1907 the cardiovascular physician has had to rely on the subjective interpretation of ECG waveforms to determine a patient's heart condition. Today, if a 12-lead electrocardiogram and/or patient's symptoms lead one to suspect a heart problem, a confirming diagnosis must be formulated with such existing clinical technology as standard treadmill stress testing, ultrasonic (echo) imaging, isotopic imaging, and, at times, angiographic imaging. These techniques have certain disadvantages. Angiographic imaging is not routine, very costly, invasive, risky, and should not be performed unless a specific descriptive ventricular or coronary anatomy is desired in preparation for an interventional or surgical procedure.

Isotopic imaging is also invasive, nonroutine, involves injections of potentially harmful radioactive chemicals, and has poor images with an accuracy that is unmatched with its very high cost. Ultrasonic (echo) imaging basically provides nonspecific structural information from which information about electrical physiologic function is inferred. The standard treadmill stress test, though widely used, is based on and limited by the standard 12-lead ECG for data acquisition and, thus, can provide incomplete and misleading information. It is unusable to provide regional myocardial information and, in many individuals, is nondiagnostic with a low level of accuracy.

CASE 2000 eliminates the need for such practices and provides more accurate and descriptive diagnostic analysis where adapted to existing technology in a less costly manner. The patient's heart data is taken by 32 sensing points instead of merely 12. The data is displayed on a high resolution, 3D screen that highlights any specific problem area. The physician is provided an ECG printout as well as the screen image which allows for an immediate crosscheck of the data by the physician. This significantly increases the speed and accuracy of the diagnosis which allows much more definitive action to be taken without the risk of subjective interpretive diagnosis.

FCD, Inc. is interested in pursuing the imaging technology and imaging market due to their knowledge base and that market's potential for exploitation and successful business entrance.

These interested people will consider FCD, Inc. a success only if and when it is sufficiently profitable to realize their expected return on investment. In start-up situations, this is normally in the range of a factor of five over a 3 to 5 year period. (Conservative projections show that FCD, Inc. will experience sales over $20 million and gross profits of approximately $5 million over 4 years. This meets the investment goal if the company goes public or is sold.)

This type of return should be realizable since the product being presented will address a known market need by replacing and augmenting the current ECG equipment, which the product will render obsolete in the future. The product introduces a new technological basis of medical imaging—imaging the electrical functioning of the image subject rather than the physical characteristics of that subject.

DEFINITION OF THE MARKET

CASE 2000 uses the same principles as the ECG monitoring devices that have been in use since 1907. However, it is based on today's new, state-of-the-art, computer workstation technology. In short, it uses the ECG data to produce a 3D video image of the electrical functioning of the patient's heart in real time.

The primary competition existing for this product is the ECG based products, which, by introduction of this product, may be rendered obsolete in the future. This product may also negatively impact the radio isotope imaging market as well as the magnetic resonance imaging (MRI) and ultrasonic imaging markets. These markets will be affected to the extent that they address the practice of cardiovascular imaging.

When the product is introduced and in production, it is expected that the company will experience a high growth period. This will be controlled by the sale of licensed production rights to meet geographic areas of demand throughout the United States and the international markets.

Sales and distribution will be in the continental United States during the Beta testing period and most of the first year after product release. This allows us to closely track the product performance under field conditions. In addition, the anticipated domestic market is such that FCD, Inc. may be hard pressed to keep up with that demand.

The sales force will be trained to act as the staff to train the Beta sites and ongoing site staffs in the proper use of the product. The sales people will be paid a base salary initially. Following product acceptance, compensation will change to the more traditional base salary plus commission/bonus.

Three to five Beta sites will be selected. These sites will be cardiovascular training hospitals and clinics. Two have already been selected in California and one site is under consideration in Utah. (All requesting sites have agreed to purchase the Beta units, which is a unique action for new products in the medical industry.)

Further advertising will be done by:

Display and demo of the product at selected medical conventions and trade shows

Print advertising in cardiovascular and hospital journals as well as health and fitness magazines

Direct mail to the cardiovascular community

Promotion of discounted software updates

Financing assistance

On-line product technical support (telephone technical advice/troubleshooting)

TV and radio news (science announcements)

Press releases

The major market advantages that FCD, Inc. has is that the company was founded by a highly respected group of medical practitioners from the cardiovascular specialty. These people lend a great deal of credibility and long-term prestige to this company and its entry product(s).

Another advantage is the fact that this imaging product is a noninvasive cardiovascular device. This greatly reduces medical risk. Thus it becomes much more attractive to the customer than those imaging products that are invasive.

A further advantage is that it is state-of-the-art equipment for alerting patients of potential heart disease dangers as well as for diagnosing the damage caused by a heart attack (i.e., latent ischemia).

The company has no perceived market disadvantage. The product is new, and, as such, it is difficult to accurately predict public and medical acceptance. All reactions have thus far been positive. The market being used for clinical study is the current ECG market which is represented by the medical application market.

FCD, Inc. expects to conservatively gain 15 percent of the ECG based market and to ship at least 100 units during the first year after product introduction and continue a minimum of 32 percent sales revenue growth rate through the first 5 years.

Industry Analysis

General Overview

The medical application market is approximately 10 years old. In 1986, the medical application:

Generated approximately 3.4 percent of the total 1986 factoryrevenue for all technical system applications

Produced an estimated 8.9 percent of the total unit shipments

Revenue in this market grew at a 16.7 percent compound rate, from $269 million in 1982 to $499 million in 1986.

Sales Trends

The medical application market will grow 11.0 percent in revenue and 29.3 percent in units, compounded over 5 years. Average system prices are decreasing as the industry moves toward the use of micro and personal computers (see Table 1).

Table 1 Factory Revenue and Unit Shipments
(5-Year Forecast)

	Year					
	1	2	3	4	5	CAGR
Revenue ($M)	569.0	643.0	709.0	785.0	863.0	11.0%
Change (%)	14.0	13.0	11.0	11.0	10.0	
Shipments (K Units)	85.1	112.4	151.7	187.2	237.7	29.3%
Growth (%)	29.0	32.0	35.0	23.4	22.0	27.0

Major Vendor Analysis

Table 2 lists the 1986 revenue, unit shipments, and market share estimates, by vendor, for the medical applications market.

Table 2 Medical Applications Vendor Analysis

1986 Revenue Analysis

Vendor	Revenue ($M)	Rank	Market Share
Hewlett-Packard	122	1	24.4%
IBM	113	2	22.6
Digital Equip.	64	3	12.8
Data General	19	4	3.8
Other	161		36.4
Total	$499		100.0%

1986 Shipments Analysis

Vendor	Shipments (K Units)	Rank	Market Share
IBM	19.5	1	29.4%
Hewlett-Packard	5.3	2	8.0
Digital Equip.	2.4	3	3.6
Data General	0.2	4	0.3
Other	39.1		54.6
Total	66.5		100.0%

Note: Columns may not add to totals shown because of rounding.

Future Industry Trends

The forces motivating the user to purchase computer tools for medical applications are:

Increasing malpractice insurance costs are causing doctors to perform as many non-surgical diagnostic techniques as possible

Sophisticated medical diagnostic equipment is becoming increasingly more complex, requiring computerization

There is a need to integrate many instruments to improve productivity and increase utilization of expensive instruments

There are shortages of medical technicians and doctors with critical skills

Labor costs are increasing

Outside Influences Facing the Industry

Medical products are subject to the following restrictions and influences:

Liability insurance

Government regulators such as FDA (Federal Drug Administration) and FTC (Federal Trade Commission)

Medical associations sales and criterion

International trade policy (for exports)

Political status of medical environment

Insurance industry regulations

Healthcare cost containment

Third party pay regulators (e.g., Medicaid and Medicare)

These outside influences have generated the following recent activities:

Liability insurance for physicians has almost doubled making them more responsive to new, no-risk, noninvasive technologies which provide early warning of an impending disaster

Medical products have relatively short lives

Hospitals, physicians, and suppliers are competing among themselves for available funds since insurance companies and the government have capped spending for health programs

Monitoring of cardiac function in all surgical patients is becoming an industry standard

The trend is toward using micro, board, and personal computers in medical applications

The U.S. government has legislated limits to the number of scanners that hospitals can purchase because doctors were overusing scanners in an effort to protect themselves against malpractice suits. (For example, a doctor might order five CAT scans at $800 each, for a total of $4000, before performing a $2000 surgical procedure.)

Pricing

The average price per unit in the medical applications market is $7500 ($499 million/ 66,500 units). However, this represents the pricing of a fully matured product base.

Advertising and Promotion Costs

Normally, 15 to 20 percent of total investment in product is spent on media by industrial firms. ("Sharing the Value Added: A Bonus Plan for a Growth Company," A. Graham Sterling, Operating Model of a Hypothetical Growth Company, *Strategic Planning and Management Handbook*, New York: Van Nostrand Reinhold Company, p. 522.)

Mini and Micro Computer industry spent an average of 15.7 percent of margin on advertising during 1985. Hospital services industry spent 12 percent of margin on advertising during 1985. (*Advertising Age*, September 15, 1986 p. 60)

CASE 2000 Marketing Potential

The medical application market is growing at a compound annual growing rate of 11.0 percent for the years 1987 to 1991. The gross national product is forecasted to grow at a rate of 305 percent during the same time period. The cardiology segment is especially strong, and the penetration in the medical application field is relatively low. Additionally, according to recent market research studies, Data General, which ranked number fourth in market share will drop out of the market. No new entries are foreseen in the medical application marketplace.

The fact that heart disease is the number one killer in America makes this product a necessity in the medical community.

The uniqueness and need for this product indicates that there is a lot of potential for it now. FCD, Inc. has the technical expertise to make this product and the medical industry specific contact and marketing experience to successfully sell it.

The imaging technology being used is new and noninvasive and shows potential for expanded use in brain scan application as well as other industries in need of scanning methodologies.

DESCRIPTION OF PRODUCTS OR SERVICES

Initial Release (proposed base user price $40,000)

Product will identify:

Specific areas of infarctions, acute injury, and ischemia. Areas include transmural and subendocardial determinations.

Localization of areas of infarction, acute injury, and ischemia despite vintrarefibular conduction delays or bundle branch blocks.

Location of accessory bypass pathways in WPW syndromes.

Localization of sites of ventricular ectopic complexes or sites of ventricular re-entry for use in mapping of ventricular tachycardia for ablation purposes.

Product will have:

- 3 to 5 minute sensor/screen refresh rate
- 32 sensor input band
- 32 sensor signal display and printout
- 3-dimensional image generation at normal size
  - Image display orientation (to be determined)
  - Interior and exterior views
  - 1 mm slicing
  - Zoom to approx. 5X
  - Full image rotation
  - Panning
- Color print of screen image
- Patient data recorded on removable hard disc
  - (60 heartbeat sample requiring less than 1 MBytes)
  - (Disk cartridge capable of 380 MBytes storage)

Ongoing Product Development (1.5 to 2 years)

	Base	Option
Ischemia mapping	✔	
Treadmill application		$5000
Angioplasty application		$2500
Digital display of ischemic and infarct volume		$1000
Stop time review		$1000
Surgical anesthesia monitoring	✔	
Intensive care unit monitoring	✔	

Free user training will be provided for each Beta unit.

Installation and training will be provided at a cost of $5000 per each production unit and option.

MANAGEMENT STRUCTURE

The management team consists of a president and chief executive officer, Mr. A. Team Builder, who is responsible for gathering resources and monitoring costs and schedules. Mr. Builder provides expertise in planning, budgeting, and quality assurance, ensuring that the required outcome is secured. He has successfully led other high-tech start-up programs and has played key management roles in several organizations.

Mr. Cantgetenuf, CPA who will perform the duties of director of accounting and will be responsible for maintaining a professional accounting system including payroll, general accounting, and periodic reports.

Dr. B. Thorough, PhD will perform the duties of vice president of marketing. Dr. Thorough has several years of medical product development, strategic planning, and marketing research experience and is well received in the medical community. She will be assisted by Dr. B. Good, PhD who has many years of experience in the computer marketing and high-tech customer support fields.

Dr. A. Barnone, MD, vice president of Technology, will be responsible for maintaining the focus of the engineering team which consists of A. Builder, J. Computer, R. Karona, W. Long, S. Short, and G. Stretch. All of these people are well known in their respective areas of expertise.

The technical team described above will be assisted in an advisory manner by a science team consisting of Dr. D.Z. Smithson and Mr. J. Computer the primary creators of the CASE 2000 database and technology.

Mr. J. Computer holds a MS in physics from California State University and has been the primary data technologist working in cooperation with Dr. Smithson.

Mr. U. Cantdoit, attorney at law is our legal and corporate attorney.

Mr. U. Betwe Candoit, attorney is our patent attorney.

Complete resumes of the key personnel are provided in the appendix (not included in this published example).

The FCD, Inc. board of directors consists of reputable and prominent individuals who have extensive knowledge of both technology and the business aspect of the medical community. The members are:

Dr. D.Z. Smithson
U. Betwe Candoit
I. Lookintoit
C. Joiner

Consultants and Advisers

Dr. I. Attractem, PhD, is an expert on magnetic resonance imaging, math modeling, and electronics in the fields of medicine, pharmacology, and micro-devices.

I. Lookforem, consultant on FDA (Federal Drug Administration) regulations.

Organization Chart

(Not included in this published example)

OBJECTIVES AND GOALS

Within 3 years FCD, Inc. plans to be well into delivery of its base product (see Product Definition). During the next 12 months, Development (Phase II), FCD, Inc. plans to develop and verify a working prototype of CASE 2000. This program will require the following actions:

- ECG sensing development
  - Testing
  - Verification
  - Issue final specification for production
- System Set Up
  - Prototype configuration
  - Product design layout
  - Issue final system design specification
- Clinical Studies
  - Equipment component evaluation
  - Equipment integration
  - Clinical application evaluation
- Marketing Program Development
  - Product profile
  - Initial product positioning

Once the above program has been accomplished an intensive 16 months program of market introduction of production models will occur. This program will consist of:

- Continued clinical feedback
- Prototype modifications
- Production facility location
  - Contract manufacturer
  - Self-manufacture
- Final design evaluation
- Marketing planning and promotion
- Limited production
- Sales and promotion

The management team at FCD, Inc. sees no obstacle in attaining the above stated goals in the time specified. They have successfully attained the Phase I goals ahead of schedule and below budget.

FINANCIAL DATA

Profits

FCD, Inc. will not be profitable until the first quarter of the fourth year of operation.

Market Share

FCD, Inc. is pursuing a market which has been relatively untapped by new technology since 1907. The goal is to gain approximately 3 percent of that market within the first year of product introduction and increase the share at a rate greater than 32 percent per year compounded until 30 to 40 percent of that market has been captured. At that time continued efforts will allow it to move at a rate slightly ahead of the projected market growth of 11 percent.

The primary concentration will then be on product profit margin rather than on market share.

Market Areas (geographic)

Initially FCD, Inc. will concentrate on satisfying the domestic market. This will take an estimated 3 to 5 years. As this satisfaction occurs FCD, Inc. will investigate the international markets for methods of penetration as well as profitability.

Services and Products

Initially FCD, Inc. will be a "systems integrator." The company will produce software that will be loaded into a hardware configuration purchased from a vendor (i.e., SiliconGraphics and/or Sun Microsystems). The company will also contract with a manufacturer (Stateside) to produce the devices necessary for sensing the patient's heart signals.

These above stated elements will be brought together under the complete direction and control of FCD, Inc., and will remain in that control until it is found advisable to move that integration process outside FCD, Inc.

Financial

FCD, Inc. has just successfully completed Phase I which was the program to prove the feasibility of the original concept using the new microprocessor workstation technology. It is now ready to proceed with Phase II which is the process of developing the production prototype of the product and begin the marketing processes.

Phase II

To start and successfully complete the Phase II process it will be necessary to raise $1.5 million to cover the expenses of operation for the next 12 months.

The following pro forma financial statements detail the need of these funds and further detail the need for funds to begin production of the product in Phase III. Also, the statements detail the ultimate reward for the successful accomplishment of this effort. During Phase II it will be necessary to support the following expenditures:

Capital Expenditures			
Computer equipment			
1 SG IRIS workstation	$ 15,000		
1 MIPS Superworkstation	120,000		
1 IBM PC system	5,000		
Office Furn. and equip.	42,000		
Total		$182,000	
Manufacturing & Assembly			
Components			
1 32 lead ECG band	40,000		
Packaging & rack des.	30,000		
Salaries			
Design consult's	250,000		
Technical & mgmt	450,000		
3 technicians	70,000		
Fringes & taxes	90,000		
Total		930,000	
Marketing			
Salaries 150,000			
Fringes & taxes	30,000		
Product profile	15,000		
Total		195,000	
Administration			
Admin. expenses	30,000		
Rent 50,000			
Travel 40,000			
Total		120,000	
Total expenditures for Phase II			1,427,000

During Phase II it is anticipated that five Beta units will be installed at about the tenth month of development. These units will be sold to the Beta sites at slightly above cost (approx. $150,000).

Phase III

During Phase III it will be necessary to support the following expenditures:

Capital Expenditures		
Computer equipment	$50,000	
Office furn. & equip.	30,000	
Assembly tables * Equip.	25,000	
Workstations	25,000	
Total		$130,000
Manufacturing & Assembly		
Components	2,000,000	
Salaries , Fabrication	400,000	
Fringes & taxes	80,000	
Total		2,480,000
Marketing		
Salaries 280,000		
Fringes & taxes	56,000	
Delivery costs	50,000	
Total		386,000
Salaries		
Technical staff	494,000	
Data analyst	134,000	
Administration	207,000	
Fringes & taxes	167,000	
Total		1,002,000
Consultants Fee	360,000	360,000
Administration		
Office expenses	50,000	
Rent	320,000	
Travel	20,000	
Total		390,000
Total expenditures for Phase III		4,748,000

The closing of Phase II on schedule will allow a cash flow carry forward of approximately $200,000. It will be necessary to have an additional cash infusion of $5 million to carry the project forward to profitability sometime during the second quarter of the second year of operation. At that time FCD, Inc. will have shipped over 200 units at the starting point of our most rapid growth period.

Projected Value Analysis

The following table provides an analysis of the projected stock value of FCD, Inc. for a 4-year growth period.

Projected Value Analysis

	1990	1991	1992	1993
Market Size of ECG units sold per year ($U.S. millions)	$465.00	$510.00	$550.00	$600.00
Concentration @ 79%	367.35	402.90	434.50	474.00
Market Penetration	1%	5%	10%	15%
Annual Sales in ($U.S.millions)	3.67	20.15	43.45	71.10
Anticipated Profit @ 30% (markup as a % of sales)	1.10	6.04	13.04	21.33
Net Income per Share	0.11	0.60	1.30	2.13
Market Share Price	6.04	13.04	21.33	

Assumptions:		
	Number of outstanding shares	10,000,000
	Earnings multiplier	10
	Risk free rate (treasuries)	7.94%
	Risk rate of return	25.00%
	Annual return rate expected	33.00%

Conclusions

The next phase of development facing FCD, Inc. is to raise sufficient capital to develop the product to completion, and eventually to market.

FUNCTIONAL CARDIAC DISPLAYS, INC.
PROJECTION OF FINANCIAL STATEMENTS
PHASE II OPERATION (12 MONTHS)
Actual Projections -->

Spread in hundreds ( )
Spread in thousands (X)

	A	1	2	3	4
PROFIT AND LOSS					
Unit Sales		0	0	0	0
Unit Sales ($40K per unit)		.00	.00	.00	.00
Training Sales ($5K per unit)		.00	.00	.00	.00
NET SALES		.00	.00	.00	.00
Less: Component Cost (30% sales)		5.83	5.83	5.83	5.83
Direct Labor (6% sales)		43.33	43.33	43.33	43.33
Fringe & Tax (20% labor)		8.67	8.67	8.67	8.67
Other Oper. Expense		.00	.00	.00	.00
COST OF GOODS SOLD		57.83	57.83	57.83	57.83
GROSS PROFIT		-57.83	-57.83	-57.83	-57.83
Less: Mktg/Sales Exp. (4% sales)		1.25	1.25	1.25	1.25
Warranty(.1% sales)		.00	.00	.00	.00
Salaries (3% sales)		12.50	12.50	12.50	12.50
Fringe & Tax (20% salaries)		2.50	2.50	2.50	2.50
Consulting Fees (.5% sales)		20.83	20.83	20.83	20.83
Admin. Exp. (.2% sales)		2.50	2.50	2.50	2.50
Cap. Equip.		15.17	15.17	15.17	15.17
Rent (1.3% sales)		4.17	4.17	4.17	4.17
Travel (.13% sales)		3.33	3.33	3.33	3.33
Deprec. (.34% sales)		3.03	3.03	3.03	3.03
OPERATING PROFIT		-123.11	-123.11	-123.11	-123.11
Less: Other Exp. or Inc. (Net)		.00	.00	.00	.00
Taxes on Income (40% operating profit)		-49.24	-34.47	-34.47	-34.47
NET PROFIT		-73.87	-88.64	-88.64	-88.64
P & L RATIO ANALYSIS					
Sales					
Cost of Goods Sold					
Gross Margin					
Net Profit on Sales					
Marketing (Sales Exp. + Wty)					
Admin. (Gen. and Admin. + Burden)					
CASH PROJECTION					
CASH BALANCE (Opening)		34.00	1289.83	1219.34	1148.50
Plus RECEIPTS: Receivable Coll.		.00	.00	.00	.00
Interest Inc. (cash bal x .06/12)		.00	6.45	6.10	5.74
Return of Net Profit		.00	.00	.00	.00
Phase II Cash Equity Infusion		1500.00			
Bank Loan Proceeds					
Total		1534.00	1296.28	1225.44	1154.24
Less: DISBURSEMENTS: Trade Payables		5.83	5.83	5.83	5.83

5	6	7	8	9	10	11	12	TOTAL
0	0	0	0	0	5	0	0	5
.00	.00	.00	.00	.00	150.00	.00	.00	150.00
.00	.00	.00	.00	.00	.00	.00	.00	.00
.00	.00	.00	.00	.00	150.00	.00	.00	150.00
5.83	5.83	5.83	5.83	5.83	105.66	5.83	5.83	169.79
43.33	43.33	43.33	43.33	43.33	43.33	43.33	43.33	519.96
8.67	8.67	8.67	8.67	8.67	8.67	8.67	8.67	6252583.48
.00	.00	.00	.00	.00	.00	.00	.00	.00
57.83	57.83	57.83	57.83	57.83	157.66	57.83	57.83	793.74
-57.83	-57.83	-57.83	-57.83	-57.83	-7.66	-57.83	-57.83	-643.74
1.25	1.25	1.25	1.25	1.25	1.25	1.25	1.25	15.00
.00	.00	.00	.00	.00	.15	.00	.00	.15
12.50	12.50	12.50	12.50	12.50	12.50	12.50	12.50	150.00
2.50	2.50	2.50	2.50	2.50	2.50	2.50	2.50	30.00
20.83	20.83	20.83	20.83	20.83	20.83	20.83	20.83	249.96
2.50	2.50	2.50	2.50	2.50	2.50	2.50	2.50	30.00
15.17	15.17	15.17	15.17	15.17	15.17	15.17	15.17	182.04
4.17	4.17	4.17	4.17	4.17	4.17	4.17	4.17	50.04
3.33	3.33	3.33	3.33	3.33	3.33	3.33	3.33	39.96
3.03	3.03	3.03	3.03	3.03	3.03	3.03	3.03	36.41
-123.11	-123.11	-123.11	-123.11	-123.11	-73.09	-123.11	-123.11	-1427.30
.00	.00	.00	.00	.00	.00	.00	.00	.00
-34.47	-34.47	-34.47	-34.47	-34.47	-20.47	-34.47	-34.47	-414.42
-88.64	-88.64	-88.64	-88.64	-88.64	-52.62	-88.64	-88.64	-1012.88
					1.00			1.00
					1.05			5.29
					-.05			-4.29
					-.35			-6.75
					.01			.10
					.04			.53
1077.30	1005.75	933.84	861.57	788.94	627.31	500.88	373.82	
.00	.00	.00	.00	.00	150.00	.00	.00	
5.39	5.03	4.67	4.31	3.94	3.14	2.50	1.87	
.00	.00	.00	.00	-88.64	-88.64	-52.62	-88.64	
1082.69	1010.78	938.51	865.88	704.25	691.80	450.76	287.05	
5.83	5.83	5.83	5.83	5.83	105.66	5.83	5.83	

FUNCTIONAL CARDIAC DISPLAYS, INC.
PROJECTION OF FINANCIAL STATEMENTS
PHASE II OPERATION (12 MONTHS)
Actual Projections -->

Spread in hundreds ( ) Spread in thousands (X)	A	1	2	3	4	5	6	7	8	9	10	11	12
BALANCE SHEET													
ASSETS: Cash (opening)		34.00	1289.83	1219.34	1148.50	1077.30	1005.75	933.84	861.57	788.94	627.31	500.88	373.82
Marketable Securities		.00	.00	.00	.00	.00	.00	.00	.00	.00	.00	.00	.00
Receivables Coll.		.00	.00	.00	.00	.00	.00	.00	.00	.00	150.00	.00	.00
Inventory (Net)		.00	.00	.00	.00	.00	.00	.00	.00	.00	105.66	.00	.00
Total Current Assets		34.00	1289.83	1219.34	1148.50	1077.30	1005.75	933.84	861.57	788.94	882.97	500.88	373.82
Fixed Assets (Net)		.00	182.00	.00	.00	.00	.00	.00	.00	.00	.00	.00	.00
Deferred Charges													
TOTAL ASSETS		34.00	1471.83	1219.34	1148.50	1077.30	1005.75	933.84	861.57	788.94	882.97	500.88	373.82
LIABILITIES: Notes Payable - Banks		.00	.00	.00	.00	.00	.00	.00	.00	.00	.00	.00	.00
Trade Payables (Comp. Cost)		187.83	5.83	5.83	5.83	5.83	5.83	5.83	5.83	5.83	109.83	5.83	5.83
Income Tax		-49.24	-34.47	-34.47	-34.47	-34.47	-34.47	-34.47	-34.47	-34.47	-20.47	-34.47	-34.47
Accruals (ins. $3500/yr.)		.29	.29	.29	.29	.29	.29	.29	.29	.29	.29	.29	.29
CURRENT LIABILITIES		138.88	-28.35	-28.35	-28.35	-28.35	-28.35	-28.35	-28.35	-28.35	89.65	-28.35	-28.35
CAPITAL STOCK SURPLUS		-104.88	1500.18	1247.69	1176.85	1105.65	1034.10	962.19	889.92	817.29	793.32	529.23	402.17
Net Worth for Ptnrship. or Indiv.													
TOTAL LIABILITIES AND NET WORTH		34.00	1471.83	1219.34	1148.50	1077.30	1005.75	933.84	861.57	788.94	882.97	500.88	373.82
BALANCE SHEET RATIO ANALYSIS													
Current Ratio		.24	-45.50	-43.01	-40.51	-38.00	-35.48	-32.94	-30.39	-27.83	9.85	-17.67	-13.19
Debt-to-Equity		-1.32	-.02	-.02	-.02	-.03	-.03	-.03	-.03	-.03	.11	-.05	-.07
Return on Assets		-3.62	-.08	-.10	-.11	-.11	-.12	-.13	-.14	-.16	-.08	-.25	-.33
Return on Equity		.70	-.06	-.07	-.08	-.08	-.09	-.09	-.10	-.11	-.07	-.17	-.22
Investment Turnover		.31	9.92	9.92	9.92	9.92	9.92	9.92	9.92	9.92	1.44	9.92	9.92
Return on Investment (ROI)		.00	.00	.00	.00	.00	.00	.00	.00	.00	.17	.00	.00
Working Capital (acid test)		.24	-45.50	-43.01	-40.51	-38.00	-35.48	-32.94	-30.39	-27.83	8.67	-17.67	-13.19

****
Worksheet for ratios

		1	2	3	4	5	6	7	8	9	10	11	12
Operating Profit		-123.11	-123.11	-123.11	-123.11	-123.11	-123.11	-123.11	-123.11	-123.11	-73.09	-123.11	-123.11
Net Profit		-73.87	-88.64	-88.64	-88.64	-88.64	-88.64	-88.64	-88.64	-88.64	-52.62	-88.64	-88.64
Cost of Goods Sold		57.83	57.83	57.83	57.83	57.83	57.83	57.83	57.83	57.83	157.66	57.83	57.83
Net Sales		.00	.00	.00	.00	.00	.00	.00	.00	.00	150.00	.00	.00

FUNCTIONAL CARDIAC DISPLAYS, INC.
PROJECTION OF FINANCIAL STATEMENTS
THREE RUNNING YEARS CASH FLOW PROJECTIONS
Projections -->

Spread in hundreds ( ) Spread in thousands (X)	BY QUARTER				BY QUARTER				BY QUARTER			
	1	2	3	4	1	2	3	4	1	2	3	4
CASH PROJECTION												
CASH BALANCE (Opening)	210.11	4701.92	4487.17	4778.39	5784.33	7964.18	9477.88	11646.35	15403.21	22535.07	29436.01	37231.02
Plus RECEIPTS: Receivable Coll.	.00	.00	450.00	1125.00	2025.00	2250.00	3375.00	5625.00	9000.00	9000.00	10125.00	11250.00
Int. Inc. (cash bal. x .06)/12												
Return of Net Profit	-215.43	9.16	270.65	597.41	810.59	1240.69	2096.13	3377.23	3377.23	3803.63	4230.02	5082.80
Phase III Cash Equity Infusion	4748.00											
Bank Loan Proceeds												
Total	4742.68	4711.08	5207.82	6500.80	8619.92	11454.87	14949.01	20648.58	27780.44	35338.70	43791.03	53563.82
Less: DISBURSEMENTS: Trade Payables	17.49	12.51	12.51	12.51	12.51	1012.50	1687.50	2700.00	2700.00	3037.50	3375.00	4050.00
Direct Labor	129.99	129.99	129.99	129.99	135.00	202.50	337.50	540.00	540.00	607.50	675.00	810.00
Other Oper. Exp.	.00	.00	.00	.00	.00	.00	.00	.00	.00	.00	.00	.00
Sales,Gen & Adm Exp	36.90	55.30	86.50	155.70	173.00	259.50	432.50	692.00	692.00	778.50	865.00	1038.00
Fixed Asset Adds	.00	20.00	20.00	20.00	20.00	20.00	30.00	.00	.00	.00	.00	.00
Income Taxes	-143.62	6.11	180.43	398.27	315.23	482.49	815.16	1313.37	1313.37	1479.19	1645.01	1976.65
Dividends or Withdrawals	.00	.00	.00	.00	.00	.00	.00	.00	.00	.00	.00	.00
Bank Loan Repaym't												
Total	40.76	223.91	429.43	716.47	655.74	1976.99	3302.66	5245.37	5245.37	5902.69	6560.01	7874.65
CASH BALANCE (Closing)	4701.92	4487.17	4778.39	5784.33	7964.18	9477.88	11646.35	15403.21	22535.07	29436.01	37231.02	45689.17

Spread in hundreds ( ) Spread in thousands (X)	1	BY QUARTER 2	3	4	TOTAL
PROFIT AND LOSS					
Unit Sales	0	10	25	45	80
Unit Sales ($40K per unit)	.00	400.00	1000.00	1800.00	3200.00
Training Sales ($5K per unit)	.00	50.00	125.00	225.00	400.00
NET SALES	.00	450.00	1125.00	2025.00	3600.00
Less: Component Cost (30% sales)	17.49	135.00	337.50	607.50	1097.49
Direct Labor (6% sales)	129.99	129.99	129.99	129.99	519.96
Fringe & Tax (20% labor)	26.00	26.00	26.00	26.00	103.99
Other Oper. Expense	.00	.00	.00	.00	.00
COST OF GOODS SOLD	173.48	290.99	493.49	763.49	1721.44
GROSS PROFIT	-173.48	159.01	631.51	1261.51	1878.56
Less: Mktg/Sales Exp. (4% sales)	.00	18.00	45.00	81.00	144.00
Warranty(.1% sales)	.00	.40	1.00	1.80	3.20
Salaries (3% sales)	30.75	30.75	33.75	60.75	156.00
Fringe & Tax (20% salaries)	6.15	6.15	6.75	12.15	31.20
Consulting Fees (.5% sales)	62.49	2.25	5.63	10.13	80.49
Admin. Exp. (.2% sales)	7.50	7.50	7.50	7.50	30.00
Cap. Equip.	47.10	47.10	47.10	47.10	188.40
Rent (1.3% sales)	12.51	12.51	14.63	26.33	65.97
Travel (.13% sales)	9.99	9.99	9.99	9.99	39.96
Deprec. (.34% sales)	9.09	9.09	9.09	9.09	36.36
OPERATING PROFIT	-359.06	15.27	451.08	995.68	1102.98
Less: Other Exp. or Inc. (Net)	.00	.00	.00	.00	.00
Taxes on Income (40% op. profit)	-143.62	6.11	180.43	398.27	441.19
NET PROFIT	-215.43	9.16	270.65	597.41	661.79 661.79
P & L RATIO ANALYSIS					
Sales		1.00	1.00	1.00	1.00
Cost of Goods Sold		.65	.44	.38	.48
Gross Margin		.35	.56	.62	.52
Net Profit on Sales		.02	.24	.30	.18
Marketing (Sales Exp. + Wty)		.04	.04	.04	.04
Admin. (Consult. Admin. Rent. Travel)		.07	.03	.03	.06
PROPOSED UNIT PRICE	40.00				
PROPOSED INSTALLATION AND TRAINING PRICE	5.00				

FUNCTIONAL CARDIAC DISPLAYS, INC.
PROJECTION OF FINANCIAL STATEMENTS
THREE RUNNING YEARS PROFIT AND LOSS
Projections -->

		BY QUARTER					BY QUARTER			
1	2	3	4	TOTAL	1	2	3	4	TOTAL	YEAR 5
50	75	125	200	450	200	225	250	300	975	1600
2000.00	3000.00	5000.00	8000.00	18000.00	8000.00	9000.00	10000.00	12000.00	39000.00	64000.00
250.00	375.00	625.00	1000.00	2250.00	1000.00	1125.00	1250.00	1500.00	4875.00	8000.00
2250.00	3375.00	5625.00	9000.00	20250.00	9000.00	10125.00	11250.00	13500.00	43875.00	72000.00
675.00	1012.50	1687.50	2700.00	6075.00	2700.00	3037.50	3375.00	4050.00	13162.50	21600.00
135.00	202.50	337.50	540.00	1215.00	540.00	607.50	675.00	810.00	2632.50	4320.00
27.00	40.50	67.50	108.00	243.00	108.00	121.50	135.00	162.00	526.50	864.00
.00	.00	.00	.00	.00	.00	.00	.00	.00	.00	.00
837.00	1255.50	2092.50	3348.00	7533.00	3348.00	3766.50	4185.00	5022.00	16321.50	26784.00
1413.00	2119.50	3532.50	5652.00	12717.00	5652.00	6358.50	7065.00	8478.00	27553.50	45216.00
90.00	135.00	225.00	360.00	810.00	360.00	405.00	450.00	540.00	1755.00	2880.00
2.00	3.00	5.00	8.00	18.00	8.00	9.00	10.00	12.00	39.00	64.00
67.50	101.25	168.75	270.00	607.50	270.00	303.75	337.50	405.00	1316.25	2160.00
13.50	20.25	33.75	54.00	121.50	54.00	60.75	67.50	81.00	263.25	432.00
11.25	16.88	28.13	45.00	101.25	45.00	50.63	56.25	67.50	219.38	360.00
7.50	7.50	11.25	18.00	44.25	18.00	20.25	22.50	27.00	87.75	144.00
47.10	47.10	47.10	47.10	188.40	47.10	47.10	47.10	47.10	188.40	47.10
29.25	43.88	73.13	117.00	263.25	117.00	131.63	146.25	175.50	570.38	936.00
9.99	9.99	9.99	11.70	41.67	11.70	13.16	14.63	17.55	57.04	93.60
9.09	11.48	19.13	30.60	70.29	30.60	34.43	38.25	45.90	149.18	244.80
1125.82	1723.19	2911.29	4690.60	10450.89	4690.60	5282.81	5875.03	7059.45	22907.89	37854.50
.00	.00	.00	.00	.00	.00	.00	.00	.00	.00	.00
315.23	482.49	815.16	1313.37	2926.25	1313.37	1479.19	1645.01	1976.65	6414.21	10599.26
810.59	1240.69	2096.13	3377.23	7524.64	3377.23	3803.63	4230.02	5082.80	16493.68	27255.24
				7524.64					16493.68	
1.00	1.00	1.00	1.00	1.00	1.00	1.00	1.00	1.00	1.00	1.00
.37	.37	.37	.37	.37	.37	.37	.37	.37	.37	.37
.63	.63	.63	.63	.63	.63	.63	.63	.63	.63	.63
.36	.37	.37	.38	.37	.38	.38	.38	.38	.38	.38
.04	.04	.04	.04	.04	.04	.04	.04	.04	.04	.04
.03	.02	.02	.02	.02	.02	.02	.02	.02	.02	.02

FUNCTIONAL CARDIAC DISPLAYS, INC.
PROJECTION OF FINANCIAL STATEMENTS
THREE RUNNING YEARS BALANCE SHEET
Projections -->

Spread in hundreds ( ) Spread in thousands (X)	1	BY QUARTER 2	3	4	1	BY QUARTER 2	3	4	1	BY QUARTER 2	3	4
BALANCE SHEET												
ASSETS: Cash (opening)	210.11	4701.92	4487.17	4778.39	5784.33	7964.18	9477.88	11646.35	15403.21	22535.07	29436.01	37231.02
Marketable Securities	.00	.00	.00	.00	.00	.00	.00	.00	.00	.00	.00	.00
Receivables (Net)	.00	.00	450.00	1125.00	2025.00	2250.00	3375.10	5625.00	9000.00	9000.00	10125.00	11250.00
Inventory (Net)	.00	.00	.00	.00	.00	.00	.00	.00	.00	.00	.00	.00
Total Current Assets	210.11	4701.92	4937.17	5903.39	7809.33	10214.18	12852.98	17271.35	24403.21	31535.07	39561.01	48481.02
Fixed Assets (Net)	.00	182.00	202.00	222.00	242.00	262.00	282.00	312.00	312.00	312.00	312.00	312.00
Deferred Charges												
TOTAL ASSETS	210.11	4883.92	5139.17	6125.39	8051.33	10476.18	13134.98	17583.35	24715.21	31847.07	39873.01	48793.02
LIABILITIES: Notes Payable: Banks												
Trade Payables	17.49	135.00	337.50	607.50	675.00	1012.50	1687.50	2700.00	2700.00	3037.50	3375.00	4050.00
Income Tax	-143.62	6.11	180.43	398.27	315.23	482.49	815.16	1313.37	1313.37	1479.19	1645.01	1976.65
Accruals (ins. $3500/yr.)	.88	.88	.88	.88	.88	.88	.88	.88	.88	.88	.88	.88
CURRENT LIABILITIES	-125.25	141.99	518.81	1006.65	991.11	1495.87	2503.54	4014.25	4014.25	4517.57	5020.89	6027.53
CAPITAL STOCK SURPLUS	335.36	4741.93	4620.36	5118.74	7060.22	8980.31	10631.44	13569.10	20700.96	27329.50	34852.12	42765.49
Net Worth for Ptnrship. or Indiv.												
TOTAL LIABILITIES AND NET WORTH	210.11	4883.92	5139.17	6125.39	8051.33	10476.18	13134.98	17583.35	24715.21	31847.07	39873.01	48793.02
BALANCE SHEET RATIO ANALYSIS												
Current Ratio (acid test)	-1.68	33.12	9.52	5.86	7.88	6.83	5.13	4.30	6.08	6.98	7.88	8.04
Debt-to-Equity	-.37	.03	.11	.20	.14	.17	.24	.30	.19	.17	.14	.14
Return on Assets	-1.03	.00	.05	.10	.10	.12	.16	.19	.14	.12	.11	.10
Return on Equity	-.64	.00	.06	.12	.11	.14	.20	.25	.16	.14	.12	.12
Investment Turnover	.00	.09	.22	.33	.28	.32	.43	.51	.36	.32	.28	.28
Return on Investment (ROI)	-1.03	.00	.05	.10	.10	.12	.16	.19	.14	.12	.11	.10

* * *

The following is the actual business plan released to the general investment and venture capital community.

This summary plan was successful in attracting a group of private investors (Angels) who negotiated a phased investment approach. This amounted to first funding the venture through beta site tests and FDA (Federal Drug Administration) approval. Then further investment would be considered based on the success or failure of the beta tests and FDA approval.

All the previous demonstrated and mentioned marketing plans and business plan material were used in the negotiations to demonstrate the market, the management teams ability to knowledgeably work in the market being addressed, and the compatibility of the product to the needs of the marketplace.

The project is currently successfully being pursued with product introduction foreseen in approximately 4 years from conception.

FUNCTIONAL CARDIAC DISPLAYS, INC.
SUMMARY
BUSINESS PLAN

FEBRUARY, 1989

Reference:
Functional Cardiac Displays, Inc.
General Program and Planning

A. Team Builder, President/CEO
3039 Cardiac Health Drive
Anytown, Anywhere 90000
999-555-1234

Contents

1.0 EXECUTIVE SUMMARY

As a result of over two decades of accumulated research, Functional Cardiac Displays, Inc. (FCD) of Anytown, Anywhere is proud to announce a successful breakthrough in the field of medical science and the resultant business opportunity.

This business plan describes Functional Cardiac Displays, Inc. a company which has currently completed feasibility studies (Phase I) for a product that addresses a particular segment of the medical applications marketplace: Cardiovascular Analysis System Evaluation (CASE 2000).

The ECG market is valued at approximately $500 million and is used here strictly for comparison purposes. FCD products represent a great advantage over ECG diagnostic procedures. Forecasts through 1991 anticipate uninterrupted growth for the industry owing to a demand for cardiac diagnostic services. This situation has evolved because of the increased longevity of the world population, especially in the industrialized nations. Worldwide revenues for 1991 are forecast at $860 million, which represents an average annual growth rate of 12 percent.

1.1 Management Team

The FCD management has a proven record of several successful start-up assignments and has guided numerous multimillion dollar programs in a timely manner. The management staff has served as executive officers of technical societies in local chapters and on a national basis.

FCD work force consists of excellent professionals who are versed in a specific array of required disciplines. Each member of the team is a significant contributor in a particular element of this project and was selected for that expertise and for his or her fit with the other members. FCD general plan provides resumes of the team that detail the experience available for this project.

The principles of FCD have a long established relation with a number of reliable technical resources that will assist through the development process of this product. Scientific reviews have been conducted with several members of reputable cardiovascular clinics and a close relation with several hospitals has now been established. These valuable resources and individuals will serve as consultants throughout the development stage of the product.

1.2 Market Environment

The general environment for the medical supply industry is still in the growth stage. The technologic complexity of this new procedure requires a team with many valued and rare abilities to be able to develop such a new concept in cardiac diagnostic techniques. The difficulty of assembling such a team and the virtual impossibility of duplicating the proprietary information which is the basis of the product makes it unlikely that a competitor would soon arrive on the scene. As a result, we at FCD believe we offer a unique opportunity to be first with a valuable advanced cardiac diagnostic tool for medical technology. A noninvasive procedure designed to provide an accurate evaluation of a patient, and at the same time allow for low cost and maximum safety.

The market for new advanced medical technology shows no direct dependency on sustained general economic status or substantial growth. the market for medical service is complex and one finds that some areas grow regardless of national economic conditions.

The cornerstone of this plan is the breakthrough mentioned earlier. This breakthrough provides a major leap forward for cardiovascular diagnostic technology using the proven ECG data sensing techniques as input to a computer system. That system compares that data with a mathematically synthesized heart model and presents a three-dimensional color display of the electrical function of the patient's heart highlighting the extent of pathologies and presenting traditional ECG electrical signals.

1.3 Financial Forecasts

Estimated sales during the first year of production are \$3.7 million (starting 1990), rising to \$20 million and \$40 million in the second and third years, respectively.

Gross margin in the first production year is calculated to be 52 percent and the after tax income is about 18 percent. Positive cash flow is expected in the mid part of the second year.

1.4 Conclusion

The business opportunity presented here is to capitalize on an information base which has taken over 20 years and uncounted hours to accumulate. The product uses this information base in such a way as to greatly benefit the cardiovascular medical services in saving lives.

The market for this product is proven by marketing survey and the enthusiasm of significant members of that potential market. The total required capital to bring the product to manufacturing prototype (Phase II) and on to production (Phase III) is estimated at \$5 million with a positive cash flow expected in the mid part of the second year.

The investors are expected to realize a return on investment in the order of 5 to 10 times that investment in approximately 3 to 5 years when the company goes public.

In summary, this plan identifies an opportunity to enter a marketplace that has enormous potential for revenue and profit growth, using an already established product technology and an experienced and seasoned management team.

2.0 INTRODUCTION

The modern science of the interpretation of the electric signals from the heart almost 100 years ago (1907) with Einthoven's application of the string galvanometer to the recording of the ECG. The next major step forward was the development of the Wilson unipolar chest leads some 50 years ago. The standardization of ECG recordings to consist of 6 precordial leads and 6 limb leads followed soon after. The electrocardiographer reading these 12 scalar ECG traces consisting of the familiar P-QRS-T waveforms reconstructs a three-dimensional (3D) image in his mind of the electrical activity in the upper and lower chambers of the heart. The result of this mental image building is the ECG interpretation, that is, "Complete Heart Block," "Left Ventricular Hypertrophy," or "Acute and Extensive Anterior Myocardial Infarction," the recording, processing, and interpretation of the ECG has been assisted by digital computers to an ever-increasing extent in recent years. The primary signal is, however, still the 12 lead set of ECG waveforms.

With the advent of high speed colorgraphic digital image technology it is now possible (in addition to the standard 12 lead ECG processing) to reconstruct a 3D color image of the electrical activity of the heart directly from multiple body surface lead measurement. The local area of "Block," "Hypertrophy," "Injury," or "Infarction," for example, can be directly imaged and shown in 3D color on a high resolution color monitor. The image can be rotated and magnified to optimize the definition of the local injury or disorder electrical activity. The enhancement of the mental image building by this direct imaging process can be expected to lead to clearer, simple, and more quantitative and diagnosis.

The development of just such a high resolution 3D color cardiac local electric field imaging system is underway at Functional Cardiac Displays in Anytown, Anywhere.

Dr. Donald Z. Smithson, MD

Prof. of Med.: University of Estonia
Dir: Biomathematics and ECG Research Group
Editor-in-Chief: *Journal of Cardiac Technology*
Dir. and Chief Scientist: Cardiac Local Field Imaging, FCD, Inc.

3.0 HISTORY

Approximately 25 years ago Dr. Smithson, MD conceived that electrical signals of the heart could be used as input data to a computer. This data could then develop an accurate image of a patient's heart. At this time, the technology did not exist that would make this economically feasible. However, the trend of technology development indicated that it would be available in the near future. Dr. Smithson with the help of J. Computer, a computer expert and physicist, began the arduous task of collecting the data necessary to develop the database (digitally recorded information) and Dr. Barnone, a Cardiologist at Cardiovascular Hospital, to construct the mathematical model of the heart. Initially, this data was gathered on a mainframe computer system.

During this period Mr. Computer took a healthy heart, dissected it, and took approximately 280,000 data point measurements to accurately define the database math model.

The resulting database and math model can now be demonstrated, in a time intensive manner, using the mainframe system. FCD is now addressing the conversion of that data to a supermini system for use with the more cost-effective, high speed, engineering workstations being produced today by companies such as Silicon Graphics and Sun Microsystems.

To date, FCD, Inc. has converted a sufficient amount of the data to prove and demonstrate the feasibility of the conversion process. This represents the successful completion of Phase I of the project. The next phase (Phase II) consists of completing the data conversion process, developing and verifying the prototype system, starting clinical studies, and beginning development of the marketing program.

Through the contributions of private investors, including many of the founders and first employees, sufficient resources of money, manpower, facilities, and equipment have been made available. FCD, Inc. is now at the point where it requires an increase in manpower and resources to accomplish the task ahead. Additional technical and marketing expertise must now be adopted in order to move the project forward to the commercial market.

4.0 PRODUCT DEFINITION

FCD, Inc. is in the "noninvasive medical imaging" business. The company has started with electrical imaging of the heart, based on the founders devoted time to cardiovascular study. The study base has given FCD, Inc. a head start in this highly specialized area of medical imaging.

Since 1907, the cardiovascular physician has had to rely on the subjective interpretation of ECG waveforms to determine a patient's heart condition. Today, if a 12-lead electrocardiogram and/or patient's symptoms lead one to suspect a heart problem, a confirming diagnosis must be formulated. Such existing clinical technology as standard treadmill stress testing, ultrasound (echo) imaging, isotopic imaging, and, at times, angiographic imaging is used. These techniques have certain disadvantages. Angiographic imaging is not routine, very costly, invasive, risky, and should not be performed unless a specific descriptive ventricular or coronary anatome is desired in preparation for an interventional or surgical procedure.

Isotopic imaging is also invasive, non routine, involves injections of potentially harmful radioactive chemicals, and has poor images with an accuracy that is unmatched with its very high cost. Ultrasonic (echo) imaging basically provides nonspecific structural information from which information about electrical physiologic function is inferred. The standard treadmill stress test, though widely used, is based on and limited by the standard 12-lead ECG for data acquisition. Thus it can provide incomplete and misleading information. It is unusable in providing regional myocardial information and, in many individuals, is nondiagnostic with a low level of accuracy.

CASE 2000 eliminates the need for such practices and provides more accurate and descriptive diagnostic analysis where adapted to existing technology in a less costly manner. The patient's heart data is taken by 32 sensing points instead of merely 12. The data is displayed on a high resolution, 3D screen that highlights any specific problem area. The physician is provided an ECG printout as well as the screen image which allows for an immediate crosscheck of the data by the physician. This significantly increases the speed and accuracy of the diagnosis which allows much more definitive action to be taken without risk of subjective interpretive diagnosis.

5.0 DEFINITION OF THE MARKET

In order to maintain a conservative marketing analysis for CASE 2000, we have selected the current ECG market as a reference point. However, it should be understood that CASE 2000 provides information far beyond the current ECG capabilities.

The primary competition existing for this product are the ECG based products. Which, by introduction of this product, may be rendered obsolete in the future. This product may also negatively impact the radio isotope imaging market as well as the magnetic resonance imaging (MRI) and ultrasonic imaging markets. These markets will be affected to the extent that they address the practice of cardiovascular imaging.

When the product is introduced and in production, it is expected that the company will experience a high growth period. This will be controlled by the sale of licensed production rights to meet geographic areas of demand throughout the United States and international markets.

Sales and distribution will be in the continental United States during the Beta testing period and most of the first year after product release. This allows us to closely track the product performance under field conditions. In addition, the anticipated domestic market is such that FCD may be hard pressed to keep up with that demand.

The sales force will be trained to act as the staff to train Beta sites and ongoing site staffs in the proper use of the product. The sales people will be paid a base salary initially. Following product acceptance, compensation will change to the more traditional base salary plus commission/bonus.

Three to five Beta sites will be selected. These sites will be cardiovascular training hospitals and clinics. One site has been approved for the clinical study at LBJ Memorial Hospital and one site is under consideration in Utah. (These sites will be requested to purchase the Beta units, which is a unique action for new products in the medical industry.)

5.1 Market Areas (Geographic)

FCD, Inc. will concentrate initially on satisfying the domestic market. This will take an estimated 3 to 5 years. As this satisfaction occurs we will investigate the international markets for methods of penetration as well as profitability.

5.2 Services and Products

Initially, FCD, Inc. will be a "systems integrator." The company will produce software that will be loaded into a hardware configuration (computer environment) purchased from a vendor (i.e., Silicon Graphics and/or Sun Microsystems). The company will also contract with a manufacturer (Stateside) to produce the devices necessary for sensing the patient's heart signals.

These above stated elements will be brought together under the complete direction and control of FCD, Inc. and will remain in that control until it is found advisable to move that integration process outside FCD, Inc.

Advertising will be done by:

- Display and demo of the product at selected medical conventions and trade shows
- Print advertising in cardiovascular and hospital journals as well as health and fitness magazines
- Direct mail to the cardiovascular community
- Promotion of discounted software updates
- Financing assistance
- On-line product technical support (telephone technical advice/troubleshooting)
- TV and radio news (science announcements)
- Press releases

The major market advantage FCD, Inc. has is that the company was founded by a highly respected group of medical practitioners for the cardiovascular specialty. These people lend a great deal of credibility and long-term prestige to this company and its entry product(s).

Another advantage is the fact that this imaging product is a noninvasive cardiovascular device. This greatly reduces the medical risk. Thus it becomes much more attractive to the customer than those imaging products that are invasive.

A further advantage is that it is state-of-the-art equipment for alerting patients of potential heart disease dangers as well as for diagnosing the damage caused by a heart attack (i.e., latent ischemia).

The company has no perceived market disadvantage. The product is new and, as such, it is difficult to accurately predict public and medical acceptance. All reactions have thus far been positive. The market being used for clinical study is the current ECG market which is represented by the medical applications market.

FCD, Inc. expects to conservatively gain 15 percent of the ECG based market and to ship at least 80 units during the first year after product introduction and continue a minimum of 32 percent sales revenue growth rate through the first 5 years.

6.0 INDUSTRY TRENDS

6.1 Future Industry Trends

The forces motivating the user to purchase computer tools for medical applications are:

- Increasing malpractice insurance costs are causing doctors to perform as many nonsurgical diagnostic techniques as possible
- Sophisticated medical diagnostic equipment is becoming increasingly more complex, requiring computerization
- There is a need to integrate many instruments to improve productivity and increase utilization of expensive instruments
- There are shortages of medical technicians and doctors with critical skills
- Labor costs are increasing
- Drastic attention has been projected in the 1990s to focus toward fitness and cardiovascular related progress

6.2 Outside Influences Facing the Industry

Medical products are subject to the following restrictions and influences:

- Liability insurance
- Government regulators such as FDA (Federal Drug Administration) and FTC (Federal Trade Commission)
- Medical associations' sales and criterion
- International trade policy (for exports)
- Political status of medical environment
- Insurance industry regulations
- Healthcare cost containment
- Third party regulators (e.g., Medicaid and Medicare)

These outside influences have generated the following recent activities:

- Liability insurance for physicians has almost doubled making them more responsive to new, no-risk, non-invasive technologies which provide early warning of impending disaster
- Medical products have relatively short lives
- Hospitals, physicians, and suppliers are competing among themselves for available funds since insurance companies and the government have capped spending for health programs
- Monitoring of cardiac function in all surgical patients is becoming an industry standard
- The trend is toward using micro, board, and personal computers in medical applications

6.3 Pricing

The price per unit, at this time, is estimated at $40,000. Increasing volume sales and contracting services will bring the price down another 10 to 20 percent. The general trend of pricing in the type of workstation that will integrate our system is continuously going down. Dun and Bradstreet analysis show price reductions of 15 percent and more every year. This is similar to the personal computer and disk drive market response of the past. ECG analysis cost and CAT scans of patients ranges between $120 and $800. The use of CASE 2000 for analysis will justify a patient cost in the middle of that range.

6.4 Advertising and Promotion Costs

Approximately 15 to 20 percent of total investment in product is normally spent on media by industrial firms. ("Sharing the Value Added: A Bonus Plan for a Growth Company," A. Graham Sterling, Operating Model of a Hypothetical Growth Company, *Strategic Planning and Management Handbook,* New York: Van Nostrand Reinhold Company, p. 522.)

Mini and micro computer industry spent an average of 15.7 percent of margin on advertising during 1985. Hospital services industry spent 12 percent of margin on advertising during 1985. (*Advertising Age,* September 15, 1986)

6.5 CASE 2000 Marketing Potential Conclusion

* FACT: Heart disease is the number one killer in the United States—makes this product a necessity in the medical community.
* FACT: The uniqueness and need for this product indicated that there is a lot of potential for it now. FCD, Inc. has the technical expertise to make this product and the medical industry specific contact and marketing experience to successfully sell it.
* FACT: The imaging technology being used is new and non-invasive and shows potential for expanded use in brain scan applications as well as other industries in need of scanning methodologies.
* FACT: In America, someone dies of cardiovascular disease every 32 seconds.
* FACT: In 1986, heart and blood vessel diseases killed nearly one million Americans, almost as many as cancer, accidents, pneumonia, influenza, and all other causes of death combined.
* FACT: Almost one in two Americans die of cardiovascular disease.

The medical application market is growing at a compound annual rate of 11.0 percent per the years 1987 to 1991. The gross national product is forecasted to grow at a rate of 305 percent during the same time period. The cardiology segment is especially strong, and the penetration in the medical application field is relatively low. No new entries are foreseen in the medical application marketplace.*

*Ref: The American Heart Association, 1989 Heart Facts

7.0 DESCRIPTION OF PRODUCTS OR SERVICES
CASE 2000
USER SPECIFICATIONS

Initial release (proposed base user price $40,000)

Product will identify:

- Specific areas and volumes of infarctions, acute injury, and ischemia. Areas include transmural and subendocardial determinations
- Localization of areas and volumes of infarction, acute injury, and ischemia despite intraventricular conduction delays or bundle branch blocks
- Locations of accessory bypass pathways in WPW syndromes
- Localization of sites of ventricular ectopic complexes or sites of ventricular re-entry for use in mapping of ventricular tachycardia for ablation purposes

Will have:

- 3 to 5 minute sensor/screen refresh rate
- 32 sensor input band
- 32 sensor signal display and printout
- 3-dimensional image generations at normal size
  - Image display orientation (to be determined)
  - Interior and exterior views
  - 1 mm slicing
  - Zoom to approximately 5X
  - Full image rotation
  - Panning
- Color print of screen image
- Patient date recorded on removable hard disk
  - (60 heartbeat sample requiring less than 1 MBytes)
  - (Disk cartridge capable of 380 MBytes storage)
- On going product development (1.5 to 2 years)

	Base	Option
Ischemia mapping	✔	
Treadmill applications		$5000
Angioplasty applications		$2500
Digital display of ischemic and infarction volume	✔	
Stop time review	✔	
Surgical anesthesia monitoring	✔	
Intensive care unit monitoring	✔	

- Free user training will be provided for each Beta unit
- Installation and training will be provided at a cost of $5000 per each production unit and option

8.0 MANAGEMENT STRUCTURE

The management team consists of president and chief executive officer, Mr. A. Team Builder, who is responsible for gathering resources, monitoring costs, and schedules. As a key executive, Mr. Builder, is involved in corporate strategies, corporate mission, and progress. He provides expertise in planning, budgeting, and quality assurance, ensuring that the required outcome is secured. He has successfully led other high-tech start-up programs and has played key management roles in several organizations.

Dr. B. Thorough, PhD will perform the duties of vice president of marketing. Dr. Thorough has several years of medical product development, strategic planning, and marketing research experience and is well received in the medical community. She will be assisted by Dr. B. Good, PhD who has many years experience in the computer marketing and high-tech customer support fields.

Dr. A. Barnone, MD, cardiologist, is responsible for maintaining the focus of the engineering team toward the end-users need.

The technical team described above will be assisted in a advisory manner by a science team consisting of Dr. Smithson and Mr. Computer the primary creators of CASE 2000 database and technology.

Mr. Computer, has a MS in physics from California State University and has been the primary data technologist working in cooperation with Dr. Smithson.

Mr. U. Cantdoit, attorney at law, is our legal and corporate attorney.

Dr. U. Betwe Candoit, PhD., Stanford University, will handle the complex technology patent matters.

The FCD, Inc. board of directors consists of reputable and prominent individuals who have extensive knowledge of and backgrounds in technology and the business aspect of the medical community. The members are:

D. Smithson	Chief scientist, chief of cardiology
U. Betwe Candoit	Attorney at law
I. Lookintoit	Cardiovascular heart surgeon
C. Joiner	Director of ASME, Western Region

As the organization moves through these planned phases of activity, the boards character and philosophies will move and focus toward business related issues. Currently we are proud to see that very reputable individuals are attracted to FCD, Inc.'s board from the business community.

8.1 Consultants and Advisors

Dr. I. Attractem, PhD, expert on magnetic resonance imaging, math modeling, and electronics in the fields of medicine, pharmacology, and micro-devices, will be assisting FCD, Inc. in CASE 2000 sensor development program.

Mr. I. Lookforem, consultant for FDA (Federal Drug Administration) regulations.

9.0 MANAGEMENT OBJECTIVES

Based on the response received from esteemed members of the medical community to the demonstrated prototype, which is the result of the feasibility study, the need and the desire for such a product is here.

FCD, Inc. long-term objectives are to develop products related to imaging technology. CASE 2000 being the first product introduced in the market is just the threshold of a huge market existing in the medical area. FCD, Inc. is currently reviewing other related product possibilities which use the same technology principles such as Trajectories of Electroencephalographic (EEG) potential which would be the next product to develop.

There are a number of advantages that arise as a result of the use of this imaging technology:

1. The components integrated in this product are proven to be reliable from an engineering standpoint, since the hardware has been in use in the medical community for a number of years. The hardware used in this product has been approved by the American Heart Association and it takes little effort to obtain FDA (Federal Drug Administration) approval.
2. The basic product (ECG) family is known in the marketplace and has an accepted reputation.
3. The product will become available at a time when the market segment is expected to expand rapidly because of the growing percentage of older people in the general world population growth pattern.
4. A greater demand for advanced technology.
5. The investment in hardware engineering required by FCD, Inc. is low in comparison to similar start-up concerns.
6. Because the product is primarily software based, FCD will act primarily as a systems integrator with software that is easily adaptable to many hardware sources. This provides the additional opportunity of licensing the software to the international market for additional revenue with little effort.

9.1 Near-Term Objectives

FCD, Inc. is now in the position to continue further clinical product development which will last 16 months. This effort now needs $1.5 million funding to move through Phase II of the plan.

At the end of Phase II, FCD, Inc. will hold a design specification for each of the hardware and software components to the system. This, by itself, provides a tangible asset. With this, FCD, Inc. could employ other vendors to manufacture/distribute the product. This would develop a selection of opportunities allowing FCD, Inc. alternatives of market approach thus securing the best advantage for the investors. This asset would also provide FCD, Inc. alternatives in financing on-going objectives.

9.2 Long-Term Objective

Manufacturing activities (Phase III) are planned to start at the end of Phase II and will require an additional cash infusion of $3.5 million if FCD, Inc. sets up a manufacturing facility. However, management is looking into other alternatives such as a strategic alliance to support manufacturing needs.

First shipments will be made during the second quarter after the start of manufacturing. In the period between start-up and shipments, the sales effort will be supported by a small quantity of CASE 2000 systems to be used for customer evaluation and demonstration at selected beta sites. The intention of management is to go public the fourth or fifth year of operation. At which time it is anticipated the company's market value will be in excess of $200 million. This will provide a return to the investor of 5 to 10 times investment.

10.0 PRODUCT DEVELOPMENT PROGRAM
(Phase II)

Within 2 years FCD, Inc. plans to be well into delivery of its base product (see Description of Products and services).

During the next 16 months, development (Phase II), FCD, Inc. plans to develop and verify a working prototype of CASE 2000. This program will require the following actions:

Testing and Verification
- Multilead ECG sensing development
- Issue final specification

System Set Up
- Prototype configuration
- Product design layout
- Issue final system design specification

Clinical Studies
- Equipment component evaluation
- Equipment integration
- Clinical applications evaluation

Marketing Program Development
- Product profile
- Initial product positioning

11.0 PRODUCT DEVELOPMENT PROGRAM
(Phase III)

Once the above program has been accomplished an intensive 16 months program of market introduction of production models will occur. This program consists of:

- Continued clinical feedback
- Prototype modifications
- Production facility location
    Contract manufacturer
    Self-manufacturer
- Final design evaluation
- Marketing planning and promotion
- Limited production
- Sales and promotion

The management team at FCD, Inc. sees no obstacle in attaining the above stated goals in the time specified. They have successfully attained the Phase I goals ahead of schedule and below budget.

12.0 FINANCIAL DATA

12.1 Market Share

FCD, Inc. is pursuing a market which has been relatively untapped by new technology since 1907. The goal is to gain approximately 1 to 3 percent of that market within the first year of product introduction and increase the share at a rate greater than 32 percent per year compounded until 30 to 40 percent of that market has been captured. At that time continued effort will allow us to move at a rate slightly ahead of projected market growth of 11 percent.

At that time, the primary concentration will be on product profit margin and cash flow rather than on market share.

12.2 Budget

FCD, Inc. has just successfully completed Phase I which was the program to prove the feasibility of the original concept using the new microprocessor workstation technology. We are now ready to proceed with Phase II which is the process of developing the production prototype of the product and begin the marketing processes.

To start and successfully complete the Phase II process, it will be necessary to raise $1.5 million to cover the expenses of operation for the next 16 months. The pro forma financial statements that follow detail the need of these funds and further detail the need for funds to begin production of the product in Phase III.

The closing of Phase II on schedule will allow a cash flow carry forward of approximately $200,000. It will be necessary to have an additional cash infusion of $3.5 million to carry the project forward to profitability sometime during the second quarter of the second year of operation. At that time FCD, Inc. will have shipped over 10 units and will be at the starting point of our rapid growth.

12.3 Projected Value Analysis

The following table is an analysis of the projected stock value of FCD for a 4-year growth period based on a very conservative assumption* (using ECG as a reference point).

	1990	1991	1992	1993
Market Size of ECG units sold per year (in $ U.S. millions)	$465.00	$510.00	$550.00	$600.00
Concentration @ 79%	367.35	402.90	434.50	474.00
Market penetration	1%	5%	10%	15%
Annual sales (in $ U.S. millions)	3.67	20.15	43.45	71.10
Anticipated profit @ 30%	1.10	6.04	13.04	21.33
Net income per share	0.22	1.20	2.60	4.26
Market share price	12.00	26.00	42.00	

*Assumptions: Number of outstanding shares 5,000,000
Earnings multiplier 10
Risk free rate (treasuries) 7.94%
Risk rate of return 25.00%
Annual return rate expected 33.00%

APPENDIX A
FINANCIAL DETAILS

FCD, INC.
Estimated Cash Requirement

	Phase I R. & D. Completed 12/88	Phase II Dev. of Prototype 3/1/89 to 6/30/90	Phase III Limited Production 7/1/90 to 10/31/91 90 Units Produced
Capital Expenditures			
Computer Equipment	0	110000	150000
Office Furn. and Equipment	0	55500	30000
Manufacturing and Assembly			
Component, Design and Assembly Labor	0	70000	1512000
Technical and Management Personnel			
Technical Salaries	0	480000	600000
Fringe and Taxes	0	96000	120000
Accountant	0	60000	70000
Technical Consultants	0	250000	200000
Marketing Staff			
Marketing Salaries	0	150000	220000
Fringe and Taxes	0	30000	44000
Product Profile/Design and Graphic	0	15000	40000
Product Promotion	0	10000	40000
Delivery	0	0	54000
Administration Expenses			
Administration Salaries	0	42000	50000
Stationery and Mail	0	8000	10000
Rent and Utilities	0	60000	180000
Fringe and Taxes	0	8400	10000
Travel	0	40000	90000
Legal Fees	0	15000	20000
Total Expenditures	completed 12/88	1499900	3440000

FCD, INC.
PROJECTED INCOME STATEMENT
PRODUCTION PHASE

	FISCAL YEAR ENDED			
	10/31/91	10/31/92	10/31/93	10/31/94
ESTIMATED SALES (SEE NOTE 1)	3600000	20210000	43362000	70890000
ESTIMATED COST OF SALES				
COMPONENT COST	1080000	5800000	11680000	19460000
LABOR	360000	2320000	5840000	11120000
FRINGE AND TAXES	72000	464000	1168000	2224000
TOTAL COST OF SALES	1512000	8584000	18688000	32804000
GROSS PROFIT	2088000	11626000	24674000	38086000
ESTIMATED OPERATING EXPENSES				
MARKETING AND DELIVERY (NOTE 2)	478000	1610000	3248000	6104400
SALARIES (NOTE 3)	600000	980000	1310000	1965000
FRINGES AND TAXES	120000	196000	262000	393000
CONSULTING FEES	200000	100000	80000	80000
ADMINISTRATIVE EXP.	70000	90000	135000	202500
RENT	180000	400000	500000	600000
ACCOUNTING FEES	70000	80000	90000	100000
TRAVEL	10000	60000	70000	80000
LEGAL FEES	20000	30000	40000	50000
DEPRECIATION	50000	50000	50000	50000
TOTAL OPERATING EXPENSES	1798000	3596000	5785000	9624900
EST. INCOME BEFORE TAXES	290000	8030000	18889000	28461100
TAXES ON INCOME	116000	3212000	7555600	11384440
ESTIMATED NET INCOME	174000	4818000	11333400	17076660

FCD, INC.
PROJECTED INCOME STATEMENT
PRODUCTION PHASE

	FISCAL YEAR ENDED			
	7/31/91	7/31/92	7/31/93	7/31/94
NOTE 1				
EXPECTED SALES				
UNITS PRODUCED AND SOLD	90	580	1460	2780
UNIT PRICE	40000	34500	29700	25500
TOTAL EXPECTED REVENUE	3600000	20010000	43362000	70890000
NOTE 2				
MARKETING AND DELIVERY				
MARKETING SALARIES	220000	600000	1160000	2300000
FRINGES AND TAXES	44000	120000	232000	460000
TRAVEL	80000	462000	900000	1600000
PRODUCT PROMOTION	80000	80000	80000	80000
DELIVERY	54000	348000	876000	1664400
TOTAL MARKETING EXPENSES	478000	1610000	3248000	6104400
NOTE 3				
SALARIES				
TECHNICAL	295000	495000	685000	1100000
SUPPORT AND ADMINISTRATIVE	305000	485000	625000	865000
TOTAL SALARIES	600000	980000	1310000	1965000

FCD, Inc.
PHASE II
Estimated Cash Requirement

	Mar-89	Apr-89	May-89	Jun-89	Jul-89	Aug-89	Sep-89
Capital Expenditures							
Computer Equipment	110000						
Office Furniture and Equipment	55500						
Sub Total	165500	0	0	0	0	0	0
Manufacturing and Assembly							
Component, Design, and Assembly		40000			30000		
	0	40000	0	0	30000	0	0
Technical Consultants							
Scientist/Computer	15625	15625	15625	15625	15625	15625	15625
	15625	15625	15625	15625	15625	15625	15625
Technical and Management Personnel							
Technical Salaries	30000	30000	30000	30000	30000	30000	30000
Fringe and Taxes	6000	6000	6000	6000	6000	6000	6000
Accountant	3750	3750	3750	3750	3750	3750	3750
	39750	39750	39750	39750	39750	39750	39750
Marketing Staff							
Marketing Salaries						13636	13636
Fringe and Taxes						2727	2727
Product Profile/Design, and Graphic						1364	1364
Product Promotion and Presentation						909	909
	0	0	0	0	0	18636	18636
Administration Expense							
Administration Salaries	2625	2625	2625	2625	2625	2625	2625
Taxes and Benefits	525	525	525	525	525	525	525
Stationery and Mail	500	500	500	500	500	500	500
Rent & Utilities	3750	3750	3750	3750	3750	3750	3750
	7400	7400	7400	7400	7400	7400	7400
Travel	2500	2500	2500	2500	2500	2500	2500
Legal Fees	938	938	938	938	938	938	938
Total Expenditures for Phase II	231713	106213	66213	66213	96213	84849	84849

Oct-89	Nov-89	Dec-89	Jan-90	Feb-90	Mar-90	Apr-90	May-90	Jun-90	Total
									110000
									55500
0	0	0	0	0	0	0	0	0	165500
									70000
0	0	0	0	0	0	0	0	0	70000
15625	15625	15625	15625	15625	15625	15625	15625	15625	250000
15625	15625	15625	15625	15625	15625	15625	15625	15625	250000
30000	30000	30000	30000	30000	30000	30000	30000	30000	480000
6000	6000	6000	6000	6000	6000	6000	6000	6000	96000
3750	3750	3750	3750	3750	3750	3750	3750	3750	60000
39750	39750	39750	39750	39750	39750	39750	39750	39750	636000
13636	13636	13636	13636	13636	13636	13636	13636	13636	149996
2727	2727	2727	2727	2727	2727	2727	2727	2727	29997
1364	1364	1364	1364	1364	1364	1364	1364	1364	15004
909	909	909	909	909	909	909	909	909	9999
18636	18636	18636	18636	18636	18636	18636	18636	18636	204996
2625	2625	2625	2625	2625	2625	2625	2625	2625	42000
525	525	525	525	525	525	525	525	525	8400
500	500	500	500	500	500	500	500	500	8000
3750	3750	3750	3750	3750	3750	3750	3750	3750	60000
7400	7400	7400	7400	7400	7400	7400	7400	7400	118400
2500	2500	2500	2500	2500	2500	2500	2500	2500	40000
938	938	938	938	938	938	938	938	938	15008
84849	84849	84849	84849	84849	84849	84849	84849	84849	1499904

INDEX

A

B

C

D

E